Dante Gabriel Rossetti
and the Limits
of Victorian Vision

Dante Gabriel Rossetti and the Limits of Victorian Vision

DAVID G. RIEDE

Cornell University Press

ITHACA AND LONDON

First published 1983 by Cornell University Press.
Published in the United Kingdom by Cornell University Press Ltd.,
Ely House, 37 Dover Street, London W1X 4HQ.

International Standard Book Number 0-8014-1552-7
Library of Congress Catalog Card Number 82-22099
Printed in the United States of America
*Librarians: Library of Congress cataloging information appears
on the last page of the book.*

The paper in this book is acid-free and meets the guidelines for permanence and durability of the Committee on Production Guidelines for Book Longevity of the Council on Library Resources.

For Natalie

Contents

Contents

Plates

Preface

ONE of the most colorful of the major Victorians, Dante Gabriel Rossetti was the kind of man to inspire legends, and consequently to inspire biographies. Much has been written about his life and career, yet misconceptions persist. I have deliberately avoided adding to the glut of biographical commentary, but my attempt to correct two persistent errors about his career has largely dictated the shape of this book. First, to combat the legend that Rossetti's imaginative vision was fully realized by the time he was nineteen, and did not significantly change, I have structured the book in a roughly chronological order, attempting to show that Rossetti struggled arduously to achieve his artistic originality, that he fully matured as a poet only in the late 1860s, when he reached forty, that his styles in both arts changed repeatedly in response to both internal and external pressures. Second, in order to refute the idea that Rossetti, as a poet-painter, was able to unify the sister arts, enhancing each with the other, I have, when possible, discussed his two careers simultaneously, arguing that though he did indeed attempt a synthesis of the two arts, the harder he tried the more he floundered on the necessary independence of each art from the other. Despite his own intentions, and despite the prevalent notions about his accomplishments, Rossetti may actually have helped to widen the gap between the two arts and contributed to the aesthetic autonomy of painting.

The attempt to follow Rossetti's career chronologically creates certain problems. First, because no variorum edition of his writings exists, and because he revised his works perpetually, it is necessary to consult early versions of the poems in manuscripts, contemporary periodicals, and various scholarly editions of single poems. A greater difficulty arises because Rossetti's careers as painter and poet do not coincide in their stylistic shifts, so that it is sometimes impossible to adhere strictly to chronology. His three major stylistic periods in painting were, roughly, 1847 to 1853, 1853 to 1859, and 1859 to his death in 1882, but in poetry he was only sporadically active, with productive periods from 1847 to 1852, 1868 to 1872, and 1878 to 1881. As a result, I have been able to study his struggles toward a personal style in both arts from 1847 to 1853 simultaneously in Part I of this book, but the chronology becomes less convenient thereafter. In Part II I have concentrated exclusively on the characteristic themes and style of Rossetti's best period as a poet, from 1868 to 1872. In Part III I have been forced to backtrack to 1859 for a discussion of his last, longest, and in some ways richest period as a painter. In this section I also discuss the poetry of his last decade, and the relation between the two arts in the Victorian period generally, and in Rossetti's theory and practice.

I am grateful to a number of individuals and institutions for their support of this project. I am indebted, of course, to previous Rossetti scholars, and particularly to Cecil Y. Lang, who first interested me in Rossetti's painting, to Robert Langbaum, who first interested me in Rossetti's poetry, and to Virginia Surtees, both for personal assistance and for her magnificent and indispensable *catalogue raisonné* of Rossetti's paintings and drawings. For their careful readings and extremely helpful suggestions, I thank George P. Landow of Brown University and four of my colleagues at the University of Rochester, George Ford, Bruce Johnson, James Rieger, and James Spenko. I thank Kay Scheuer for spotting many errors and infelicities. I am also very grateful to Katharine Macdonald for permission to reproduce Rossetti's drawing for "The Raven" from her collection, and to Imogen Davis for permission to publish passages from Rossetti's manuscripts. And I am indebted to Betty A. Riede for frequent timely assistance, and to Natalie, Benedict, and Austin Riede for frequent restorative distractions. In addition, I thank the Mellon Foundation and the University of Rochester for a grant that gave me time to finish the book and the National Endowment for the Humanities for a stipend that made possible my study of the paintings and manuscripts in England. Finally, I am grateful for permission to reproduce materials from the collections of the Firestone Library at Princeton University; the British Library; the Fitzwilliam Museum, Cambridge; the Ashmolean Museum, Oxford; the British Museum; the Tate Gallery; the City Art Gallery of Manchester; the Birmingham Museums and Art Gallery; the Victoria and Albert Museum; and the Delaware Art Museum. I appreciate the gracious assistance of the many helpful librarians, curators, and other staff members at these institutions. I am especially obliged to Phyllis Andrews of the Rush Rhees Library, University of Rochester, and T. A. J. Burnett of the British Library.

Citations of works in the text generally refer to Oswald Doughty's convenient edition in the Everyman's Library series, *Dante Gabriel Rossetti: Poems* (London: Dent, 1961), abbreviated in the text as *Poems.* I am grateful to J. M. Dent & Sons Ltd. for permission to quote from this edition. Works not included in Doughty are cited in William Michael Rossetti's edition, *The Works of Dante Gabriel Rossetti* (London: Ellis, 1911), abbreviated in the text as *Works.* The sources of many works not to be found in either of these editions are provided in the footnotes. I also thank Oxford University Press for permission to quote from the *Letters of Dante Gabriel Rossetti*, ed. Oswald Doughty and John Robert Wahl, 4 vols. (London: Oxford University Press, 1965–1967), abbreviated in the notes as *Letters.* The paintings discussed are identified by their catalogue numbers in Virginia Surtees's *Dante Gabriel Rossetti: 1828–1882. The Paintings and Drawings: A Catalogue Raisonné*, 2 vols. (Oxford: Oxford University Press, 1971).

DAVID G. RIEDE

Rochester, New York

13

PART I

In Search of a Center

painting from Ford Madox Brown.[2] Further, his works at this time reflect experimentation, not a clearly defined purpose. What is most remarkable about Rossetti's work from the 1840s and the early 1850s, in fact, is the variety of forms he experimented with. In poetry he ranged from translations and imitations of the early Italians through satires and burlesques to dramatic monologues *à la* Browning and dreamy languorous romance *à la* Keats; in drawing from illustrations of Shakespeare, Goethe, and other writers to assorted medieval and religious topics.[3] Rossetti would eventually gain the respect and admiration of his contemporaries for finding his own small but original imaginative realm, but in 1847 and well into the 1850s his realm and range were enormous, but somewhat derivative. Far from reaching precocious maturity in 1847, Rossetti was then and for years afterward seeking to define himself as a painter and poet.

Rossetti's difficulty in finding a truly original artistic vision is evident from the affinity of his early work with that of his near predecessors, and the cause of his difficulty in getting started can be best appreciated with reference to Matthew Arnold's contemporaneous comments on the "perplexity" that "Keats Tennyson et id genus omne" must cause young poets: "They will not be patient neither understand that they must begin with an Idea of the world in order not to be prevailed over by the world's multitudinousness: or if they cannot get that, at least with isolated ideas: and all other things shall (perhaps) be added unto them." Rossetti's very versatility and diversity can be seen as an index of such multitudinousness. In a world growing increasingly relativistic and philosophically incoherent, an "Idea of the world" was difficult to come by, yet necessary to an ambitious artist who sought a large, yet original, vision. In this regard the influence of Browning and Keats on

[2]See William Bell Scott, *Autobiographical Notes,* ed. W. Minto, 2 vols., (New York: Harper and Brothers, 1892), I:245–246, and *Family Letters,* I:123.

[3]The earliest versions of poems influenced by the early Italians, "Ave," "On Mary's Portrait," "My Sister's Sleep," and "The Blessed Damozel," date from 1847, as does the burlesque "Jan Van Hunks." From 1848 to 1850 Rossetti worked on primitive versions of the dramatic monologues "Jenny," "A Last Confession," and the somewhat Keatsian "The Bride's Prelude" as well as on a kind of ballad-narrative, "Dante at Verona." For Keats's influence on Rossetti, see George H. Ford, *Keats and the Victorians* (New Haven: Yale University Press, 1944).

Rossetti's early work is especially suggestive, since according to Arnold, both, like Rossetti, lacked a clear "Idea of the world"[4] by which to order their artistic efforts. Significantly, both Browning and Keats had epic ambitions, but lacked epic themes and so accepted less grand, if no less great, artistic roles. The poetic form that most influenced the young Rossetti, the dramatic monologue, is a self-consciously limited one, which revels in multitudinousness, as Browning's gallery of characters illustrates, and which requires no clear "Idea of the world."[5] Despite his early success with the form in an ur-version of "Jenny" and in "A Last Confession," Rossetti was evidently not satisfied with it—partly, perhaps, because he did not want to be regarded as an epigone of Browning, and probably more because he still could not accept a fragmented view of the world, still sought a unifying theme and voice. And if his poems were to express a limited sensibility, Rossetti, ambitious and vain of his originality, wanted that sensibility to be his own.

Rossetti must have been aware that his early works were more remarkable for diversity than for expressing a coherent world view, but he nevertheless attempted to impose unity on them by simply labeling himself, first an "Art-Catholic" and shortly afterward a "Pre-Raphaelite." The act of labeling is in itself significant, since it is the most facile form of self-definition, and the labels chosen are especially revealing. Both suggest a desire to escape the flux and uncertainty of nineteenth-century skepticism and relativism, to return to the certainties of dogma and the simplicity of an earlier era. Labeling himself did not, of course, solve Rossetti's problems. In the first place, he was never a believing Catholic; in the second, no one ever really understood what the tag "Pre-Raphaelite" meant. In fact, though the three most important members of the Pre-Raphaelite Brotherhood, Rossetti, Holman Hunt, and John Everett Millais, agreed in principle on an aesthetic creed of "truth to nature," they soon found that, without an "Idea of the world" to begin with, neither "truth" nor "nature" were easy terms to com-

[4]*The Letters of Matthew Arnold to Arthur Hugh Clough*, ed. Howard Foster Lowry (London: Oxford University Press, 1932), p. 97.
[5]For an extended discussion of Browning's dramatic monologues as a "diminished" form, see James Richardson's excellent chapter on Browning in *Thomas Hardy: The Poetry of Necessity* (Chicago: University of Chicago Press, 1977).

prehend. In fact, none of the Pre-Raphaelite Brothers ever successfully established an aesthetic platform that the others all felt comfortable on. Nevertheless, the determination with which they tried
to fit their disparate planks into a cohesive structure is informative,
for it demonstrates the general need of Victorian artists to find
some fixed values on which to build their art. What the Pre-
Raphaelites really had in common was not a program for art, but a
desire to find one that could replace the worn-out conventions of
the Royal Academy. Consequently, from 1848 into the 1850s,
their works, especially Rossetti's, reveal a constant experimentation, a continual search for an Idea of art and the artist in a
multitudinous world. The label alone had not solved the problem.

The label "Art-Catholic," as I have suggested, could not be
much help either, though it was largely Art-Catholicism that
Rossetti had contributed to the Pre-Raphaelite endeavor. In some
ways Art-Catholicism seems a natural result of Rossetti's Italian
heritage, his love of Dante and the *stilnovisti*, his poetic apprentice-
ship as a translator of the early Italians. In Art-Catholicism, perhaps, he believed that he had found an original means to express
his love for medievalism, his love of an ideal of woman, and his
mixed inheritance as an Italian Englishman. The difficulty implicit
in Rossetti's Art-Catholicism, however, was that the emphasis fell
too heavily on the Art, to which he was genuinely devoted, and
slighted the Catholicism, in which he seems never to have had any
genuine faith.[6] He could follow Dante and the *stilnovisti* just so far,
but without the faith that inspired and sustained them, his own
work would necessarily remain academic—exercises in galvanizing
a dead art form. The frequent criticism of Rossetti's Art-Catholicism has often been directed at the lyric "My Sister's Sleep," on the
grounds that the religious imagery of the poem is ornamental, not
functional. The criticism does not fairly describe the much revised

[6]This view, however, has been recently challenged by D. M. R. Bentley,
especially in his article, "Rossetti's 'Ave' and Related Pictures," *Victorian Poetry*,
15 (1977), 21–35. But Bentley's argument, based on the apparent "sincerity" of
some of the Art-Catholic works and on Rossetti's exposure to Anglo-Catholicism,
is far from conclusive, and must be countered with William's repeated claims that
his brother never had a real religious faith, and by Rossetti's own lack of interest in
religious issues that did not directly feed his art.

poem that Rossetti published in 1870, but it is not far from the mark concerning the versions of this poem and others written in 1847. These early poems consistently suffer from a disjunction between imagery and belief, not because sincerity is a necessary artistic criterion, but only because a superimposed grid of implausible imagery naturally leads to problems. In the earliest extant version of "My Sister's Sleep," such superimposed imagery does create problems, since the symbolism plainly suggests a religious truth, yet when the speaker attempts to express any kind of religious sentiment, the result is absurdly banal:

> I said, "There is a sleep like death;
>   There also is a death like sleep:
>   Things it is difficult to keep
> Apart when one considereth."[7]

As a reviewer later said of Rossetti, when "he seeks to treat either a purely intellectual or a purely spiritual subject, he fails almost inevitably. . . . Like Antaeus, if he is held off the earth too long his strength fails him."[8]

"Art-Catholicism" invited other problems too. When Rossetti did succeed in establishing a consistent tone of religious fervor and faith, as in "Ave," the poem became a dramatic monologue without drama, or worse, an anachronism. Similarly, in the Marian paintings, effective as they are in various ways, the expression of faith seems quaint rather than impassioned, and the viewer who chooses to take the religious symbolism seriously is relegated to a severe aesthetic distance to contemplate it. David Masson, writing on Pre-Raphaelitism, recognized this danger as early as 1852.

> How shall artists now tell of heaven and hell as emphatically as these old Italians,—now that the earth is not, as they fancied it, an infinitely extended mass of brown mineral matter, with a sulphurous hell

---

[7]The earliest extant version was first published in *The New Monthly Belle Assemblée*, 29 (September 1848), 140–142. For a discussion of this version, see D. M. R. Bentley, "The *Belle Assemblée* Version of 'My Sister's Sleep,'" *Victorian Poetry*, 12 (1974), 321–334.

[8]The remark, by Harry Quilter, is quoted in *Family Letters*, p. 303.

21

somewhere in the chasms beneath, and a heaven of light as close above, as seemed the upper sky with its stars; but a little orb poised in infinite azure, with a serene and unfathomable firmament beneath, and a firmament above as serene, and where equally the telescopes descry nought but new removes of suns and galaxies?[9]

Masson's question nicely defines the problem facing not only Rossetti and the Pre-Raphaelites, but all poets and artists in an enlightened, scientific, and therefore perplexing age. Yeats, much later, was to say that "all symbolic art should arise out of a real belief, and that it cannot do so in this age proves that this age is a road and not a resting place."[10] This conviction, coupled with his admiration of Rossetti, led him to claim elsewhere that Rossetti, "though his dull brother once convinced him he was an agnostic," was a devout Christian.[11] But though his art fooled Yeats, little evidence exists to support the notion of Rossetti's belief. Consequently, Art-Catholicism, plainly, could not come to grips with problems that meant anything to him or to the nineteenth century. Even the most celebrated of his early poems—perhaps the most celebrated of all his poems—seems strangely impersonal and detached. "The Blessed Damozel," especially as it appeared in 1850, before being revised and deepened with the sorrows of personal experience, attempts to describe heaven, though not hell, in the terms of the old Italians. The poem is unquestionably beautiful for its exquisite metrical control, occasionally stunning descriptive imagery, and even for inspiring a kind of sentimental nostalgia for the ages of belief, but its religious sentiment and symbolism can sometimes ring ludicrously false:

> "We two will lie i' the shadow of
> That living mystic tree

[9]David Masson, "Pre-Raphaelitism in Art and Literature," reprinted in James Sambrook, ed., *Pre-Raphaelitism: A Collection of Critical Essays* (Chicago: University of Chicago Press, 1974), p. 82.

[10]W. B. Yeats, "Discoveries," in *Essays and Introductions* (New York: Macmillan, 1968), p. 294.

[11]W. B. Yeats, "The Trembling of the Veil," in *Autobiographies* (New York: Macmillan, 1927), p. 387.

Within whose secret growth the Dove
   Sometimes is felt to be,
While every leaf that His plumes touch
   Saith His name audibly."[12]

Still, as Ronnalie Roper Howard has convincingly shown, Rossetti's ultimate achievement in the poem was far more complex and far more successful than a mere depiction of an aesthetic heaven could be. The poem's real success lies in the intersecting dramatic monologues of the speaker and his envisioned damozel, and its real concern is not with a depiction of the Christian heaven, but with the apparently unbridgeable gulf that separates the heavenly maiden and the earthly lover.[13] Nevertheless, the weakness of the poem, especially in the early versions, is the overemphasis on Art-Catholic detail in the damozel's speech, since such detail, as generations of readers have felt, dominates the poem and distracts attention from its more complex purposes. Unfortunately, Rossetti's Art-Catholic work is never wholly successful, since his lack of real faith is never completely hidden by the superficial imagery. It is an aesthetic problem that he himself later perceived, not in his own work, but in William Bell Scott's tale *Anthony,* which he praised, but with an important qualification: "It is full of the real thing, only seems to be . . . a little lacking in basic faith. One can't help seeing Scotus's *grin* all through Anthony's terror."[14] A still more serious problem with faithless Art-Catholicism becomes evident in the strictures of a genuine Catholic, Newman, against taking the forms of ritual and belief as sufficient in themselves. Without "the one idea of worship," said Newman, "the whole pageant becomes a mummery," and further, without "the lifting up of the heart to God," the forms of belief are as a "body without a soul."[15]

[12]Quoted from *Dante Gabriel Rossetti: The Blessed Damozel: The Unpublished Manuscript, Texts and Collation,* ed. Paull Franklin Baum (Chapel Hill: University of North Carolina Press, 1937), p. 13.

[13]Ronnalie Roper Howard, *The Dark Glass: Vision and Technique in the Poetry of Dante Gabriel Rossetti* (Athens: Ohio University Press, 1972), pp. 40–49.

[14]*Letters of Dante Gabriel Rossetti,* ed. Oswald Doughty and John Robert Wahl, 4 vols. (London: Oxford University Press, 1965–1967), II:663.

[15]Newman, *Discourses on the Scope and Nature of University Education, Addressed to the Catholics of Dublin* (Dublin: James Duffy, 1852), pp. 146–147.

Rossetti's early labels for himself, particularly "Art-Catholic," only isolated certain not altogether successful strains in his art. Both terms, "Art-Catholic" and "Pre-Raphaelite," oversimplify Rossetti's early career by suggesting an exclusive concern with medieval subjects and styles, and with an archaic and unconvincing spiritualism. In fact, his self-definitions have led to comparative neglect of a formative influence at least as important as the early Italians. He was indeed nurtured on medieval Italian literature, but he also reveled from an early age in northern gothic, the "modern gothic" of Meinhold, Chamisso, Maturin, Monk Lewis, and Poe. The original source of most of Rossetti's concerns—and most of his imagery—is this combined stream of genuine southern medievalism and sham northern gothic. William Rossetti's description of his brother's youthful enthusiasms shows that he was drawn to the chaste love poetry of the southern tradition, but perhaps even more to the tales of the supernatural and macabre from the northern. And remarkably, though Rossetti was never able to exploit the spiritual values of medieval Christianity, he was able to find images of soul that corresponded to his own experience and sensibility in the far less revered supernaturalism of gothic tales. He was evidently more comfortable using the versions of the supernatural presented in Chamisso's *Peter Schlemihl* than he was using Dante's Christianity. In fact, though he certainly never accepted gothic supernaturalism as *true,* he did find in it images that corresponded to the truth as he knew it, and that he used from his earliest poetry to his latest.

The influence of gothic tales on Rossetti's imagination, actually, was probably greater than the influence of medieval Christianity, if only because the supernatural machinery did not advance the same claims to be taken seriously, but did provide metaphors for poetry— and handles for coming to grips with various modern dilemmas. In the first place, the gothic tales provided a release from the Catholicism of the early Italians, since the Catholicism they featured was usually mocked—monks were corrupt, monasteries were dens of sadism and masochism, and the church itself was a massive Inquisition. Rossetti could consequently enjoy the archaism of medieval Christianity without concern about extending his faith fully. Gothic tales must have had a twofold attraction for him—he would have enjoyed both the "strong savours" of sensationalism and the moral judgment that gothic supernaturalism, like Christianity, meted out according to a rigid moral scheme.[16] He could vicariously enjoy the debaucheries of gothic antiheroes, and simultaneously appreciate a moral universe governed by a transcendent God. This double appreciation is deeply significant, since it involves a strong impulse to join the devil's camp and an equally strong moral constraint. As Masao Miyoshi has shown, this duality inherent in gothic tales reflects a sense of a "divided self"—a split between soul and body—that increasingly troubled nineteenth-century writers.[17] The ideas that remained with Rossetti from his reading of gothic tales were almost entirely concerned with this problem—from Chamisso's *Peter Schlemihl* he took the image of the shadow as the soul, and the absence of a shadow as the body's division from the soul; from Poe's "William Wilson," Godwin's *Caleb Williams,* and from other stories of *döppelgangers,* he took the image of the double as a chastening or instructing soul; from Walpole's *The Castle of Otranto* and, more especially, from Maturin's *Melmoth the Wanderer,* he took the idea of the living portrait as an image of soul. All these images affected and were transformed by the Romantic poets, especially Byron and Shelley, and were consequently available to Rossetti in subtler forms than the original romances. But though these subtler forms were eventually an important influence on Rossetti, in his early career, he drew his imagery almost directly from the originals—mixing them, of course, with ideas and images from the Italians.

The mixed influence of genuine Italian gothic and the late northern "gothic" on the young Rossetti is immediately evident in the drawings. By 1849 he was working within the chaste, ascetic conventions of early Christian art to produce his first major paintings, *The Girlhood of Mary Virgin* and *Ecce Ancilla Domini!,* but in the years preceding, his sketches were obsessively concerned with the

[16]For William's account of his brother's reading, see *Family Letters,* I:83. William Allingham, describing Rossetti's interests two decades later, states that Rossetti still sought "strong savours, in art, in literature, and in life": *A Diary,* ed. H. Allingham and D. Radford (London: Macmillan, 1907), pp. 162–163.

[17]Masao Miyoshi, *The Divided Self: A Perspective on the Literature of the Victorians* (New York: New York University Press, 1969).

supernatural of gothic romance. Most of his early sketches are illustrations of scenes from literature, usually supernatural literature,
and they very often represent experimental efforts to draw the spirit
world. His characteristically Victorian interest in drawing scenes
from literature began with childish drawings of scenes from Shakespeare. More particularly, his lifelong effort to find ways to represent the supernatural through natural imagery is apparent in such
very early works as a drawing of Macbeth and the "aerial dagger,"
and especially in a series of drawings from *Faust* from 1846 to 1848,
in which he represented the devil—sometimes, in William's words,
as a "human being with a tale."[18] Other drawings from 1846 and
1847 indicate their concerns in their titles: *The Shadowless Man*
(28), *The Sleeper* (after Poe's poem, 29), *Two Female Figures with
Cross and Serpent* (probably an illustration to Meinhold's *Sidonia the
Sorceress*, 22). Perhaps the most interesting of his early sketches are
a series of illustrations to works of Poe, since these clearly show his
experiments with representing the supernatural in natural forms.
His three alternative designs for "The Raven" (Plate 1) intriguingly
anticipate many of Rossetti's later themes. The earliest of these,
dated June 1846, presents a swirl of activity as the supernatural
rudely bursts into the room in the form of leaping, dancing fairies,
an angel, and a skeleton. The composition is neatly fitted into the
classical S recommended by the Royal Academy. The two slightly
later designs, probably executed in 1847, are far more interesting
and far less conventional. Rossetti's peculiarly angular style of
drawing is here becoming apparent and the composition of both is
more characteristically Rossettian, depending on balanced vertical
lines intersected by horizontals to give the odd impression of a
composition based on the balancing of boxes. In one of these a man
rises slowly and incredulously from his seat as a procession of angels
passes solemnly before him. The angels, far more "human" than
the tiny fairies of the previous picture, are not rude and boisterous
but melancholy and seemingly questioning. The third angel in the
procession leans forward and stares intently into the man's eyes.
Rossetti's lifelong concern with the idea of the *döppelganger* is here
clearly set forth, for not only do the female angels look curiously

[18]*Family Letters*, I:67, 99.

Plate 1a. First illustration to "The Raven." Pen and brown ink, 13-⅜ × 9-½. Photograph by A. C. Cooper. Reproduced by permission of Mrs. Katharine Macdonald.

Plate 1b. Second illustration to "The Raven." Pencil, pen with brown and black ink, 8-¾ × 6-⅞. By courtesy of Birmingham Museums and Art Gallery.

Plate 1c. Third illustration to "The Raven." Pen and wash, 9 × 8-½. By courtesy of the Victoria and Albert Museum.

like one another, and like the man, but behind them are two spectral males, who are plainly doubles of the startled man. Poe apparently deserves much of the credit for Rossetti's fascination with doubles, since his next use of them was an illustration of Poe's "Ulalume" (Plate 2). The third of the designs also anticipates Rossetti's later concerns. Again a procession of identical spirits passes by, but now the man, increasingly at home with the supernatural, remains seated. Here the spirits are, strangely, both more spectral and more human—more spectral because more transparent, more human because without the extraterrestrial mechanism of wings. In the background, just above the procession of spirits, is a portrait of the girl who now appears in multiplied spirit form. These images—the portrait and the multiple specters of the beloved—were to be central to Rossetti's art for the rest of his life.

In Rossetti's early drawings, the impulses of the Art-Catholic and of the neogothicist are usually kept separate, though some of his illustrations to *Faust* enabled him to sketch the architecture of a gothic cathedral, and though he was developing an archaic or "early Christian" style. In his drawing for "Ulalume" however, the two influences merge to create a picture that is quintessentially Rossettian. In the center of the picture stands a young man, the speaker of the poem, staring off to the left, past "an alley Titanic / Of Cypress." At his feet kneels Psyche, his soul, "letting sink her / Wings until they trailed in the dust," and to the right stands his double, staring through the alley of cypress, and the double of his psyche. The winged angels of early Christian art are—with the help of Poe's poem—transformed from messengers of God to almost secular manifestations of the soul. They become external images of interiority. The use of doubles is still more interesting, since there is no precedent for them in Poe's poem, and since it is unclear what Rossetti meant by them. Most likely the *döppelganger* is meant to represent the speaker at a different point in the poem, since the standing Psyche at the right illustrates the first four stanzas of the poem, whereas the central, kneeling Psyche represents the last four. If so, the picture is an early example of Rossetti's efforts to overcome the limitations of his medium, which Lessing had said was incapable of expressing movement in time. The representation, moreover, anticipates Rossetti's later characterizations of past

Plate 2. "Ulalume." Pen and brown and black ink, 8-⅛ × 7-¾. By courtesy of Birmingham Museums and Art Gallery.

selves in memory, hovering near the present as gloomy wraiths. On the other hand, the double may well represent another image of the soul, as it does in a later, much more famous picture, *How They Met Themselves* (118). In this case, Rossetti is having the supernatural both ways, using the Christian imagery of angels, and the gothic of doubles—a somewhat confused mixture that became clearer, though more complex, as he secularized his Christian imagery in later works. In *How They Met Themselves*, the female figures have lost their wings, and have become the representations of the soul not as Psyche, but as the beloved, the Epipsyche.[19]

The subject of *Ulalume*, from Poe, is plainly a gothic tale, yet the winged angels suggest the other tradition, as does their startling anticipation of the features of the Virgin in *The Girlhood of Mary Virgin* and *Ecce Ancilla Domini!*. This anticipation also suggests, of course, that the style of drawing has now become completely Rossetti's own, from the angular features to the poses of the characters. The male, in fact, closely resembles several much later males—most conspicuously the *döppelgangers* in *How They Met Themselves* and two drawings of Hamlet with Ophelia (152, 189). But then, these resemblances, too, may be more than a matter of stylistic consistency, since the doubles of *Ulalume* and *How They Met Themselves*, and Hamlet, all suggest the same thematic concern with the divided self, the irreconcilability of soul and body. By 1847, however, such concerns were not yet entirely clear to Rossetti, though the images to deal with them were already impressed on his consciousness.

The convergence of southern and northern traditions in Rossetti's early work is more easily seen in his writing than in his graphic art. "On Mary's Portrait, Which I Painted Six Years Ago," written in 1847, shows not only the influence of the early Italian Jacopo da Lentino, but also that of Maturin and Chamisso, and the very modern influence of Browning. The poem, which was later drastically recast as "The Portrait," is the dramatic monologue of a

[19]The word "epipsyche" has no official sanction—it is not in the *OED*—but has become a critical commonplace, especially among Shelleyans, to denote the object of the mind's or soul's quest for its own highest ideal of beauty and good. See, for example, Carlos Baker's use of the term throughout his *Shelley's Major Poetry: The Fabric of a Vision* (Princeton: Princeton University Press, 1948).

painter musing upon his portrait of his beloved, who has since died, and thinking back to the day on which he painted it. Formally, at least, the strongest influence is plainly Browning's "My Last Duchess," as the occasional casual tone and the implied auditor make clear:

> Your pardon,—I have wearied you;
> To you these things are cold and dead
> But I look round and see nought else
> Alive.[20]

And the subject, too, a description of a miraculously lifelike portrait, also reveals a debt to Browning. But Rossetti was also familiar with the conceit from his efforts as a translator, particularly from Lentino's "Canzonetta: Of His Lady, and of Her Portrait." In both poems the speaker, inspired by his love and desire to paint a portrait of his beloved, has executed one that was miraculously lifelike, and has found that, even so, the portrait cannot replace its absent subject. The debt, moreover, is partially affirmed by a slight verbal parallel, since Rossetti's line, "Gaze hard, and she shall seem to stir," seems a likely recollection of his own translation of Lentino's lines, "I gaze, till I am sure / That I behold thee move" (*Works*, 440). Rossetti's debt in this poem to the Italian poets goes beyond his particular debt to Lentino. The "mystic courts" of the speaker's reverie strongly recall many mystic groves of the *stilnovisti,* and lines alluding to the sitter's namesake are pure Art-Catholicism:

> So, along some grass-bank in Heaven,
> Mary the Virgin, going by,
> Seeth her servant Rafaël
> Laid in warm silence happily.

But gothic supernaturalism is at least as evident, and considerably more convincing in the poem. The whole idea of a mysterious,

---

[20]Quotations from this poem are from the 1847 version, printed in *Dante Gabriel Rossetti: An Analytical List of Manuscripts in the Duke University Library, with Hitherto Unpublished Verse and Prose,* ed. Paull Franklin Baum (Durham: Duke University Press, 1931), pp. 67–71.

almost living, portrait recalls a tradition that begins in Walpole's
The Castle of Otranto and gathers strength in Maturin's *Melmoth the
Wanderer*, and beyond this the tone of much of the poem suggests
the naive surprise of the gothic narrator, not the reverential awe of
neoplatonic lovers:

> It seems to me unnatural
> > And a thing much to wonder on,
> As though mine image in the glass
> > Should tarry when myself am gone.
> While her mere semblance (I would say)
> Has for its room, from May to May,
> > The open sunwarm library
> > Where her friends read and think, is she
> In the dark always, choked with clay?

The emphasis is on unnaturalness, not spiritual awe, and the
strange image of lines three and four suggests both the gothic concern with doubles, and the dilemma of Peter Schlemihl, who could
walk away from his shadow. Even the revulsion of the last lines
suggests eighteenth-century, not medieval, inspiration. The point
is that the two traditions are being forced, with some success, to
work together. The poem does communicate the loving reverence,
the spiritual adoration, of the *dolce stil nuova,* but at the same time
it expresses a far more secularized sense of the uncanny, superstition
rather than religion. The partial fusion of the traditions again results in some confusion of purpose (the Marian allusions, for example, are hard to make sense of) and an impression of facile image-
mongering, but it also results in a poem that, despite its faults, does
successfully evoke both a sense of reverence and the counterbalanc-
ing sense of uneasiness. The balance of bloodlessly "aesthetic" Art-
Catholicism and sensationalistic gothic was necessarily precarious—even its successes, as in this case, show signs of strain.

Gradually, Rossetti was beginning to distill a personal style and
voice from the multitudinous mass of literary and artistic precedents
and from his own mixed ethnic heritage, but despite his uneasy
balancing of traditions, he remained uncertain about his artistic
direction and purpose. For this reason, in both his writing and his

painting, his best works of the late 1840s and early 1850s are all attempts to explore or expound the relation of the artist to his art, to nature, to society. The prose tales "Hand and Soul" and "Saint Agnes of Intercession" and the linked sonnets "Old and New Art" were all, directly or indirectly, aesthetic manifestos, and his famous early paintings *The Girlhood of Mary Virgin* (Plate 3) and *Ecce Ancilla Domini!* (Plate 4) subtly examine and pronounce upon his aesthetic perplexities. Rossetti reportedly referred to the most ambitious of his programmatic statements, "Hand and Soul," as an "artistic *confessio fidei*,"[21] but as a confession of artistic faith it raises more questions than it answers. "Hand and Soul" is the story, narrated by a contemporary lover of art, of a fictional Pisan painter of the thirteenth century, Chiaro dell'Erma, who, after achieving great success and renown while painting "for the race of fame" (*Works*, 551), decides that his art must serve God, and devotes himself to the production of labored, uninspired religious allegories. He realizes that he has failed in this aim when, following a "great feast in Pisa, for holy matters," the two principal families of Pisa emerge from mass through an entry decorated by a "moral allegory of peace" painted by Chiaro. As Chiaro watches from his studio, a fight breaks out in which "there was so much blood cast up the walls on a sudden, that it ran in long streams down Chiaro's painting" (*Works*, 552). The painter, understandably, despairs, but a vision of a woman, the image of his own soul, appears to him, telling him that he should not take it upon himself to interpret God to man, for "God is no morbid exactor" (*Works*, 554), but should serve God by painting what it is in his heart to paint. He should paint his own soul, as she herself commands: "Chiaro, servant of God, take now thine Art unto thee, and paint me thus, as I am, to know me: weak, as I am, and in the weeds of this time; only with eyes which seek out labour, and with a faith, not learned, yet jealous of prayer. Do this; so shall thy soul stand before thee always, and perplex thee no more" (*Works*, 555).

The tale, both in its setting and its archaic diction, clearly owes much to Rossetti's Art-Catholicism, his love of medieval Italian

[21]William Sharp, *Dante Gabriel Rossetti: A Record and a Study* (London: Macmillan, 1882), p. 297.

35

poetry and painting—his inspiration, in fact, is evident in the epigraph, a quotation from Bonaggiunta Urbiciani:

> Rivolsimi in quel lato
> Là onde venìa la voce,
> E parvemi una luce
> Che lucea quanto stella:
> La mia mente era quella.
> [*Works*, 545]

Rossetti's rather free translation renders these lines:

> I turn to where I heard
> That whisper in the night;
> And there a breath of light
> Shines like a silver star.
> The same is mine own soul.
> [*Works*, 456]

The translation of "mia mente" as "mine own soul" is significant, of course, for much of the point of "Hand and Soul" is that the artist must look not upon his mind, but his heart, to find the soul ("not thy mind's conscience, but thine heart's" [*Works*, 553]). The inspiration was indeed from the early Italians, but only as Rossetti misunderstood them, replacing intellect with emotion, and conceiving the soul not in a rigorous religious sense, but only as the "heart's conscience."

Though the tale is filled with the worship of God, it is, like "On Mary's Portrait," more unsettlingly uncanny than worshipful. The appearance of the soul itself as a physical presence owes much to, say, Dante's personifications of Love, but it has an added strangeness, perhaps because the vision is explicitly subjective and personal—not a mythical being, but his very self: "he knew her hair to be the golden veil through which he beheld his dreams" (*Works*, 553). She is, moreover, in some mysterious way both within and without:

As the woman stood, her speech was with Chiaro: not, as it were, from her mouth or in his ears; but distinctly between them.

36

"I am an image, Chiaro, of thine own soul within thee. See me, and know me as I am." [*Works*, 553]

Adding to the uncanniness is the narrator's description of the portrait as he saw it in 1847, and of his reaction: "the most absorbing wonder of it was its literality. You knew that figure, when painted, had been seen; yet it was not a thing to be seen of men" (*Works*, 555). To emphasize that the story is not one of religious awe so much as of gothic mystery, Rossetti provides the obviously inadequate response of an excessively rational French student, and forces the reader to disagree with it:

"Je dis, mon cher, que c'est une spécialité dont je me fiche pas mal. Je tiens que quand on ne comprend pas une chose, c'est qu'elle ne signifie rien."

My reader thinks possibly that the French student was right.

[*Works*, 556][22]

Forcing the reader to admit that he cannot understand the extremely significant mystery accomplishes two things—it moves the tale squarely into the realm of gothic, and more important, it exempts Rossetti from the need to understand the full implications of the tale or, at least, from the need to express a belief in anything in particular beyond a kind of vague supernaturalism.

In some senses "Hand and Soul" surely was an "artistic *confessio fidei*." The injunction to paint one's own soul is a demand for a subjective, Romantic art that Rossetti clearly believed in. Further, the tale was written after the Pre-Raphaelite Brotherhood had been formed and its members had committed themselves to the rigorous honesty of medieval art, and after Brown had, in all likelihood, shown Rossetti the merits of the Nazarenes and their early Christian art. Also, the tale was written—apparently in one night—for inclusion in *The Germ*, a journal designed to promote the Pre-Raphaelite *confessio fidei*. And of course, even before the Brotherhood had formed, Rossetti had been trying in various ways to paint

[22]"I say, my Friend, that that's a specialty I couldn't care less about. I hold that when you can't understand something, it's because it doesn't mean anything."

the soul, though not necessarily his own. But two important points must be made about Rossetti's assertion that the story was a manifesto of his artistic principles. First, he made the claim many years later, when he was trying to paint his own soul in portraits of women, and second, if "Hand and Soul" is an artistic *confessio fidei*, it is a very uncertain one.[23]

It is even difficult to tell whether the tale is an affirmation or a rejection of Art-Catholicism. Some of Rossetti's own works, like Chiaro's, might be regarded as allegories of the head, rather than the passionate expressions of the heart, and some of his other works at this time, especially his sonnets for pictures, make it clear that he was opposed to intellectual allegory. In that case, however, his manifesto seems to subvert itself, both because it is Art-Catholic in some respects, and because it is certainly abstractly cerebral. In addition, the tale can hardly be seen as a palinode if only because Rossetti's immediately succeeding works showed no apparent change in artistic direction. On the other hand, if the tale was meant as an affirmation of Art-Catholicism, Rossetti must not have fully perceived how allegorical his Art-Catholic works were, or he must have been trying to convince himself that his use of the archaic symbolism of an alien religion sprang from his heart.

In general, "Hand and Soul" seems not so much a statement of artistic principles as a search for artistic purpose. Rossetti was still groping for his own theme and style, and the idea of painting his own soul, though perhaps a good enough idea, was far too vague to be very useful. *How* should he paint his own soul, if it would not, like Chiaro's, present itself for a sitting? Besides, his *confessio fidei* was at cross-purposes with itself. Painting his own soul would involve honest introspection, a close examination of what he truly believed in, yet if he closely examined the Christian trappings of this tale—which made the soul's appearance plausible—would he in fact believe in them? Chiaro could not paint well with only an intellectual faith, but he needed faith of some kind to paint at all, yet Rossetti did not have the Christian faith that sustained Chiaro. Rossetti's dilemma, then, was that his inspiration in early Italian

---

[23] Joan Rees points out (p. 40) that the vision of the soul is most notable, despite its confusing implications, for its suggestion of "the earnestness with which the young author was facing questions about his role as artist."

poetry and painting was hardly introspective and, far from being centered in faith, involved a disjunction between faith and artistic impulse.

Though Rossetti evidently believed that "Hand and Soul" was the most important artistic manifesto for himself and, presumably, for Pre-Raphaelitism, his brother William reserved that honor for the three sonnets of "Old and New Art." "This trio of sonnets," he said, "forms a manifesto—perhaps the best manifesto that it ever received in writing—of the Praeraphaelite movement" (*Works*, 656). Like "Hand and Soul," however, the sonnets really reflect only Rossetti's concerns, and they reflect his uncertainty, his desire for a manifesto, rather than constitute an explicit statement of an artistic creed. The second and third sonnets, written in 1848, are explicitly about the modern artist's difficulty in finding his true path. Number II, "Not as These," is a rebuke to the young poets and painters who contemptuously deny kinship with their mediocre contemporaries, and an injunction in the sestet, to look to their own artistic futures with the ambition to rival the luminaries of the recent past:

> Unto the lights of the great Past, new-lit
> Fair for the Future's track, look thou instead,—
> Say thou instead, "I am not as *these* are."
> > > [*Poems*, 231]

The sonnet presents not an artistic creed, but an artistic challenge; it does not clear a path, "the Future's track," but, in fact, in its implicit assumption that modern artists are not moving forward, and in its strange advice to look to the future by looking at the past, it emphasizes—accidentally, I think—the artist's dilemma. The third sonnet, "The Husbandmen," similarly enjoins young artists to get to work, while simultaneously emphasizing the problems that beset them. The sonnet alludes to the parable of the vineyard to make its forceful point:

> Stand not ye idle in the market-place.
> Which of ye knoweth *he* is not that last
> Who may be first by faith and will?
> > > [*Poems*, 232]

The advice is characteristically Victorian—the advice of Carlyle and later of George Eliot and a host of others to do the work that lies closest to hand. But again, the advice underscores the problem, for the poem strongly implies that the previous toilers in the vineyard have left so little to do that the latecomers cannot find their labor. In artistic terms, the poem implies that the "lights of the great Past" shine so brightly that the modern artist can but hold his feeble candle in sunshine. Or, to change metaphors again, the past has become not a guide but a burden.

Of the "Old and New Art" sonnets, only "St. Luke the Painter" (printed as Number I, though actually written last, in 1849) makes any very clear statement about art. And even here the injunction to work grows out of a sense of the extreme difficulty of doing so:

> Give honour unto Luke Evangelist;
>   It was this Luke (the aged legends say)
>   Who first taught Art to fold her hands and pray.
> Scarcely at once she dared to rend the mist
> Of devious symbols: but soon having wist
>   How sky-breadth and field-silence and this day
>   Are symbols also in a deeper way,
> She looked through these to God and was God's priest.
>
> And if, past noon, her toil began to irk,
>   And she sought nostrums, and had turned in vain
>   To soulless self-reflections of man's skill,—
>   Yet now, in this the twilight, she might still
>   Kneel in the latter grass to pray again,
> Ere the night cometh and she may not work.[24]

The closing line alludes to John 9:4, but more significantly it parallels the closing line of Carlyle's "The Everlasting Yea": "Work while it is called Today, for the Night cometh, wherein no man can work." Once again, the evident need for such encouragement is

---

[24]Since the poem was not published until over twenty years after it was written, I quote from the earliest known manuscript, which is in the Fitzwilliam Museum, Cambridge University. The published version differs only slightly, but significantly, in its use of the more uncertain phrase "some deeper way" in place of "a deeper way."

perhaps more important than the encouragement itself. The burden of the past and the old age of the world again make themselves felt, and again the poet's counsel is difficult to follow. The advice is fine for a Christian, but the one thing a skeptical Art-Catholic cannot do is "Kneel in the latter grass to pray again." Rossetti desperately wanted to put soul back into art, but as long as he devoted himself to Christian art, he was forced to content himself with the forms without worship, the body without the soul. The octave of "St. Luke the Painter," however, does offer some useful advice, and a partial way out of the dilemma. The painter—the artist in any medium—need not devote himself to devious symbols, the intellectual allegory that had distracted Chiaro dell'Erma, but should serve God by serving and honoring his creation. The painter cannot paint what he cannot see, but he can regard the material world as the apparent symbol of the spiritual. Even the skeptic can perceive "sky-breadth and field-silence and this day" as "symbols also in a deeper way," and such a symbolist art will be, for him, far more meaningful than the "devious symbols" and allegorical counters of a religion he does not believe in. Still, the poem's insistence on prayer and on seeing through natural symbols to God plainly indicates that Rossetti was not yet willing to abandon his Art-Catholicism, to unmoor his symbols and let them drift to more personal, more subjective, bearings.

The program for art expressed in "St. Luke the Painter" was precisely carried out in *The Girlhood of Mary Virgin* and *Ecce Ancilla Domini!* Both paintings combine "devious symbols" with natural symbols in a way that Yeats was later to admire: "I quoted the lily in the hand of the angel in Rossetti's *Annunciation,* and the lily in the jar in his *Girlhood of Mary Virgin,* and thought they made the more important symbols, the women's bodies, and the angels' bodies, and the clear morning light, take that place, in the great procession of Christian symbols, where they can alone have all their meaning and all their beauty."[25] Yeats is surely right, since the traditional Christian symbols in the paintings, though far more deviously complex than Yeats suggests, are plainly subordinate to the "more important" natural symbols. *The Girlhood of Mary Virgin* is simply

[25]Yeats, "Symbolism in Painting," in *Essays and Introductions,* p. 147.

41

crammed with Christian *figurae*, but its success as a painting is far less dependent on these than on the strangely affecting portraits of Rossetti's mother and sister as Saint Anne and the Virgin. Yet these portraits would surely not be so affecting without the "devious symbols," less complementary than contrasting, that place the flesh and blood of the women in an awesome spiritual context. Rossetti wrote two sonnets to accompany the painting, one of which epitomizes its devious symbolism, and the other, first written, its psychological tenor. The first sonnet describes not the painting, but only its subject:[26]

> 'This is that blessed Mary, pre-elect
> God's Virgin. Gone is a great while, and she
> Was young in Nazareth of Galilee.
> Her kin she cherished with devout respect:
> Her gifts were simpleness of intellect
> And supreme patience. From her mother's knee
> Faithful and hopeful; wise in charity;
> Strong in grave peace; in duty circumspect.
>
> So held she through her girlhood; as it were
> An angel-watered lily, that near God
> Grows, and is quiet. Till one dawn, at home,
> She woke in her white bed, and had no fear
> At all,—yet wept till sunshine, and felt awed;
> Because the fulness of the time was come.'

The sonnet, like the picture and like the image of Mary that both project, is profoundly simple in diction and in theme. It describes, with naïve awe, the wonder of an ordinary woman suddenly made part of a divine plan. The closing lines, especially, express beautifully the awesome meeting of the temporal and the eternal, the human and the divine, not with devious symbols but with the touchingly natural image of Mary's weeping. The second sonnet

---

[26]The sonnets were later much revised, but I quote from the early versions, printed by Virginia Surtees in *Dante Gabriel Rossetti 1828–1882, The Paintings and Drawings: A Catalogue Raisonné*, 2 vols. (London: Oxford University Press, 1971), I:10.

written for the picture, however, reveals that Rossetti was still drawn to more devious symbols:

> 'These are the symbols. On that cloth of red
> I' the centre is the Tripoint: perfect each,
> Except the second of its points, to teach
> That Christ is not yet born. The books—whose head
> Is golden Charity, as Paul hath said—
> Those virtues are wherein the soul is rich:
> Therefore on them the lily standeth, which
> Is Innocence, being interpreted.
>
> The seven-thorn'd briar and the palm seven-leaved
> Are her great sorrow and her great reward.
> Until the end be full, the Holy One
> Abides without. She soon shall have achieved
> Her perfect purity: yea, God the Lord
> Shall soon vouchsafe His Son to be her Son.'

The two sonnets contrast sharply, as is evident even in the two openings, "This is that blessed Mary" and "These are the symbols." Read together, the sonnets, like the painting, establish a perilously balanced juxtaposition of two orders of reality and of two ways of perceiving reality. The result is, I think, undeniably effective in *The Girlhood of Mary Virgin* and its accompanying sonnets, and also in *Ecce Ancilla Domini!*, but for various reasons it is a difficult aesthetic mode to sustain. In the first place the balance *is* precarious— the two pictures, especially *The Girlhood*, come extremely close to being weighed down by the devious symbols. Also, the use of Christian typology, though it does add a temporal dimension to a spatial art form, creates problems for an artist lacking in basic faith. Rossetti could, through typological symbols, recapitulate theological tradition, but such sciolism was misdirected if his real concern was with the girl, the young Mary, and the human emotions of awe, worship, and acceptance. The symbols succeeded, as Yeats said, in placing the "more important symbols" within the rich Christian tradition, but Rossetti, enamored of such easy symbolism, needed to beware of making it an end in itself. Finally, and most important, if Rossetti were truly interested in expressing and exploring

43

Christian doctrine, he might have continued exclusively in this mode (he did, in fact, continue to paint figurally rich Marian pictures for the next eight years, but they were neither his most ambitious nor his most frequent paintings),[27] but if he had a personal, non-Christian theme to express, he could not usefully go on placing everything in the Christian tradition.

Rossetti's artistic efforts after 1850, of course, indicate that he was still looking for a personal theme, but his continuing search is evident even in the Marian pictures, which have impressed many viewers as experiments in form rather than devout expressions of faith. Timothy Hilton, noting such problems as the lack of perspective, has observed that "stylistically, *The Girlhood of Mary Virgin* is composed with a kind of simple-minded originality, in which it is difficult to distinguish the parts played by calculation and by sheer lack of ability."[28] Even though the painting, somehow, works, it does give the impression of having been designed to make it easier for a novice to execute. The structural pattern consists of intersecting vertical and horizontal lines that divide the canvas into a balanced pattern of boxes—almost as though the design were being transferred on graph paper. The lack of perspective also helps—even in such simple matters as enabling Rossetti to draw nearly parallel lines for the floorboards. But most significant, the Christian symbolism, however effective it admittedly is, was also a convenient way to make sure the painting "meant" something. The stunning originality of the picture, whatever else it does, also caters

---

[27]See Bentley, "Rossetti's 'Ave' and Related Pictures." For a discussion of Rossetti's typological symbolism, see also George P. Landow, " 'Life touching lips with immortality': Rossetti's Typological Structures," *Studies in Romanticism*, 17 (1978), 247–265, his *William Holman Hunt and Typological Symbolism* (New Haven: Yale University Press, 1979), pp. 148–161, and Herbert L. Sussman's *Fact into Figure: Typology in Carlyle, Ruskin, and the Pre-Raphaelite Brotherhood* (Columbus: Ohio State University Press, 1979), pp. 115–136.

[28]Timothy Hilton, *The Pre-Raphaelites* (New York: Oxford University Press, 1970), p. 40. According to Holman Hunt, Rossetti himself defended the errors in perspective in *The Girlhood of Mary Virgin*, and attempts at correction seemed only to reinforce his distaste for science: "In general terms he denounced the science, and objected strongly to each result of its application, declaring that what it proved to be wrong was obviously better": *Pre-Raphaelitism and the Pre-Raphaelite Brotherhood*, 2 vols. (New York: Macmillan, 1905), I:118.

Plate 3. The Girlhood of Mary Virgin. Oil, 32-¾ × 25-¾. By courtesy of The Tate Gallery, London.

to Rossetti's technical inabilities and contributes to the impression that the painting was experimental in both form and meaning.

The experimental nature of the design is related, as Martin Meisel has pointed out, to the fundamental issue of the Pre-Raphaelite program for art—the relation of art to nature. Rossetti was determined to paint this and subsequent pictures from nature, with absolute fidelity, and so he sought out real ivy, a real lily, and a series of real, fidgety children to represent the angel, and yet the picture can hardly be said to show the iconography of the natural world—the real boy does, after all, have wings. Still, as Meisel has said, the difficulty of the Pre-Raphaelite aesthetic, which insisted on absolute mimesis, was that as long as the artist's goal was to represent nature exactly, art must necessarily fall short of nature—nature could do it better. In *The Girlhood*, Meisel notes, Mary is engaged in a work of mimetic art, embroidering a lily from nature, but the natural lily is far more impressive than the artistic one.[29] Similarly, as I have noted, the iconographic details in the picture, the devious symbols, lack the life and expressiveness of the "natural" images. Rossetti never believed that absolute fidelity to nature could, by itself, point to the spiritual, but he was plainly uneasy with traditional symbolism alone. *Ecce Ancilla Domini!* makes the uneasiness still more apparent, for here the iconographic art of the Virgin, folded and thrust to the side, is pointedly transcended by the *spiritual* reality of the *natural* lily held by the angel. The angel's lily, Meisel points out, is more schematized, more perfect, than the natural lily of the previous picture, and more natural than the schematized lily of Mary's embroidery. The lily now has a "*primary symbolic character*" as a "*spiritual reality*": "a scepter and wand, with the third bloom of their trinity appropriately still in bud."[30] Rossetti has, in this picture, evidently found the compromise between the devious symbolism and the naturalism that had been uneasily yoked together in *The Girlhood of Mary Virgin*.

What is more, the paintings are both concerned with the anxiety

[29]Martin Meisel, "'Half Sick of Shadows': The Aesthetic Dialogue in Pre-Raphaelite Painting," in *Nature and the Victorian Imagination*, ed. U. C. Knoepflmacher and G. B. Tennyson (Los Angeles: University of California Press, 1977), pp. 314–315.
[30]Ibid., p. 317.

of the aspiring artist. That the assumed superiority of nature to art could be a problem for the ambitious artist is well illustrated by the artistic career of Ruskin, who had done so much to promote the notion. Believing, as he did, that the trees of the forest were more beautiful "than Gothic tracery, more than Greek vase-imagery, more than the daintiest embroiderers of the East could embroider, or the artfullest painters of the West could limn,"[31] Ruskin, not surprisingly, never fully exploited his great artistic gifts. Rossetti's concerns in the Marian pictures with the relation of art to nature represent, in part, an attempt to come to terms with the Ruskinian position without sacrificing ambition. Further, the anxiety is not only that art cannot compete with nature, but still more emphatically that it cannot, as an alternative, represent things spiritual. Meisel's most brilliant insight is, I think, into the anxiety of the young artist still seeking his proper path. He points out that in *The Girlhood*, Saint Anne is in the same relation to the Virgin as Holman Hunt was in to Rossetti, that of artistic mentor, but in *Ecce Ancilla Domini!* the angel, fortuitously but relevantly named Gabriel, "is not a mentor to the artist of the lilies, but an agent of revelation." With this in mind, the emotional center of the painting, the Virgin's expression, takes on added significance:

> There is nothing fortuitous . . . in the dual focus of the Virgin's look—on the spiritual lily, and deep within—and in the psychological *contraposto* between the look and the body, shrinking against the wall. The artist's anxiety over himself and his art is in that pathos. It is to feel the doubtful power of the material—mere flesh and blood and mere cloth and color—to sustain and ultimately contain the revelation of the Spirit. Art that is the mirror of Nature has been diminished and seemingly transcended; but Art that is the counterpart image of a subjective reality has a terror that even in the moment of promise threatens any hope of achievement.[32]

Had Rossetti fully believed in Christianity, "subjective reality" would have presented no problems—faith would present an "objec-

---

[31]*Praeterita*, in *The Complete Works of John Ruskin*, ed. E. T. Cook and Alexander Wedderburn, 39 vols. (London: George Allen, 1903–1912), 38:315.
[32]Meisel, p. 317.

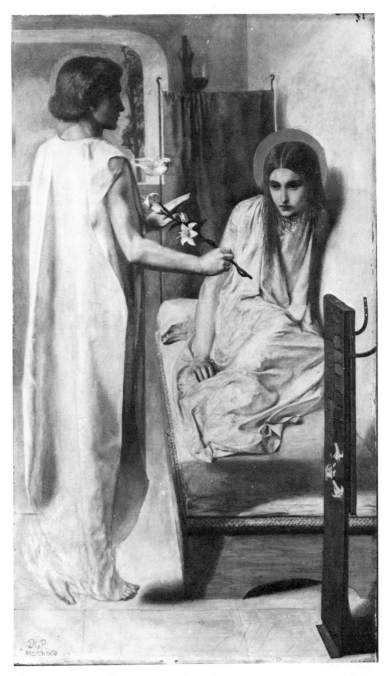

Plate 4. Ecce Ancilla Domini! Oil, 28-⅝ × 16-½. By courtesy of The Tate Gallery, London.

tive" reality for which iconographic symbolism would have been fully sufficient. But what symbolism, what art, could express the not fully apprehended realities of his own subjective vision?

Rossetti's aesthetic dilemma is apparent in the curious, unfinished tale "Saint Agnes of Intercession," written in 1850. It is the story of an aspiring painter who includes a portrait of his beloved in a painting that he hopes will establish his fame. The painting is in accord with Pre-Raphaelite doctrine (though not usually Rossetti's) in its modernity, and it is particularly in accord with Rossetti's aesthetic belief that the artist must paint his soul: "The subject was a modern one, and indeed it has often seemed to me that all work, to be truly worthy, should be wrought out of the age itself, as well as out of the soul of its producer, which must needs be a soul of the age" (*Works*, 558). The artist, he says elsewhere in the tale, submits "his naked soul" (*Works*, 559) to other men. But the naked soul he presents is, in this case, recognized by a critic as similar to a little-known painting by a Florentine artist of the fifteenth century, named Angiolieri. Upon investigating, the artist discovers that the Florentine painting, an engraving of which had enthralled him as a child, represented the exact likeness of his beloved, and more, that Angiolieri's self-portrait represented an exact likeness of himself. Further, the Florentine's beloved had died young, leaving him to mourn, and the story breaks off with the strong implication that the modern artist is about to find his own beloved dead or dying.

The implications of "Saint Agnes of Intercession" are extraordinarily complex. First, and most simply, the tale expresses the anxiety of the artist who labors to express himself, to expose his own soul, only to discover that he has been anticipated, that his work is not as original, that he is not as fully individualized as he had hoped. If even his own soul is not original, then truly there is nothing new under the sun: the burden of the past becomes unbearable. But beyond this, the tale suggests that in expressing the soul the artist endangers it—the beloved, analogous to the soul itself in "Hand and Soul," sits for the portrait that expresses the artist's soul, and dies. The suggestion that the artist preys upon himself was not new—Coleridge had suggested the idea in "Dejection: An Ode":

49

> . . . to be still and patient, all I can;
> And haply by abstruse research to steal
> From my own nature all the natural man—
> This was my sole resource, my only plan:
> Till that which suits a part infects the whole,
> And now is almost grown the habit of my soul.

The danger to the Romantic artist who produces art from his own soul is that he may rob from himself to provide for his art. The fear expressed by Rossetti in "Saint Agnes of Intercession" lies in the tradition from Wordsworth, who turned his childhood into a work of art, to Wilde, who turned his whole life into a work of art, and whose Dorian Gray gave his soul over to be a portrait. The same fear is implicit, though far less self-consciously, in "Sister Helen," probably written at some point in 1851 or 1852. Sister Helen, having been betrayed by her lover, makes a waxen doll in his image and kills him by melting it. The work of art, the waxen man, is inspired by strong emotions—"Hate, born of love," in this case— and is again an image of the soul. In fact, "Sister Helen," much influenced by the old ballad tradition, provides a reminder that neogothic imagery has its origins in folk beliefs and primitive magic. As Frazer made clear throughout *The Golden Bough*, the belief that a manufactured image of a man (like his shadow, reflection, or double) might correspond closely to his soul is all but universal in primitive and folk cultures. The artistic impulse is, again, destructive, since it is a desire to substitute a controllable artifact for life itself, to rob from life to supply the needs of art and, most obviously, to escape from the vicissitudes of life by replacing it with art. Also, as in "Saint Agnes," the poem suggests a complex relation between love and art, since both the lover and the artist seek complete control, even at the expense of exposing and endangering the soul.

The main inspiration for "Saint Agnes of Intercession" was Poe, both for the style of the narration and for the themes. In fact, the closest analogues to the tale are Rossetti's pictures *Ulalume* and *How They Met Themselves*, for in all of these the artist's quest for his own soul results in the discovery of a quartet. First he finds for his soul a female *anima*, a beloved woman who is his epipsyche. These two, the artist and his epipsyche, then expand to four as they encounter their *döppelgangers.* All of this is certainly more suggestive than definitive, and one would be hard pressed to say precisely what it means. Nevertheless, the multiplication of selves and souls produces an eerie sense of the uncanny and, in artistic terms, a distressing sense of a lack of an artistic center, since the self is spread out over four selves, and at the same time, a distressing sense that escape from the self is impossible. Rossetti, of course, was exploiting gothic traditions, not expressing a metaphysical belief, but at some level this repeated theme must have suggested to him the profound difficulty of the introspective artist, who is presented with no definitive point of view but with the multiple perspectives of his various hopes and fears.

Finally, "Saint Agnes of Intercession," though it announces no aesthetic program, does reveal the increasingly narrow and assured path of Rossetti's art. The young artist's portrait of his own soul echoes the concern of "On Mary's Portrait," of "Hand and Soul," and to a very considerable extent, of the Marian pictures, in which the figure of Mary is in some respects a surrogate for the artist. Over the next several years Rossetti's paintings and drawings repeatedly reveal the same motif. A series of pictures represent Dante looking upon either a living or a dead Beatrice, his epipsyche, and more significant, Dante drawing an angel—an act clearly analogous to Chiaro painting his soul. Most significant of all, Rossetti repeatedly, compulsively, drew sketches of his own beloved, Elizabeth Siddal.

Though much experimentation lay ahead, Rossetti's complex but, by 1851, fairly consistent symbolism anticipated the direction his art would take. First, Art-Catholicism was certainly dead. Rossetti would paint many more pictures on religious themes, would even improve on his typological symbolism, but Christianity was no longer at the center of his art. Second, the supernaturalism of the gothic tradition, the weird tales of doubles and living portraits, was germinating in his mind to produce a subtle symbolism for exploring his most personal concerns as an artist. Rossetti's artistic development over the years is fascinating in the way it shows the dilemma of any mid-nineteenth-century artist who seeks spiritual values for his art, but cannot find them in the traditional source, Christianity. His Art-Catholicism shows the temptation, which became increasingly powerful toward the end of the century, to embrace Christianity, particularly Catholicism, for the sake of its aesthetic tradition, and his growth beyond Art-Catholicism illustrates the inadequacy of adopting a set of beliefs for the sake of a ready-made symbolism and a set of associations. His obsession with more secular symbols for spiritual values reveals the dilemma of the skeptical artist who still seeks some meaning beyond material appearances, and the particular symbols he relies upon—portraits, doubles, epipsyches—suggest both the increasingly necessary inward gaze of the artist, and the need to find images capable of externalizing inner states. In short, Rossetti's early career epitomizes the transition of art from faith to skepticism as it illustrates the groping of the young artist toward a modern, symbolist art adapted to express not religious truths, but the psychological need for and perception of some spiritual value.

2

Skepticism and the Abandonment of Poetry (1853–1868)

ROSSETTI's lack of sincere religious faith is evident from the ease with which he dropped his Art-Catholic stance. There was no personal religious crisis, but only a change of aesthetic direction. William Bell Scott, to whom he had sent the *Songs of the Art-Catholic,* came to realize that Rossetti "had never thought of pietistic matters except as a sentiment," and that by 1853 even the sentiment was no longer part of his inspiration, that by this time "the spirit that had made him choose 'Songs of the Art-Catholic' as a general title died out."[1] In "The Church-Porches," a pair of sonnets written in 1853, Rossetti acknowledged the attraction of an aesthetically beautiful religion but affirmed that it must be left behind. The first sonnet, addressed to his sister Maria, describes the entrance into church as a solemn and sacred thing, but emphasizes that the solemnity is achieved largely by artistic means: the paintings, sculptures, "gothic church-door," music of the bells, and the echoing silence of the gothic vault. The second sonnet, addressed to Christina, is as David Sonstroem has pointed out, a "literal

---

[1]William Bell Scott, *Autobiographical Notes,* ed. W. Minto, 2 vols. (New York: Harper and Brothers, 1892), I:290–291.

departure from church,"[2] but it is a departure filled with regret and trepidation:

> Sister, arise: We have no more to sing
>> Or say. The priest abideth as is meet
>> To minister. Rise up out of thy seat,
> Though peradventure 'tis an irksome thing
> To cross again the threshold of our King
>> Where His doors stand against the evil street,
>> And let each step increase upon our feet
> The dust we shook from them at entering.
> Must we of very sooth go home? The air,
>> Whose heat outside makes mist that can be seen,
>> Is very clear and cool where we have been.
>> The priest abideth ministering, Lo!
> As he for service, why not we for prayer?
>> It is so bidden, sister, let us go.
>
> [*Poems*, 308]

The tone of regret results from a fear of the evil and dust of the world outside the sanctuary, but the implication throughout is that the church, though a great comfort, is an escape from life—life must be faced.

For the deeply religious Christina, the departure from church would have been a severe religious crisis, but for Rossetti it was only an abandonment of a certain sensibility. Still, even without a religious crisis, the rejection of Christian art as a model did create an artistic crisis. For the next fifteen years, without his old themes, Rossetti wrote very little poetry, and what he did write reflects a lack of confidence and a flailing about for a sense of direction. The sonnet "Lost Days" (1854) laments that the poet wasted his efforts, and states that with each wasted day he has murdered a part of himself:

[2]David Sonstroem, *Rossetti and the Fair Lady* (Middletown: Wesleyan University Press, 1970), p. 49. The phrase "gothic church-door" is from an early manuscript in the Janet Camp Troxell collection at Princeton University. The published version, "carven church-door," emphasizes artistry to a still greater extent.

I do not see them [the lost days] here; but after death
   God knows I know the faces I shall see,
Each one a murdered self, with low last breath.
     'I am thyself,—what hast thou done to me?'
  'And I—and I—thyself,' (lo! each one saith,)
     'And thou thyself to all eternity!'

                       [*Poems,* 124]

Earlier, in "Saint Agnes of Intercession," Rossetti had seemed to fear that the morbid introspection of an artist might be self-destructive, but "Lost Days" implies just the reverse—that the artist's failure to redeem each passing moment in art may be self-destructive. Rossetti's regret that he had not been a more sincerely introspective artist is expressed far more clearly in another sonnet of 1854, "The Landmark":

Was *that* the landmark? What,—the foolish well
   Whose wave, low down, I did not stoop to drink,
   But sat and flung the pebbles from its brink
In sport to send its imaged skies pell-mell,
(And mine own image, had I noted well!)—
   Was that my point of turning?—I did think
   Proud piles should mark my station, link with link,
As altar-stone or ensigned citadel.[3]

Art-Catholicism had at least provided a clear, well-marked path—Rossetti later revised the poem to indicate that the path had seemed as clear as the ritualized stations of the cross: "I had thought / The stations of my course should rise unsought" (*Poems,* 119). But the real landmark for an artist without genuine faith is the well in which he sees his own image, which is, like the doubles of "Lost Days," a symbol of his inner self, the proper source of Romantic art. He had neglected, even distorted, that image, and so lost his path. "The Landmark," however, concludes more optimistically than "Lost Days" with the notion that though "the

[3]The early version is quoted from a manuscript in the Fitzwilliam Museum, Cambridge University.

55

path is missed," the poet can return to it, thankful that "the same goal is still on the same track."

Perhaps it was in this spirit of optimism that Rossetti wrote, also in 1854, his most ambitious poem of the period, "Nocturn" (later revised and retitled "Love's Nocturn"), a poem that invokes his most frequent image of inwardness, the double. The poem is addressed to the god of sleep, asking him to send the speaker's dream-double to his beloved's dream to achieve "the one dream mutually / Dream'd in bridal unison." But as the central conceit indicates, the poem is extraordinarily forced, and becomes confused and obscure. Moreover, the setting of the poem in dreamland, though it might conceivably have been used to explore the subconscious mind, is too self-consciously artificial:

> Thence are youth's warm fancies: there
> Women thrill with whisperings
> Valleys full of plaintive air;
> There breathes perfume; there in rings
> Whirl the foam-bewildered springs;
> Syren there
> Winds her dizzy hair and sings.[4]

Even the image of Adam's dream, which for Keats had suggested "the holiness of the Heart's affections and the truth of Imagination—What the imagination seizes as Beauty must be truth,"[5] is brought unconvincingly into a poem that has already conceded the relative inadequacy of dream visions: "Half-formed visions" that are "Less than waking ecstasy." The poem, consequently, reveals that the Romantic path was a very difficult one for Rossetti to return to, partly because he lacked the confidence to look honestly within himself, and partly because he lacked confidence in the visionary mode.

[4]Quotations from "Nocturn" are from an early manuscript in the Fitzwilliam Museum. The poem was much revised in proof in 1869, when Rossetti changed the first two lines of this stanza, significantly heightening the artificiality. In the published "Love's Nocturn," the lines are "Poet's fancies all are there: / There the elf-girls flood with wings . . ." (*Poems*, 7).

[5]*The Letters of John Keats, 1814–1821*, ed. Hyder Edward Rollins, 2 vols. (Cambridge: Harvard University Press, 1958), I:184.

In fact, it was only when Rossetti entirely abandoned the visionary mode that he could write confidently and entirely successfully. His fine lyric "The Woodspurge" pointedly refuses to carry vision beyond the material world. The poem describes a state of grief in which passivity, lack of volition ("I had walked on at the wind's will,—/I sat now, for the wind was still"), coincides with a state of acute mental awareness:

> My eyes, wide open, had the run
> Of some ten weeds to fix upon;
> Among those few, out of the sun,
> The woodspurge flowered, three cups in one.
>
> From perfect grief there need not be
> Wisdom or even memory:
> One thing then learnt remains to me,—
> The woodspurge has a cup of three.
>
> [*Poems*, 134]

The Art-Catholic, of course, could exploit the obvious trinitarian potential of the natural symbol—the woodspurge would point to a consoling but unapprehended reality beyond itself. To the agnostic, however, the woodspurge itself is the very carefully apprehended reality. The poem is not concerned with the unseen, except in the blatancy of its disregard for the convenient symbol, but with the seen, and especially with the act of seeing. Because the natural image does not point outward, the reader is forced to realize that the direction of the poem is inward, to the psychological effects of grief.[6]

"The Woodspurge" embodies in a peculiarly pure form one kind of poetry that may result from a loss of faith in the visionary. It is a poetry of nonstatement. A fact is presented, but the fact suggests nothing, means nothing. The poem's refusal to locate significance anywhere movingly expresses the hopelessness of deep grief, but at the same time it implies a very limited role for poetry. Rossetti's ambition, I think, was not to be satisfied with the terribly limited

---

[6]For an excellent discussion of "The Woodspurge" along these lines, see Jerome McGann, "Rossetti's Significant Details," *Victorian Poetry*, 7 (1969), 42.

poetic position that the facts could speak for themselves, if they had anything to say. "The Woodspurge" represents a kind of minimalist poetry that not only abandons the role of the poet as *seer*, but even brings into question his role as maker, since the poem not only implies that the natural symbol has no special significance, but even that the insignificant symbol is discovered by chance, is a kind of *objet trouvé*. In fact, of course, "The Woodspurge" is a highly wrought, highly self-conscious work of art, but it is nevertheless a work of art that implies an extremely limited scope for the poet to work in.

The honesty of "The Woodspurge," which results in discovering that meaning cannot be found beyond the reach of the senses, may well have increased Rossetti's uneasiness about his role as a poet. His anxiety necessarily became pressing once he rejected the too easy symbolism of Art-Catholicism and of latter-day gothic, and accepted the burden of speaking honestly and for himself, once he accepted, that is, the fundamental principle of Romanticism. The difficulties of an aesthetic of sincerity, already evident in the Romantic poets of the first third of the century, were compounded for the belated Romantic. He faced, with the earlier Romantics, the challenge of honest introspection and the danger that what he found within himself might be neither original nor valuable in art, so he put not only the value of his art, but the value of his very identity, on the line.[7] But he also faced the immense obstacle of the earlier Romantics themselves. He must compete with them on their own ground, and he must anticipate the inevitable though odious comparisons that his critics would make. Worse, he had to compete with the great Romantics in an increasingly rationalist age, an age that was openly hostile to what Carlyle, among others, regarded as the diseased self-consciousness of Romanticism. Carlyle's attack on Romanticism, in fact, sums up Rossetti's dilemma, for he saw clearly that the loss of the "Faith" whereby "man removes mountains" paralyzes life and art: "Doubt, which . . . ever hangs in the background of our world, has now become our mid-

---

[7]In "Saint Agnes of Intercession" the young painter comments that an artist submitting a painting to the public, particularly to critics, is "submitting to them his naked soul, himself" (*Works*, 559).

dleground and foreground; whereon, for the time, no fair Life-picture can be painted, but only the dark air-canvas itself flow round us, bewildering and benighting." Rossetti's pseudo-Catholicism had, for a time, put off the paralysis of doubt, though not in a way that would have satisfied Carlyle, who might have compared him to "a noble Friedrich Schlegel," who, "stupefied in that fearful loneliness, as of a silenced battlefield, flies back to Catholicism; as a child might to its slain mother's bosom, and cling there."[8] But once he rejected this false comfort, he was depressingly confronted with the "dark air-canvas" of doubt. His efforts between 1852 and 1868 were almost entirely directed at covering that canvas with paint. Abashed by the massive obstacle of the Romantic achievement, he essentially gave up writing poetry, remarking that "if a man has any poetry in him he should paint, for it has all been said and written, and they have hardly begun to paint it."[9] And by 1856, the year of "The Woodspurge," Rossetti was stating flatly that he had "given up poetry as a pursuit of my own."[10]

In painting, Rossetti's departure from Art-Catholicism represents a conversion from the idea that painting should have a purpose to the idea that painting should be a purpose. In a curiously precise way, his aesthetic conversion anticipates a remark made thirty years later by G. F. Watts, who cited Cennini's advice that a painter, before beginning a painting, should "go down on [his] knees and implore the aid of the Virgin," and remarked that in the all-questioning nineteenth century, such "religious fervor" ought to be transferred to faith in the nobility and beauty of art.[11] Certainly in the paintings that followed his quasi-devotional pictures of the Virgin, Rossetti was greatly concerned with the ability of art to cover the "dark air-canvas," and the literal canvas, with the nobility and beauty of pattern and color. He did not entirely reject the

[8]Carlyle, "Characteristics," in *Critical and Miscellaneous Essays*, 5 vols. (New York: Scribner, 1900), III:28, 31–32.

[9]Quoted by Graham Hough, *The Last Romantics* (1947; rpt. London: Methuen, 1961), p. 42. See also Georgiana Burne-Jones, *Memorials of Edward Burne-Jones* (New York: Macmillan, 1906), p. 145.

[10]*Letters*, I:299.

[11]G. F. Watts, *The Present Conditions of Art,*" *The Nineteenth Century*, 1880, p. 242.

idea that art ought to be morally purposeful, but his experiments with combining literary and graphic arts show an increasing doubt that either art can, independently, make a significant statement, and his increasing desire to cram his pictures with visual detail reveals at least a formal urge to cover the dark air-canvas of doubt, to spread a veil over it.

The mid-to-late 1850s was certainly a period of experimentation. Rossetti worked in a variety of media, including pencil, pen and ink, oils, and watercolors, and with a variety of different themes, ranging from Dantean to biblical to illustrations of contemporary literary works. Though his attempts to combine poetry and painting during this period have been regarded as his most successful interpenetration of the two arts, they seem instead to represent a balancing of uncertainties in both arts. His study for a now lost painting called *Giotto Painting the Portrait of Dante* (Plate 5) is also a study of the possibility of combining poetry and painting. Not only does the sketch bring together the poet, Dante, and the painter, Giotto, but it adds another poet, Cavalcanti, leaning over Dante's shoulder and reading to him, and another painter, Cimabue, looking over Giotto's shoulder to study the portrait. These four are all elevated on scaffolding above a crowd of women, among whom Dante sees Beatrice. The elaboration of all this seems to suggest that the relation of the sister arts must be very complex indeed, but in fact no clear relation is established. The poets are to the right, the painters to the left, and the meeting of the twain is only in the portrait that occupies the space between them. Consequently, the meaning of the picture may be only that the painter must take his inspiration from poetry (as Rossetti did during the 1850s, when his paintings were frequently illustrations of poetic texts), but this neither very complex nor very sophisticated idea makes painting the servant of poetry. It is as though Rossetti, who was soon to give up poetry partly because "it has all been said and written," were convinced that he could serve art only by translating the ideas and poetry of other men into a different art form.

The sketch, however, is far more complicated than this, and though it never clarifies a relation between the sister arts, it raises a number of questions about each art. First, what is the ultimate source of inspiration? Giotto's is the face of Dante, but Dante is

60

"Credette Cimabue nella pintura
Tener lo campo; ed ora ha Giotto il grido,
Sì che la fama di colui s'oscura.
Così ha tolto l'uno all'altro Guido
La gloria della lingua; e forse è nato
Chi l'uno e l'altro caccierà di nido.

Vede perfettamente ogni salute
Chi la mia donna; tra le donne vede

Plate 5. Study for *Giotto Painting the Portrait of Dante.* Pen and ink, 8 × 7. By courtesy of The Tate Gallery, London.

gazing raptly on his own source of inspiration, Beatrice. Is art inspired by life and love, or by art? Also, is Dante the main influence on Giotto's painting or is Cimabue, his teacher, who looks over his shoulder? For that matter, is Beatrice the source of Dante's inspiration, or is his rapt expression produced by Cavalcanti's reading of poetry? The confusion is only compounded by Rossetti's further merger of painting and poetry, his appending to the picture two separate verses from Dante. The first, from the *Purgatorio*, draws together the painters and poets of the picture, but only to bring into question whether either art is worthwhile:

> "Credette Cimabue nella pintura
> Tener lo campo; ed ora ha Giotto il grido,
> Sì che la fama di colui s'oscura.
> Così ha tolto l'uno all'altro Guido
> La gloria della lingua; e forse è nato
> Chi l'uno e l'altro caccierà di nido."[12]

Presumably the purpose of appending lines of poetry is to elucidate the meaning of the picture, but even the poetry does not tell the whole story, which is made clearer in a private letter in which Rossetti explains that Guido Cavalcanti is, in the picture, reading aloud the poems of Guido Guinicelli, whom, according to Dante's lines, he has robbed of his glory as a poet. In a way, the addition of all this material makes Rossetti's pictorial intention clearer—Giotto and Dante, the poet already born to replace Cavalcanti, represent the culmination of early Italian art; their presence together on a raised platform represents a celebration of art and Rossetti's act of homage to the masters of the tradition that has formed him. But here the implications become more disturbing than ever, for Dante's lines confidently imply that poetry and painting con-

---

[12]Rossetti translated the passage in his Introduction to *Dante and His Circle*:

> Against all painters Cimabue thought
>   To keep the field. Now Giotto has the cry,
> And so the fame o' the first wanes nigh to nought.
>   Thus one from other Guido took the high
> Glory of language; and perhaps is born
>   He who from both shall bear it by-and-bye. (*Works*, 300)

tinually get better as pupils surpass their masters, but Rossetti, enthroning the masters on high, strongly implies that the heights have long since been reached, that the modern artist cannot hope to surpass, or even equal, his predecessors. The tradition that has been a source of inspiration has become a source of inhibition.

The second appended quotation, from the *Vita Nuova*, calls the two arts into question in a wholly different manner:

> Vede perfettamente ogni salute
> Chi la mia donna—tra le donne—vede.[13]

The question implicit in the Marian pictures, whether art can surpass nature, is answered negatively. If to see Beatrice is to see the highest perfection, then the attention of Giotto on Dante's face, and still more the attention of Cimabue on the portrait, seem misguided. Dante and Cavalcanti (who is, in fact, looking at the procession of women, not at the volume of poetry), looking at the thing itself, at the beloved woman, are seeing a higher vision than can be rendered in art. Yet Rossetti, the painter, has scanted the ultimate image of perfection, pushing Beatrice nearly out of the picture into the lower right corner, almost as if to say that he cannot aspire to the highest visions, can only pay his respects to those who could. Rossetti is in the place of Giotto in this respect, for his back is turned on the highest ideal, and he can only catch the vision as it is reflected in another man's features.

Far from reconciling the two arts, then, *Giotto Painting the Portrait of Dante* seems only to express the disconcerting notion that painting, Rossetti's chosen profession, may be dependent upon and derivative from poetry, the art he had abandoned. The abstracted, verbalized meaning of the two quotations reinforces the idea that Rossetti was coming to terms with his belatedness, in both arts, by simply accepting severe diminution, and to an extent this idea is confirmed by the formal qualities of the drawing, and even by Rossetti's plans for the painting. In the first place, it was to be a small watercolor, even though Rossetti shared the prejudice of his

---

[13]Rossetti translated the lines: "For certain he hath seen all perfectness / Who among other ladies hath seen mine" (*Works*, 334).

age that the greatest art must be in oil on large canvases. More important, the formal design gives the impression that Rossetti was attempting to make up in density for what he had relinquished in breadth, since all available space is crammed with significant detail. The claustrophobic effect is still further increased by the painting's lack of depth: everything is pushed into the foreground, so that no breathing room is suggested by receding distances. And, of course, the superimposed poetic "meanings" jam still more into the picture. All in all, the effect is one of artistic entrenchment, since the diminution in scope is accompanied with so much fortification of theme. Rossetti's entrenchment, however, enabled him to build confidence, to consolidate his strength, and to develop a strong individual style that resulted, by the mid-to-late 1850s, in some remarkably original and impressive paintings.

Some of the stylistic qualities of Rossetti's watercolors were already developing well before *Giotto Painting the Portrait of Dante*. His cramming in of significant detail and his apparent contempt for perspective are evident in *The Laboratory* (1849), *Beatrice Meeting Dante at a Marriage Feast, Denies Him Her Salutation* (1851), *Borgia* (1851), and even in the oil painting *"Hist!" Said Kate the Queen* (1851). In all these paintings, however, the uneasy alliance of poetry and painting creates problems. Because the paintings were ostensibly designed to *illustrate* lines of poetry, a viewer looks for narrative significance and mimetic accuracy, so he is disturbed by distorted perspectives and by the multiplicity of detail that distracts him from the central event. Yet, detached from the burden of illustration, these tendencies toward almost abstract pattern turn out to be Rossetti's greatest strength. One of his finest pictures, *The First Anniversary of the Death of Beatrice* (Plate 6), exhibits all the thematic confusion of *Giotto Painting the Portrait of Dante*, but viewed simply as a design it is a splendid achievement. Once again, a significant comment is evidently intended about the relations of poetry and painting, as the painter-poet Dante Rossetti paints the poet-painter Dante Alighieri painting a picture that he verbally described himself drawing in the *Vita Nuova*. The sources of confusion about "meaning" are obvious, but Rossetti's drawing succeeds in spite of them, and in ways that have little or nothing to do with the literary text that is being illustrated. It succeeds, essentially, as

64

Plate 6. The First Anniversary of the Death of Beatrice. Watercolor, 16-½ × 24. By courtesy of the Ashmolean Museum, Oxford.

a richly textured decoration of a two-dimensional surface (the perspective, not surprisingly, is utterly ludicrous—where and how the walls join, for example, is a mystery), on which the muted color harmonies of the interior and the robes are balanced against the bright blues and greens seen through the doorway and the window, and against the surprisingly prominent haloes of the Madonna and Child in the upper center of the picture. Though Rossetti has clearly chosen many of his details for their symbolic value, the effect of the picture depends very little on precise interpretation of the symbolism. As Herbert L. Sussman has said, many of the details in the painting, such as the lute, the lilies, the hour-glass, the religious icons, "demand figural reading," but the style, the use of watercolor, the lack of direct illumination, soften "the materiality of these objects."[14] Consequently, rather than functioning fully as typological symbols, as they might if their materiality were insisted upon, the objects remain only suggestive, half-defined adjuncts of a dream vision.

Other works of this period, however, indicate that Rossetti was not entirely willing to unmoor his symbols and let them drift into dreamy visions. He continued to work with the typological symbolism of his Marian pictures, using figural images very precisely in such paintings as *The Passover in the Holy Family* (78), *The Seed of David* (105), and *Mary in the House of St. John* (Plate 7). Ruskin, in fact, described *Mary in the House of St. John* as the most representative "in purity and completeness" of all Pre-Raphaelite figural paintings.[15] The painting represents Saint John sitting and Mary standing, filling a lamp, before a window looking out on a sunset. The expressions of the two, the somber twilight, and the spareness of the domestic setting all suggest the loneliness, the patient waiting, that Mary must have endured after the ascension, but as in all successful figurative art, the ordinary incidents of life are pregnant with spiritual significance. In this case, the lamp that Mary fills, as D. M. R. Bentley has said, "recalls the parable of the ten Virgins (Matthew 25: 1–3) who likewise 'trimmed their lamps' in order to

---

[14]Herbert L. Sussman, *Fact into Figure: Typology in Carlyle, Ruskin, and the Pre-Raphaelite Brotherhood* (Columbus: Ohio State University Press, 1979), p. 128.

[15]*The Complete Works of John Ruskin*, ed. E. T. Cook and A. Wedderburn, 39 vols. (London: George Allen, 1903–1912), 33:270.

Plate 7. Mary in the House of St. John. Watercolor, 18 × 14. By courtesy of the Delaware Art Museum.

go 'forth to meet the bridegroom' (who is allegorically interpreted as Christ)"[16] and so her action both fulfills the scriptural type and anticipates further fulfillment when Mary will go forth to meet Christ. And of course, the painting is dominated by the cruciform window bars, which plainly suggest the crucifixion, but the empty cross and the twilight also suggest the temporary absence of Christ, and recall His words, as recorded by Saint John: "Yet a little while is the light with you" (12:35) and the more hopeful words from John that Rossetti actually included on the frame, "A little while, and ye shall not see me: And again, a little while and ye shall see me, because I go to the Father" (16:16). The figural and dramatic depiction are entirely unified: both symbol and event express sorrow for the sufferings of Christ, and patient faith and hope in restoration to the light. Unquestionably such brilliantly successful figural art solves the problem of providing "meaning" within the picture, but it must be a specifically Christian meaning—as Ruskin observed, Rossetti could create such art only when "on pilgrimage in Palestine,"[17] and he was less and less frequently inclined to go on pilgrimage. Typology fascinated Rossetti, as George Landow has argued, because it "provides a means of redeeming human time, of perceiving an order and causality in human events,"[18] but ultimately Rossetti must have realized that it could do so only from a Christian point of view that he would not accept.

Rossetti's other works of the 1850s and 1860s indicate that he was uncomfortable with Huntian, Ruskinian, figural art not only because it expressed a faith he did not accept, but also because he was being increasingly drawn away from the mimetic realism demanded for the portrayal of material types. With *Arthur's Tomb* (73), painted, apparently, late in 1855, Rossetti executed his first Arthurian watercolor, his first picture in which formal tendencies were completely liberated from illustrative or mimetic constraints. The painting, which shows Launcelot leaning over the effigy of King Arthur on his tomb and staring into the eyes of the kneeling

[16]D. M. R. Bentley, "Rossetti's 'Ave' and Related Pictures," *Victorian Poetry*, 15 (1977), 30.

[17]*Works*, 33:270.

[18]George Landow, *William Holman Hunt and Typological Symbolism* (New Haven: Yale University Press, 1979), p. 150.

Guinevere, almost pointedly flouts the idea of mimetic realism. Its absolute lack of depth—there is no background, only foreground—combined with impossibly bright colors, stylized dwarf trees, and the ludicrous posture and impossible physical proportions of Launcelot all indicate that Rossetti was becoming more interested in stylized pattern than in representational art. It is as if he had simply exaggerated all his worst failings as a representational artist, and found himself moving toward abstraction. In such subsequent paintings as *The Blue Closet* (90), *The Tune of the Seven Towers* (92), *How Sir Galahad, Sir Bors, and Sir Percival Were Fed with the Sanc Grael; but Sir Percival's Sister Died by the Way* (94. R.I), *The Wedding of St. George and the Princess Sabra* (97), *A Christmas Carol* (98), *Chapel before the Lists* (99), and *Before the Battle* (106), Rossetti carried the tendencies still further, and with greater success. In fact the success of these pictures fully justifies Lucien Pissarro's remark that "most of the critics who have written on Rossetti deplore the fact that he did not learn to paint, but to artists one of the greatest charms of his pictures (especially the early ones) is the unexpectedness of their composition."[19] The paintings all have such great stylistic affinities that a description of any one of them seems to do for them all; Quentin Bell's description of *The Wedding of St. George* (Plate 8) sums up their characteristics succinctly: it "looks as though it had been cut from a manuscript; it makes no pretence at realism, it is filled to the bursting point, the figures packed into their frame, objects willfully distorted in order to develop the surface-pattern; and the pattern is all-important. . . . It is a very odd conception of painting in which detail seems to be made deliberately alien to the main design of the picture."[20] The details, moreover, are frequently decorative works of art, such as tapestries, richly painted clothes, or painted furniture, which exaggerate the decorative tendency of the painting and allow more opportunity for rich coloring. Their coloring, in fact, their unusual luminousness that invites comparison with stained glass, is perhaps their most remarkable feature.

[19]Lucien Pissarro, *Rossetti* (London: T. C. & E. C. Jack), p. 78.
[20]Quentin Bell, *Victorian Artists* (Cambridge: Harvard University Press, 1967), pp. 66–67.

Plate 8. The Wedding of St. George and the Princess Sabra. Watercolor, 13-½ × 13-½. By courtesy of The Tate Gallery, London.

All the stylistic effects of these paintings combine to cover as completely as possible the "dark air-canvas" of doubt and even to lighten it. The luminousness of Rossetti's surface implies that the painted veil refracts the white light of eternity rather than covers the darkness of the void. Or, to put it less fancifully, the paintings seem to represent a genuine switch of allegiance from an art that worships and instructs to an art that exists for the sake of its own nobility and beauty. Rossetti's watercolors are not merely exercises in aesthetic escapism, but raise serious questions about the role of the artist, and the relation of the viewer to the work of art. They restore the painter's independence from the poet, and simultaneously prevent the normal nineteenth-century viewer's habit of merely "reading" the picture. In addition, they seriously disorient the viewer since, as W. F. Axton has argued, the "exploration—nay, exploitation—of these ambiguities concerning surface and depth, volume and flatness, pattern and representation . . . seriously undermines and complicates the process by means of which a spectator goes about apprehending and understanding such paintings." The final result of the emphasis on pattern, Axton argues, is that the spectator's "comprehension is baffled by the plethora of glaring details, each and every one of which is crying out for narrow inspection. The spectator is thus forced out of his comfortably static, distant relationship to the picture-surface and into a succession of radically different, constantly altering perspectives, as he tries to read detail, comprehend masses, and gradually build up some sense of how everything works together."[21] Rossetti's watercolors of the mid-to-late 1850s, then, would seem to express formally the dislocation from a single, comprehensive point of view that his skepticism and his abandonment of Art-Catholicism had brought about. They perfectly reflect the multitudinousness of the age, the problem of discovering the key to the whole.

But Rossetti was not satisfied with reflecting the problem, however brilliantly. The difficulty with this aesthetic was that there might be no key to make everything work together, and that if

---

[21]W. F. Axton, "Victorian Landscape Painting: A Change in Outlook," in *Nature and the Victorian Imagination,* ed. U. C. Knoepflmacher and G. B. Tennyson (Los Angeles: University of California Press, 1977), pp. 304–305.

everything is equally significant, everything is equally insignificant. When Rossetti had confronted the same problem in poetry, he abandoned poetry, and in fact he abandoned these medieval water-colors in 1859, perhaps realizing that he had come to the familiar impasse. Rossetti had, I think, as deep a need as any spectator of his art to find meaning, so that even while he was producing minor masterpieces of nonrepresentational art, he was still struggling with ways to express complex theological issues through typological sym-bolism, still trying to cope with modern issues in a realistic way in *The Gate of Memory* (100), and still struggling with pictures that would both illustrate and explicate literary texts in a series of en-gravings for Tennyson's poems (83–86) and in *Hamlet and Ophelia* (108). In short, he was still experimenting, still seeking a style and a theme, and still attempting to unify the sister arts.

The subject that was to absorb Rossetti's attention for the rest of his career was, in a sense, one of the many glaring details of the medieval watercolors. Malory, it has been said, must have been a great erotic poet in Rossetti's eyes, for sexual love is at the center of painting after painting in this period. Gradually, during the late 1850s and early 1860s, the theme of passionate love, and the image of the beautiful, sexually inviting—or intimidating—woman, came to replace the medievalizing tendency and the thematically confus-ing formalism of the watercolors. With the production of *Bocca Baciata* (114) in 1859, Rossetti's art entered its final and longest phase, a phase in which he returned to oils to paint portraits and half to three-quarter length studies of beautiful women. Since they were often pictures of women he loved, he was returning to the theme he had long ago been concerned with in "Hand and Soul," "Saint Agnes of Intercession," "On Mary's Portrait," and his many studies of Lizzie Siddal, but he was returning to it with a difference. The pictures were now frankly sensual, unlike the delicate, almost ethereal drawings of Lizzie.

The shift to greater sexual explicitness in Rossetti's paintings of this time, and in his poetry from the mid-1850s to 1872, may well have resulted partially from developments in his personal life, and from a general historical trend that was releasing the arts from the worst excesses of Victorian prudery, but it is also a natural and seemingly inevitable development of his art. He had begun his career with the ascetic purity of Art-Catholicism and Mariolatry, and had progressed to the chivalric romances of Malory and Froissart. But asceticism and the chivalric code were both, as Blake had seen, such obvious ways of repressing and replacing sexuality that they actually called attention to it. Certainly Swinburne, Morris, and Pater, the Victorians who have most in common with Rossetti, were aware of the ambivalent sexuality of medieval religion and romance. Swinburne, for example, believed that the "church has always naturally and necessarily been the mother of 'pale religious lechery' (as Blake with such grand scorn labels the special quality of celibate sanctity 'that wishes but acts not'), of holy priapism and virginal nymphomania."[22] Also, his parody of courtly love in "The Leper" clearly shows that he saw through the ascetic pretension of the chivalric code. Morris, though less outrageously than Swinburne, sets forth a picture of a violently, passionately sensual medieval world in *The Defence of Guenevere and Other Poems*. Finally, Pater, writing specifically of Morris, but with an eye to Rossetti (and probably Swinburne), argued that the only possible nineteenth-century view of the Middle Ages was one that frankly dwells on the latent sensuality in the "monastic religion . . . [which] was, in fact, in many of its bearings, like a beautiful disease or disorder of the senses." Pater's discussion of the modern treatment of Arthurian legends, interestingly, describes Rossetti's transition from Christian to chivalric themes: "In truth these Arthurian legends, in their origins prior to Christianity, yield all their sweetness only in a Christian atmosphere. What is characteristic in them is the strong suggestion of a deliberate choice between Christ and a rival lover."[23] Throughout the 1850s Rossetti gradually made the deliberate choice, producing less and less Christian art, more and more sensual art.

The choice was, unquestionably, deliberate. Like Swinburne, Rossetti had been much influenced by Blake's writings about the repressed sensuality brought about by the medieval, and enduring, religion of chastity. And as Richard Stein has pointed out, he was

[22]*The Swinburne Letters*, ed. Cecil Y. Lang, 6 vols. (New Haven: Yale University Press, 1959–1962), III:116–117.
[23]"Aesthetic Poetry," in *Selected Writings of Walter Pater*, ed. Harold Bloom (New York: Signet, 1974), p. 191.

73

also influenced by the sensual gothic of Blake's art, in which Rossetti said, the women "are no flimsy, filmy creatures, drowsing on feather-bed wings, or smothered in draperies."[24] By 1869, when he had returned to writing poetry, and when he had devoted his art almost entirely to large, ambitious paintings of sensually beautiful women, Rossetti was able to state outright that he had made his choice, like a chivalric lover, between God and a rival lover. After criticizing Tennyson's handling of the Arthurian tales, he told Swinburne that he was seriously considering writing a poem to be called "God's Graal," "wherein God and Guenevere will be weighed against each other by another table of weights and measures." The choice, inevitably, was the rival lover, since his theme was deliberately, as he said, "chosen to emphasize the marked superiority of Guenevere over God."[25]

The clarity of Rossetti's decision in 1869 and 1870 only ratifies what had become obvious by 1859. For a decade he had experimented with various styles and themes in poetry and painting, but despite all the different directions his art took, the theme of sexual love was always just below the surface. By 1859, however, it had surfaced completely in both arts.[26] The few poems Rossetti wrote from 1859 to 1868 show a radical departure from his earlier work in their frank handling of sexual themes, and they help to show, also, why the theme of sexual love was congenial to a poet who had lost faith in the visionary mode. "Even So," "A Little While," and "A New Year's Burden," all written in 1859, broke a three-year drought in Rossetti's writing of poetry. All three poems, melan-

[24]Richard Stein, *The Ritual of Interpretation: The Fine Arts as Literature in Ruskin, Rossetti, and Pater* (Cambridge: Harvard University Press, 1975), p. 127.

[25]*Letters*, II:779, 812.

[26]Even when Rossetti deliberately gave the impression that his theme was something other than sexual love, his real interests were sometimes obvious. The "political" sonnet "After the French Liberation of Italy," written in 1859, actually consists of an octave describing the aftermath of sexual climax and a sestet that merely tacks on a political moral. According to Swinburne, Rossetti admitted that the political purpose was at best secondary: "The application of the description (of a man & a woman copulating) as a political metaphor was, he told me, an afterthought to excuse it. The sestet was to apologize for the quatrains, which were written simply through a wish to do into verse his experience of the animal sensation": *The Swinburne Letters*, V:176.

choly lyrics of lost love, are well characterized by the last stanza of
"A New Year's Burden":

> The boughs are dark above our eyes,
>   The skies are in a net:
> And what's the worst beneath the skies
>   We two would most forget?
>   Not birth, my love, no, no,—
>   Not death, my love, no, no;—
> The love once ours, but ours long hours ago.[27]

The opening image implicitly accepts the necessarily sublunary nature of human passion—love will not bring the lovers heavenward,
as it did for Dante. But at the same time the tone of the stanza
expresses a deep sense of loss, since with the abandonment of faith
in spiritual, eternal love, the end of mortal love is not an apotheosis
but a disillusionment and a desire simply to forget. These three
poems, which seem to bid farewell to the spiritual ideal of love,
were followed in 1860 by the frankly sensual "Song of the Bower,"
in which the speaker daydreams about the pleasures of entering his
mistress's bedroom:

> What were my prize, could I enter thy bower,
>   This day, to-morrow, at eve or at morn?
> Large lovely arms and a neck like a tower,
>   Bosom then heaving that now lies forlorn.
> Deep in warm pillows, (the sun's kiss is colder!)
>   Thy sweetness all near me, so distant to-day;
> My hand round thy head and thy hand on my shoulder,
>   My mouth to thy neck as the world melts away.[28]

---

[27]Quoted from a manuscript in the Fitzwilliam Museum. The published version
shows various revisions. Originally the poem was headed "Three Songs: I.
Belcolore."

[28]Quoted from a manuscript in the Fitzwilliam Museum. The published version
eliminated the vampirism of the last line, substituting a simple kiss: "My mouth to
thy mouth as the world melts away" (*Poems*, 132). Joyce's Stephen Dedalus was
perhaps recalling the published line as he pondered a poem in the making in
chapter two of *Ulysses:* "My tablets. Mouth to her kiss. No. Must be two of 'em.
Glue 'em well. Mouth to her mouth's kiss" (New York: The Modern Library,
1934), p. 48.

In the end, however, the speaker resists the temptation, not out of religious fear, but out of a sense of dim foreboding. The significant point about both "The Song of the Bower" and the melancholy lyrics that preceded it is that they all refrain from visionary statements about transcendent love, and face the question of whether love is ennobling with honest perplexity. The direction of Rossetti's thoughts on love, however, was plainly toward a Blakean appreciation of passionate physical love and away from ascetic spiritual love. But the ambivalence of these poems is important, for Rossetti never ceased to believe that love must involve the whole soul, especially after he had decided that it must also involve the whole body. From 1859 on, virtually all his major work in both painting and poetry sought to express, in one way or another, the spiritual value of sexual love. Rossetti, at last, had found his theme.

3

Aestheticism to Experience:
Revisions for *Poems* (1870)

B Y the time he returned to the writing of poetry at the end of
1868, Rossetti had been all but silent for well over a decade.
During this period he had established himself as an artist—
not gaining widespread public recognition, since he refused to exhibit, but acquiring a number of wealthy patrons and considerable
renown within artistic circles. The reasons for the revival of his
poetic ambitions are not entirely clear, though a number may be
suggested. First, he began having trouble with his eyes and feared
going blind, as his father had done. Painting became temporarily
impossible and, he feared, might become permanently so, but perhaps he could turn to poetry. In addition, he was continually en-
couraged by his friends, particularly by William Bell Scott, to write
and to publish, and he himself had always viewed poetry as a higher
art than painting. Besides, his financial success as a painter seems
to have soiled the art, as he saw it—he painted "pot-boilers" for
"tin," but he would write poetry in a more lofty spirit of dedication
to Art. And as a diary entry by William Rossetti suggests, it is likely
that he was beginning to feel inadequate as a painter, and to hope
that he might achieve immortality in the sister art: "He seems more
anxious just now to achieve something permanent in poetry than in

painting—in which he considers that at any rate two living Englishmen, Millais and Jones, show a higher innate *executive* power than himself."[1] Perhaps most important of all, he began to see more of Jane Morris in 1868, and for the first time since the death of Lizzie he was passionately in love, so a new source of inspiration was available to him.[2]

But for whatever reason, in the late fall of 1868 Rossetti began writing poetry again, and he was soon determined to publish a volume. To this end he began looking through his earlier poems and revising them. Many of them were not available to him, however, since in his grief and remorse at Lizzie's death he had buried the sole copies of many poems in her coffin. In order to have enough material for a substantial volume, he arranged for the exhumation of the coffin, and in October 1869 the poems were retrieved. He greatly revised these poems, as well as the other early works, combined them with the new poems, and finally went to press with his first original volume of poetry in April 1870.

The shape of Rossetti's career and his long struggle to find his own voice have long been overlooked because his extensive revisions of early poems have been neglected—even in chronological studies of Rossetti's development, critics have frequently attributed poems like "The Blessed Damozel" and "The Portrait" to the late 1840s without, apparently, realizing that lines cited as written in, say, 1847, were not in fact written until 1869. "The Portrait," for example, a radically transformed version of a poem written in 1846 or 1847, clearly belongs, formally and thematically, to the year 1869, yet the best of the chronological studies of Rossetti places it in 1847.[3] Such haphazard dating encourages the impression, which

[1] William Michael Rossetti, *Rossetti Papers: 1862 to 1870* (New York: Scribner, 1903), p. 408.

[2] See Oswald Doughty, *A Victorian Romantic: Dante Gabriel Rossetti* (London: Frederick Muller, 1949), pp. 369–392.

[3] Ronnalie Roper Howard, *The Dark Glass: Vision and Technique in the Poetry of Dante Gabriel Rossetti* (Athens: Ohio University Press, 1972), pp. 12–18. Howard acknowledges, in a note, that the poem was substantially revised, but nevertheless uses the late version to illustrate Rossetti's early thought and technique. She follows much the same procedure in discussing "My Sister's Sleep," pp. 2–5 (though here her footnote is more specific about the early version), and "The Card

Rossetti was always eager to foster, that the poet emerged full-blown as a precocious master in 1847, and obscures the important point that *Poems*, 1870, represented not merely a collection of early and middle works, but a new departure, in which the Art-Catholic themes are eliminated and new themes are consolidated. And finally, ignoring the revisions leads to a false estimation of the nature of the 1870 volume by undervaluing the great labor Rossetti exerted to achieve a uniform level of craftsmanship and, more important, a consistent thematic outlook. He conscientiously labored to make *Poems*, in his own words, "studied work, where unity is specially kept in view."[4]

The most important of Rossetti's revisions were designed to eliminate any impression of religious faith in his book. William Bell Scott, who noted that Rossetti "had never thought of pietistic matters except as a sentiment," observed that by 1853 even the sentiment was no longer part of Rossetti's inspiration, that by this time "the spirit that had made him choose 'Songs of the Art-Catholic' as a general title died out."[5] Rossetti, however, was not content merely to let the spirit die out, but took active steps to make certain that he could not be regarded as an adherent of Christian faith. In 1865, for example, he wrote to the fervently Christian James Smetham to inform him not only that he was not a believer, but that even discussion of Christianity was "painful" to him.[6] And in 1869 he expressed his chagrin that most of his early work revealed a "mental condition" that was "discouragingly an-

---

Dealer," pp. 8–12. Howard should not be singled out, however, since many others have made similar errors. Robert D. Johnston, for example, in his *Dante Gabriel Rossetti* (New York: Twayne, 1969), quotes a passage from "The Portrait," which he dates 1847, and notes that it anticipates lines written in 1869 and 1871 (p. 57). The passage in question, however, was written in 1870 (see Robert N. Keane, "Rossetti: The Artist and 'The Portrait,'" *English Language Notes*, 12 [1974], 96–102). A more careful study of Rossetti's poetic development is Florence Saunders Boos's *The Poetry of Dante G. Rossetti: A Critical Reading and Source Study* (The Hague: Mouton, 1976).

[4]*Letters*, II:823.

[5]William Bell Scott, *Autobiographical Notes*, ed. W. Minto, 2 vols. (New York: Harper & Brothers, 1892), I:291, 290.

[6]*Letters*, II:582.

gelic," and suggested that he would now write "better things."[7] His revisions for 1870 were, for the most part, designed to eliminate the "angelic."

While preparing his poems for publication, Rossetti was especially eager to mitigate the effect of the "Art-Catholic" poems "Ave" and "My Sister's Sleep." He was so eager to kill the Art-Catholic that he "hesitated much to print *Ave*, because of the subject." Nevertheless he "thought it well done, and so included it," though he gave prolonged consideration to accompanying it with a note described by Swinburne as "disclaiming a share in the blessings purchased by the blood of your Redeemer."[8] The note was intended to claim that the Christianity of the speaker was entirely dramatic: "This hymn was written as a prologue to a series of designs. Art still identifies herself with all faiths for her own purposes: and the emotional influence here employed demands above all an inner standing-point."[9] Though Rossetti revised "Ave" extensively, he could not possibly eliminate its Christianity, but he could, and did, eliminate Christian faith from other poems. He did not particularly want to include "My Sister's Sleep" in the volume at all, but felt compelled to because it had recently been publicly praised.[10] Once committed to it, he radically transformed it, sending the revised draft to his brother with the comments that "The thing is very distasteful to me as it now stands, and I have quite determined on all changes made in pen and ink. In pencil I indicate a very radical change in the omission of two more stanzas which would eliminate the religious element altogether."[11] In fact Rossetti eliminated four of the original nineteen stanzas, including two following stanza nine in which the speaker and his mother pray,

[7]Quoted by Robert S. Fraser, "The Rossetti Collection of Janet Camp Troxell: A Survey with Some Sidelights," in *Essays on the Rossettis*, ed. Robert S. Fraser (Princeton: Princeton University Library, 1972), p. 169.

[8]*Letters*, II:714. Swinburne is quoted in a footnote to the letter.

[9]*Works*, p. 661. William Rossetti quotes the aborted footnote as evidence of his brother's agnosticism, and observes that though it would be erroneous to infer from "Ave" that Rossetti was a Roman Catholic, it is "of all Rossetti's poems . . . the one which seems most to indicate definite Christian belief, and of a strongly Roman Catholic kind."

[10]*Letters*, II:722.

[11]*Letters*, II:731.

and two following stanza six in which the speaker finds clear religious consolation:

> Silence was speaking at my side
>   With an exceedingly clear voice:
>   I knew the calm as of a choice
> Made in God for me, to abide.
>
> I said, "Full knowledge does not grieve:
>   This which upon my spirit dwells
>   Perhaps would have been sorrow else:
> But I am glad 'tis Christmas Eve."[12]

The poem, published in 1870, contains a reminiscence of this idea
in stanza thirteen: "I heard / The silence."[13] But without the
earlier stanzas the phrase has no specifically Christian significance.
In 1850, however, the phrase had been italicized, emphatically
underscoring the "religious element" near the end of the poem.
Except for several stylistic revisions, the only other alteration
Rossetti made in the poem was to change the image of an "altar-
cup" to a secular "icy crystal cup" (*Poems*, 97), so eliminating even
the sense that the speaker's range of associations was influenced by
Christianity.

The revisions of "My Sister's Sleep" were clearly intended to
eliminate the "religious element," but they transform the poem
entirely in other ways as well. The early poem is a straightforward
religious lyric, whether or not Rossetti himself believed in its consolation. It exhibits no special psychological insight, but only a
traditional Christian point of view. The close observation of detail,
for which the revised poem is justly celebrated, had been present
but subsumed in the Christian idea. In the 1870 version, the details
are unmediated by a mythic structure and must carry their own
significance. Consequently, the poem becomes a psychological lyr-

---

[12]*The Germ: Thoughts Towards Nature in Poetry, Literature and Art* (rpt., Port-
land, Maine: Thomas B. Mosher, 1898), pp. 21–22.

[13]Quotations from Rossetti's 1870 volume are all from *Poems by Dante Gabriel
Rossetti, 1870*, Section One of *Dante Gabriel Rossetti: Poems*, ed. Oswald Doughty
(London: Dent, 1961, rpt., New York: Dutton, 1974). Doughty's text, actually of
1872 rather than of 1870, is taken from the sixth edition.

ic in which close observation itself reveals the speaker's state of mind. Without the intellectual conception of a redeeming faith, the speaker must seek significance in direct experience, in sensory observation heightened by emotional stress. As Richard Stein has said, the "subject is consciousness itself, the hyperaesthesia experienced under the pressure of strong emotion."[14] Even though the last stanza is overtly religious, ending with "Christ's blessing on the newly born" (*Poems*, 98), the effect, in the absence of explicit Christian faith earlier in the poem, is to reinforce the reader's sense of the mother's and son's psychological groping for meaning. Jerome McGann has rightly said that "the blessing at the end does not point to a religious truth, does not serve the symbolic function that it might, but rather emphasizes the emotional state of the mother and son, the measure of comfort that they derive from a traditional religious truth at a moment of deep personal loss."[15] Rossetti changed the lyric from one that adopted the "inner standing-point" of the Christian to one that reveals the psychological pressures that lead to such an "inner standing-point." The revised poem is about unmediated experience, sensory experience, rather than about the fruits of experience, the faith evolved from human need. And of course the 1870 poem is darker, more somber, more skeptical than the early version. In this respect the revisions of "My Sister's Sleep" characterize Rossetti's consistent attempt, in preparing the 1870 *Poems* for the press, to treat all experience directly, to be a "fleshly" poet to the extent that the experiences of the senses are direct and unquestionable, though not necessarily consoling. In a sense, the revised "My Sister's Sleep" is a poem about the body, whereas the early version had been about the soul.

Aside from some sonnets for his own pictures, the only other poem in the 1870 volume that was, or seemed, explicitly Christian in theme and treatment was "The Blessed Damozel." This poem, more than any other, has given Rossetti his reputation for astonishing precocity, a reputation not wholly unearned, since the early

[14]Richard Stein, *The Ritual of Interpretation: The Fine Arts as Literature in Ruskin, Rossetti, and Pater* (Cambridge: Harvard University Press, 1975), p. 204.
[15]Jerome McGann, "Rossetti's Significant Details," *Victorian Poetry*, 7 (1969), 42.

versions are very fine, but somewhat exaggerated, since several inconsistencies and crudities were eliminated as the poem was repeatedly revised before 1870. The revisions were mostly for the sake of structural coherence or stylistic felicity, but some change the meaning and tone of the poem radically. Four stanzas about the rigors of religious faith and the peace and serenity of heaven were deleted from the 1850 version, and three entirely new stanzas were added by the time it was republished in 1870.[16] The general effect of the revisions and additions was to change the "Dantesque" heavens,[17] as Leigh Hunt called them, to heavens of more fully human love, to incorporate autobiography, and to add sorrow.[18] Two simple revisions characterize the changed tone. In 1850 the damozel had asked of Christ

> To have more blessing than on earth
> In no wise; but to be
> As then we were,—being as then
> At peace. Yea, verily.[19]

But in 1870 she asks not for peace, but specifically for earthly love:

> Only to live as once on earth
> With Love,—only to be,
> As then awhile, for ever now
> Together, I and he.
> [*Poems*, 6]

[16]The earliest known text of "The Blessed Damozel" is the Morgan manuscript, dated 1847, but as J. A. Sanford has argued, the text was almost certainly fabricated by Rossetti at a much later date, perhaps to help advance the idea of his precocity. For the various texts of the poem, see *Dante Gabriel Rossetti: The Blessed Damozel: The Unpublished Manuscript, Texts and Collation*, ed. Paull Franklin Baum (Chapel Hill: University of North Carolina Press, 1937). For the argument against the validity of the 1847 manuscript, see J. A. Sanford, "The Morgan Library Manuscript of Rossetti's 'The Blessed Damozel,'" *Studies in Philology*, 35 (1938), 471–486.

[17]*Letters*, I:39.

[18]For a fuller discussion, see K. L. Knickerbocker, "Rossetti's 'The Blessed Damozel,'" *Studies in Philology*, 29 (1932), 485–504.

[19]*The Germ* text, Baum, p. 15.

Similarly, the earthly lover had pondered, in 1850, his worthiness in the eyes of the Lord, but in 1870, at the same point in the poem, he recognizes explicitly that he loves not God, but the damozel:

> But shall God lift
> To endless unity
> The soul whose likeness with thy soul
> Was but its love for thee?
> [*Poems*, 5]

The hope in these lines for the bare possibility that earthly love may be continued after death has little to do with any Christian heaven, but it places the poem thematically with poems written in 1869 and 1870. "The Stream's Secret" (1869–70) and many of the sonnets for *The House of Life* express the same faint hope, without Christian overtones. The stanza added to "The Blessed Damozel," then, helps to fit the poem into the volume without disturbing its overall thematic unity. Even in the early version, of course, "The Blessed Damozel" had not represented a genuinely spiritual view of heaven—the damozel had always been hot-blooded enough to warm the gold bar of heaven, and the emphasis had always been on human love. But the version printed in *The Germ* had sufficient religious trappings at least to suggest "Dantesque heavens" and genuine faith, whereas the 1870 version, despite its retention of medieval religious symbolism, more fully emphasizes human love and religious doubt. Reading the 1850 version, we scarcely doubt that the lovers will be reunited, but reading the 1870 poem, we are tempted to associate the damozel's assertion,

> 'I wish that he were come to me,
> For he will come,' she said
> [*Poems*, 5]

with the despairing assertion of Tennyson's Mariana,

> Then said she, "I am very dreary,
> He will not come," she said.
> [ll. 81–82]

As is true of "My Sister's Sleep," the revision replaces faith with skepticism, optimism with pessimism, and expresses not the "inner standing-point" of the Christian, but the grief that leads to adopting it.

Rossetti's revisions went beyond merely eradicating the impression that he himself was a Christian. The changes he made in "My Sister's Sleep" and "The Blessed Damozel" were necessary in part because those poems might be taken as utterances of a personal faith, but also because they needed to be compatible with other poems in the volume. "The Staff and Scrip," an old-fashioned ballad telling of a medieval love story, could easily include Christian belief as part of the dramatic framework, but even this poem was revised to show a darker and more skeptical view of Christianity. The story remained essentially unchanged; a pilgrim in a far-away land offers his services in war to Queen Blanchelys, whose lands have been ravaged. He is armed by the queen, sends his staff and scrip to her for safe keeping, and wins a battle for her, though despite the prayers of the queen and her court, he is killed. The queen dies ten years later, and is reunited with the pilgrim in heaven. "The Staff and Scrip" was not as extremely revised as other poems in the volume, partly, perhaps, because it was so impersonally conventional, but the few revisions make it a more somber poem. One stanza in the first published version of 1856, which had described the pilgrim's "joy to fight,"[20] for example, was replaced by a far gloomier stanza:

> Born of the day that died, that eve
> Now dying sank to rest;
> As he, in likewise taking leave,
> Once with a heaving breast
> Looked to the west.
> [*Poems*, 30]

Not only are the images of the dying day and evening ominous, but the suggestion of natural cycles, the natural perspective, implies a

[20]*The Oxford and Cambridge Magazine for 1856* (London: Bell and Dalby, 1856), p. 773.

view of mortality without conjuring up ideas of redemption. In fact, the religious element is altogether more ambivalent in the revised poem, as a stanza added to the description of the queen and her court in prayer and fasting illustrates:

> Lo, Father, is thine ear inclin'd
> And hath thine angel pass'd?
> For these thy watchers now are blind
> With vigil, and at last
> Dizzy with fast.
>
> [*Poems,* 31]

The addition emphasizes the idea, already latent in 1856, that the ascetic ritual is faintly ridiculous, blunting the senses of the watchers but irrelevant to the fortunes of the pilgrim. Other revisions, though slight, undercut the idea of true love between the queen and pilgrim by emphasizing the queen's willingness to send the pilgrim to his death. Originally, the queen comments ambiguously on the broken sword of the slain pilgrim:

> "O soft steel that could not withstand!
> O harder heart unstay'd,
> That pray'd and pray'd!"[21]

In 1870 the ambiguous "O harder heart" is clarified with the change to "O my hard heart" (*Poems,* 32). In the following stanza the queen commenting on the "bloodied banner" (*Poems,* 32) had originally said

> "Fair flew these folds, for shame,
> To guide Death's aim!"[22]

but in 1870 "these folds" was replaced with "my web," underscoring the queen's complicity in the pilgrim's death. The first of these changes was made, apparently, in the interest of clarity, but the second radically alters the tone. The effect is to change the charac-

[21]Ibid., p. 774.
[22]Ibid.

86

terization of the queen, who now appears less a wronged but innocent maiden, and more a fatal woman. Her character has been
adjusted to become comparable with such *femmes fatales* of the 1869
writings as Lilith in "Eden Bower" and Helen in "Troy Town." The
important point, I think, is that Rossetti's stylistic revisions were
necessarily written from his sensibility of 1869 and 1870, and so
necessarily change the tone of the poem—this one and others. And
in the process of eliminating awkward or ambiguous passages,
Rossetti gained an altered insight into the poems and consequently
changed other passages to express his more mature view.[23]

"The Staff and Scrip" had always, from its earliest conception,
been an ironic comment on chivalry and religion, but as the added
emphasis on the uselessness of religion suggests, the irony is much
sharper in the revision. Changes made in a stanza near the end of
the poem make this very clear. In 1856, Rossetti had written:

> And she would wake with a clear mind
> That letters writ to calm
> Her soul lay in the scrip; and find
> Pink shells, a torpid balm,
> And dust of palm.[24]

The sheer silliness of the religious objects she finds where she had
sought human love was certainly intended to be ironic, but Rossetti
revised the stanza as though to be certain no one missed the point.
In the early version the queen's inspection of the scrip is apparently
habitual, but in the revision she examines it only once, evidently
on the night of her death:

> And once she woke with a clear mind
> That letters writ to calm
> Her soul lay in the scrip; to find
> Only a torpid balm
> And dust of palm.
>
> [*Poems*, 33]

[23]Rossetti's avowed intention in revising "The Staff and Scrip" was to clarify
the structure and story: "In S[taff] and S[crip] there was something added where the
damsel gives her the relics to develop this incident and help the transition":
Letters, II:721.
[24]*The Oxford and Cambridge Magazine*, p. 775.

The word "Only" now emphasizes the queen's distress, and more significant still, her death, described two stanzas later, now seems related to the disappointment attendant upon her single inspection of the scrip. The closing lines of the poem, addressed to the pilgrim, had also been ironic from the start:

> Not tithed with days' and years' decease
> He pays thy wage He owed,
> But in light stalls of golden peace,
> Here in His own abode,
> Thy jealous God.[25]

The religious consolation is clearly ambivalent, as the conjunction "But" implies by suggesting that the terms were not exactly what the pilgrim had in mind, and as the negative connotations of the phrase "Thy jealous God" confirm. Nevertheless, in 1870 Rossetti reinforced the irony, substituting the phrase "with imperishable peace" for "in light stalls of golden peace" and so replacing a vision of heaven with an image that may connote nothing more than the eternal rest of clodlike death. The poem and its revision indicate that though Rossetti was inclined to be ironic about religion by 1856, by 1870 he was adopting a tougher, more unmistakable tone.

"The Burden of Nineveh," conceived as early as 1850 and first published in 1856, was revised for 1870 in much the same ways as "The Staff and Scrip." "The Burden of Nineveh" was plainly conceived from the start as an ironic comment on religion since its concern, the common nineteenth-century one most familiar from Heine, Nietzsche, and Swinburne, is the changing of the gods. The poet contemplates a statue of a "winged beast from Nineveh," recently brought to London, envisions its past as a religious idol, realizes that though all else of Nineveh is long dead, its God survives, and concludes ironically with the thought that some future archaeologist may dig up the beast, "a relic now / Of London not of Nineveh," and so

> shall hold us for some race
> That walked not in Christ's lowly ways,

[25]Ibid.

> But bowed its pride and vowed its praise
> Unto the God of Nineveh.
>
> [*Poems*, 18]

The ironic point that Christianity is no more, and possibly far less, enduring than the religion of Nineveh was abundantly clear in the 1856 version, but there the tone had been light-hearted and whimsical, opening, for example, with

> I have no taste for polyglot:
> At the Museum 'twas my lot,
> Just once, to jot and blot and rot
> In Babel for I know not what.[26]

The most obvious point of Rossetti's revisions was to remove such hilarity; the opening lines became

> In our Museum galleries
> To-day I lingered o'er the prize
> Dead Greece vouchsafes to living eyes,—
> Her art for ever in fresh wise.
> From hour to hour rejoicing me.
>
> [*Poems*, 14]

The most immediate effect of the altered tone is that the irony must now be taken more seriously—the tone of the whole poem is changed. Characteristically, however, the change in tone becomes a change in substance as well; in making stylistic changes Rossetti saw a deeper significance in his poem than he had originally put there, and so changed his entire conception. The opening emphasis on the endurance of art and its refreshing quality draws attention to the relic of Nineveh not just as the god of a dead civilization, but as a living work of art. The idea inherent in Rossetti's original conception, that man's works live on though his faiths die, is now clearly enunciated. Again, Rossetti revised the poem to articulate his skepticism more clearly, but in doing so he found a replacement for religion in art.

[26]Ibid., pp. 512–516.

89

The nature of Rossetti's revisions for 1870 is still more clear in one of the volume's most radically revised poems, "The Portrait," adapted from an 1847 poem called "On Mary's Portrait Which I Painted Six Years Ago." The poem had originally been a dramatic monologue, in which an auditor had been clearly implied from the opening two words, "Why yes,"[27] to the concluding question, but Rossetti eliminated the auditor and consequently eliminated the dramatic setting. The effect was to make the poem less a casual utterance and, as with the changes made to "The Burden of Nineveh," to make the tone more serious and contemplative. Further, the elimination of the dramatic framework makes the poem seem more personal and introspective. In addition to the formal change, from dramatic monologue to introspective lyric, the tone was made more somber by the removal of passages about the beloved in life and increased emphasis on the loneliness of the poet-painter and on the inadequacy of the portrait as a substitute for the living woman. The portrait, in 1870, remains a wonderful likeness, but it is now

> alas!
> Less than her shadow on the grass
> Or than her image in the stream.
> [*Poems*, 73]

The various revisions, as Robert N. Keane has said, reveal a poet "taking an imaginative, youthful poem of light and love and turning it into a darker, more melancholy poem filled with suggestive allusions to the personal experience of the mature poet."[28]

Not surprisingly, the increased sadness of the poem results from an increased skepticism. In 1847 the inadequacy of the portrait, its transformation of a "Once joyous" brow to one "grown stately,"[29] had been an image of hope. Looking into the eyes of the portrait, the speaker thought of the eyes of the woman in death, and envisaged her as serene and wise in an afterlife:

[27]The poem is printed in *Dante Gabriel Rossetti: An Analytical List of Manuscripts in the Duke University Library, with Hitherto Unpublished Verse and Prose*, ed. Paull Franklin Baum (Durham: Duke University Press, 1931), pp. 67–71.

[28]Keane, p. 97.

[29]Baum, *An Analytical List*, p. 68.

> And if I look into the eyes
> I think they are quite calm and wise;
> For while the world moves, she knows how.[30]

In 1870 the beloved is no longer in a heaven of omniscience, but lying in dark death, oblivious to the speaker's sorrow:

> O heart that never beats nor heaves,
> In that one darkness lying still,
> What now to thee my love's great will
> Or the fine web the sunshine weaves?
>
> [*Poems*, 74]

The faith in an afterlife in 1847, moreover, had been specifically Christian, a belief expressed in the suggestion that the past union of lovers had been a type of heavenly peace, as Rossetti's simile makes clear:

> So, along some grass-bank in Heaven,
> Mary the Virgin, going by,
> Seeth her servant Rafaël . . .[31]

In general, the quasi-Christian mysticism of 1847 was replaced with a melancholy awareness that only the artifact and the memories it inspires remain of the beloved. The revised poem, nevertheless, concludes with a vision of a Christian paradise that had not been present in the early poem:

> Here with her face doth memory sit
> Meanwhile, and wait the day's decline,
> Till other eyes shall look from it,
> Eyes of the spirit's Palestine,
> Even then the old gaze tenderer:
> While hopes and aims long lost with her
> Stand round her image side by side,
> Like tombs of pilgrims that have died
> About the Holy Sepulchre.
>
> [*Poems*, 75]

[30]Ibid.
[31]Ibid., p. 70.

91

The stanza at first seems to anticipate union with the beloved in heaven, but actually the poet is looking back, in memory, not ahead, and the beloved remains only an image. Even the long-lost hopes and aims are not fulfilled in death—they merely become, like the beloved, artifacts. Much more sadly than in "The Burden of Nineveh," Rossetti has replaced faith with art, realizing all the while that the substitution can offer only small consolation.

Other revisions also help to align "The Portrait" with the other poems of the 1870 volume. As in "The Blessed Damozel" and many of the sonnets for *The House of Life*, heaven was revised, Keane has pointed out, to represent no more than union with the lady's soul—God himself is left out.[32] More striking, the Christian myth has been replaced with the personal symbolism that pervaded Rossetti's poems from the mid-1850s onward. Conventional faith gives way to strange personal forebodings, which are symbolized here and in many other of Rossetti's poems of this period, by imagery of *döppelgangers*, echoes, and mirror images. In 1847, for example, the mystic glade represented in the painting was filled with "wet dew, / And red-mouthed damsels meeting you"[33] but in 1870 the glade is far stranger, characterized by "old dew, / And your own footsteps meeting you" (*Poems*, 73). And Rossetti added to the poem a description of past love that exactly corresponds to imagery used throughout "The Stream's Secret" and *The House of Life*, especially the "Willowwood" sonnets. In those poems the speaker looks into or drinks from a reflecting pool, or sits beside one with his beloved. The myth of Narcissus and Echo is consistently evoked, with the neoplatonic notion that both the reflection in the water and the echo are images of the soul. The lines added to "The Portrait" play on at least one of these ideas, and symbolically suggest the others:

> And with her
> I stooped to drink the spring-water,
> Athirst where other waters sprang;

[32]Keane, p. 102, notes that even after 1869 significant revisions were made: "Where the 1869 poem depicted the arrival of the lady's soul in Heaven where it would know 'the silence there for God,' the 1870 version envisions the artist's own arrival in a Heaven composed of his lady's soul. As in much of Rossetti's work, Paradise is the union of lovers forever."

[33]Baum, *An Analytical List*, p. 69.

And where the echo is, she sang,—
My soul another echo there.

[*Poems*, 74]

Since he regarded his volume as "studied work, where unity is specially kept in view," Rossetti would, I think, have expected that the symbolism here would be seen in the light of his other allusions to Narcissus and Echo throughout the book. In any case, the image here reinforces the image of the portrait as a mirror (present in both 1847 and 1870), the image of *döppelganger* selves, and the image of "her shadow on the grass / Or . . . her image in the stream." The cumulative effect within the poem is to strengthen the sense of mystery, of things unreal, or at least insubstantial—suggestive shadows, reflections, echoes—without abandoning actual observations and experience. In short, the vaguely mystical, gothic imagery that had been too literary and perhaps too confused and confusing in Rossetti's early works was finally becoming effective in expressing genuine personal emotion. As in other poems, the revised version of "The Portrait" discards assertions of faith, and replaces them with an account of the mystery and wonder, inspired by grief, memory, and art, that leads to assuming a faith. Like the other poems, "The Portrait" was revised to replace speculation with experience.

Precisely the same can be said of the revision of "Nocturn" to "Love's Nocturn." In the version written in 1854 the speaker is in love with the idea of love, and pleads for a dream that will bring him the image of an imagined lover. The seventh stanza, eliminated entirely in 1869, indicates plainly that the speaker sought not one particular lover, but a platonic ideal of Love:

As, since man waxed deadly wise
Secret somewhere on this earth
Unpermitted Eden lies,—
So within the world's wide girth
Hides she from my spirit's dearth,—
Paradise
Of a love that cries for birth.[34]

[34]Quoted from a manuscript in the Fitzwilliam Museum, Cambridge University.

But in 1869 such idealizing of the form without the substance, the wish for experience rather than the thing itself, was no longer adequate, so revisions and added stanzas both make it clear that a specific flesh-and-blood lover is envisioned and change the tone, as in "The Portrait," to one of deeper melancholy and more distressing eeriness:

> Vaporous, unaccountable,
>> Dreamland lies forlorn of light,
> Hollow like a breathing shell.
>> Ah! That from all dreams I might
>> Choose one dream and guide its flight!
>> I know well
> What her sleep should tell to-night.
>
>> > [*Poems,* 7]

The fantasy of "dreamland" remains at the center of the poem, but now the dream is put to the service of sensual experience rather than to the service of another dream, an idealization of an unborn love.

Rossetti's changed emphasis, from faith to sensation, is revealed in interesting ways in his revisions of "Jenny." The earliest known version of "Jenny" was produced in 1847 or 1848, but it was so substantially revised in 1858 and again in 1869 that the poem printed in 1870 is vastly different from Rossetti's first conception. All versions are dramatic monologues in which the speaker addresses a dozing harlot in her rooms, but unlike "The Portrait," the later version of "Jenny" draws more, not less, attention to the dramatic setting—not surprisingly, since Rossetti feared moral censure of the poem and wanted to make sure that the compromised speaker was not understood to be himself. Nevertheless, as with "The Portrait," the revisions do emphasize the origin of the speaker's thoughts in experience, since the experience itself is more fully developed, with additional details about Jenny's room and about the speaker's character. In fact, the late version consciously calls attention to the disparity between conceptual thought and actual experience. The speaker recognizes his own absurdity as his "thought runs on like this / With wasteful whims more than enough" (*Poems,* 64), characterizes his contemplation as "mere

words" and an "empty cloud" (*Poems,* 66), and even, after a particularly fanciful simile comparing lust to a "toad within a stone,"
rebukes himself for replacing sense with thought:

> Come, come, what use in thoughts like this?
> Poor little Jenny, good to kiss,—
> You'd not believe by what strange roads
> Thought travels, when your beauty goads
> A man to-night to think of toads!
>
> [*Poems,* 70]

The speaker's realization that his thoughts do not well fit his
situation, however, does not signify a change in Rossetti's original
conception, but a new way of expressing it. Indeed, a main point of
the earlier poem had been that nineteenth-century man's attempt
to replace sense with thought was ridiculous hypocrisy. One of the
two original mottos for "Jenny" had been an ironic quotation from
Shelley's translation of Goethe:

> What, still here!
> In this enlightened age too, since you have been
> Proved not to exist![35]

The body of the poem had satirized the nineteenth-century idea of
progress, of evolutionary meliorism in which man would shed his
gross, earthy nature and "perfect Man" would "be mind throughout."[36] The comparison of lust to a "toad within a stone," a fossil,
had been part of this original conception, an assertion that centuries of geological change and human progress had altered much
but had left man his atavistic desires. Further, the speaker had fully
realized the irony of his situation as he addressed Jenny:

> Thou call'st on Sense,—that's past and o'er,
> Surely, and shall not hold us more;

---

[35]The early version is printed in Paull F. Baum, "The Bancroft Manuscripts of
Dante Gabriel Rossetti," *Modern Philology,* 39 (1941), 48–52.
[36]Ibid., p. 50

> Yet to thy call, in earth and air
> Thou find'st an answer everywhere,
> And stickest even to me, thou bur,
> Who'd write myself philosopher.

And he had concluded his reverie with an elaboration on the idea that "Man gropes, but Matter clings to him."[37]

Rossetti's satire was pointed, in both versions, at man's foolishness in attempting to separate thought and sense, but the revised version, nevertheless, reveals a very changed conception. The early poem is a direct satiric attack on a popular philosophic idea and, as satire often does, it seems itself an intellectual, almost schematic, exercise. But in 1870 the irony is less pointed as both the speaker and Jenny emerge as more fully human characters. Jenny, for example, is no longer merely a harlot, but a woman like other women, as the speaker's rather sentimental comparison of her with his Cousin Nell reveals. Her childhood and probable misfortunes are described to enable the reader to feel sympathy for her, and to understand her true nature. Rossetti is no longer attacking an idea so much as examining the psychology of a man who develops such ideas in the chambers of a woman whose dishonor is a result of them. Further, the original version decries the hypocrisy that would deny man's sensual nature, but does not attack the notion that man's sensuality is an unfortunate part of his nature. In the revised poem, however, sensuality is so much a part of the characters and the characters are so sympathetic that the reader accepts it and them without question. When near the end of the poem the speaker compares Jenny to a wise virgin, the irony is obvious but it has no sting, implies no harsh judgment. The new motto for the poem, Mrs. Quickly's "Vengeance of Jenny's case! Fie on her! Never name her, child" (*Poems*, 63) was used, in fact, to make the point that such judgments are absurdly foolish. Rossetti's reason for acknowledging Mrs. Quickly as the speaker makes his intentions, for the motto and for the poem, very clear: "I want to put Mrs. Q. (instead of *Merry Wives* etc.) at end of the sentence to remind the virtuous reader strongly whose words they are that his own mind is echoing at the

---

[37]Ibid., p. 51.

moment."[38] Rossetti's clear intention was to defend the harlot, to defend the senses. And the new acceptance of sensuality, and especially of sexuality as extremely, and possibly dangerously, attractive helps, of course, to make "Jenny" compatible with other poems in the volume.

The revision of "Jenny," however, does not only incorporate ideas about the psychological development of false philosophic ideas and a defense of sensuality. The new emphasis on experience leads to a consideration of how art and faith themselves may evolve. The speaker's most serious and most pained consideration of Jenny's state results from a recognition that desecration of her beauty is no less than sacrilege:

> Fair shines the gilded aureole
> In which our highest painters place
> Some living woman's simple face.
> And the stilled features thus descried
> As Jenny's long throat droops aside,—
> The shadows where the cheeks are thin,
> And pure wide curve from ear to chin,—
> With Raffael's or Da Vinci's hand
> To show them to men's souls, might stand,
> Whole ages long, the whole world through
> For preachings of what God can do.
> What has man done here?
>
> [*Poems*, 68–69]

The speaker's Christian morality is not, of course, Rossetti's, but his realization that the proper response to beauty is akin to worship assuredly reflects Rossetti's own notion. In fact, the description of the painting that an artist might produce from Jenny precisely describes many of Rossetti's own paintings—the stilled features, long throat, thin cheeks and "pure wide curve from ear to chin" are typical of his painted women. The proper response to Jenny's beauty, then, is not a moral sermon, but an artistic appreciation that would speak directly to men's souls. Sensual appreciation becomes the basis for man's highest achievements in art. With the speaker's

---

[38]*Letters*, II:774.

notion that Jenny's beauty is evidence of God's work, Rossetti is again showing the basis of myth in direct sensual experience. He is not endorsing his character's conclusions, but is showing how such conclusions come about, how faiths are evolved. Again the emphasis is on experience and psychological process. When at the end of the poem the speaker whimsically compares Jenny to two mythic women, the Paphian Venus and then to Danae, his playful irony is evidently an attempt to detach himself from an otherwise painful situation, but once again Rossetti's point is more serious than his speaker's. The myths of the Paphian Venus and of Danae did result, in less self-conscious and ironic ages, Rossetti implies, from an appreciation of the exalted mystery of sensual beauty. The sensuality of human nature, repressed in the nineteenth century, is the basis of myth. The poverty of faith in the modern ages paradoxically results, as Nietzsche argued, from the elevation of faith over sensation.

Perhaps the most startling of Rossetti's late revisions of early poems occurs in the 1870 volume's other major dramatic monologue, "A Last Confession." One of the most memorable moments in the published poem occurs when the speaker, the murderer of a young woman he had raised and then fallen in love with, recalls his earlier gift to her:

> A little image of a flying Love
> Made of our coloured glass-ware, in his hands
> A dart of gilded metal and a torch.
> And him she kissed and me, and fain would know
> Why were his poor eyes blindfold, why the wings
> And why the arrow. What I knew I told
> Of Venus and of Cupid,—strange old tales.
>
> [*Poems*, 37]

The incident is evidently a kind of initiation into love—still more evidently an initiation into sexual love when the girl breaks the Cupid and is cut by its dart: "The dart had entered deeply and drawn blood" (*Poems*, 38). Since "A Last Confession" is dated 1847, these lines have generally been understood as characteristic of Rossetti's precocity in handling psychosexual themes, but in fact the whole passage was added late. His original image was, not surprisingly, far more characteristic of his actual concerns at that time:

> I brought her from the city, one such day,
> The earliest gift I mind my giving her,—
> A little image of great Jesus Christ
> Whom yet she knew but dimly. I had not
> Yet told her all the wondrous things of Faith
> For in our life of deadly haste, the child
> Might ill be taught that God and Truth were sure.[39]

The substitutions of Love for "great Jesus Christ" and of "strange old tales" of Venus and Cupid for "all the wondrous things of Faith" epitomize the ways in which Rossetti revised his early poems. Sexual love replaces religious faith, the somewhat empty rhetoric about "God and Truth" is eliminated, and a previously absent level of psychological penetration is added to the poem.

In one way or another, all of the substantial revisions altered the significance of poems in similar ways. Even such small changes as the alteration of "God's grace" to "Time's Grace" in the 1853 sonnet "A Dark Day" consistently reveal the same intention. In fact, the substitution of Time for God is characteristic of a number of changes that indicate how Rossetti had come to regard all such abstractions as interchangeable. His changes to "Love-Lily," not written until 1869, seem almost whimsical in this respect: he changed "soul" to "mind," "Love" to "Truth," and "God" to "Love" without, I think, changing his conception of the poem.[40] The revised poems consistently show a more pronounced skepticism, an emphasis on sensation rather than thought, and a consequent appreciation of sexual love and of woman as symbol of man's desire. But Rossetti did not attempt to achieve a unified volume only by revising his early poems to bring them into line with his mature views. His concern, frequently expressed in his letters, to

[39]Quoted from the manuscript in the Fitzwilliam Museum, Cambridge University.

[40]There are manuscripts of "Love-Lily" in both the Janet Camp Troxell collection at Princeton University and the Fitzwilliam Museum, Cambridge University.

arrange the order of his poems reveals that he was as eager to achieve a significant sequence throughout the volume as he was to order the sonnets of *The House of Life* into a coherent pattern. Futher, he carefully reviewed his poems before publication, selecting those which fitted, or could be made to fit, his mature views and rejecting others. The third section of the completed volume, "Sonnets for Pictures, and Other Sonnets," for example, draws heavily on his early work, opening with four sonnets for pictures, much revised, that had originally been published in *The Germ*. The sonnets he reprinted express no religious point of view—one, "For An Allegorical Dance of Women, by Andrea Mantegna," expresses, especially in its revised form, the view that whatever the artist intended, art communicates by sensation rather than by abstract allegorical thought. The sonnets he rejected, on two paintings by Hans Memling, had both been about religious mystery, the first beginning "Mystery: God, Man's Life, born into man/ Of woman" and the second "Mystery: Katharine, the bride of Christ."[41] The only early sonnets on religious themes that Rossetti retained, in fact, were sonnets for his own early pictures, "Mary's Girlhood," "The Passover in the Holy Family," and "Mary Magdalene at the Door of Simon the Pharisee." Just as he had included "My Sister's Sleep" because he thought it might do him some good with the reviewers, one of whom had singled it out for praise, so he may have felt that these sonnets might usefully enlist the sympathies of readers who knew his painting, or, on the other hand, might attract the attention of readers not familiar with his painting. The religious sonnets, in other words, may well have been included as a matter of business even though they do not wholly fit the tone of the volume.

Without discussing every poem in the volume in relation to the others, it would be impossible fully to investigate Rossetti's arrangement, but some general comments can be made. The work is divided into three parts, "Poems," "Sonnets and Songs: Towards a Work to be called 'The House of Life'" and "Sonnets for Pictures, and Other Sonnets." Most of the first section consists of revisions of early work. The arrangement of this section seems deliberately

[41]*The Germ*, p. 199.

designed to undercut the lighter, optimistic and, in the case of "Ave," religious implications that remained in these poems even after revision. The opening poem, "The Blessed Damozel," somewhat optimistically envisages a heaven of lovers as consolation for the death of the beloved, but it is immediately followed by the darkly skeptical "Love's Nocturn," which echoes the situation of the bereaved lover, and in which the only alternative world envisaged is one of dreams and "poets' fancies." The conjunction of poems not only implies that the heaven of "The Blessed Damozel" is an empty dream, but even that dreams dreamed in grief will take their coloring from that emotion:

> Reft of her, my dreams are all
> Clammy trance that fears the sky.
> [*Poems*, 8]

"Love's Nocturn" is then followed by "Troy Town," a poem about destructive, fatal beauty that further undercuts the idea of the beatific maiden in "The Blessed Damozel," and then by "The Burden of Nineveh," which fully enunciates Rossetti's ironic skepticism. Consistently, doubts about the soul in Rossetti's poetry lead to an affirmation of the flesh, so the next poem, appropriately, is "Eden Bower," a poem about the soulless, inhuman Lilith, the sensuous serpent-woman who was Adam's first wife. Only after the Christian ideal has been well laid to rest, and after Rossetti has established his "inner standing-point" with respect to all myths, does he then print "Ave," which can no longer possibly be regarded as representing the poet's own beliefs. Similarly, the other poem that Rossetti was concerned about, "My Sister's Sleep," is printed immediately after "The Card Dealer," a poem in which death is the province of inscrutable fate. After this, the reader cannot easily believe the possible implication of "My Sister's Sleep" that the death on Christmas Eve was providentially ordained.

Each of the three parts of the volume closes with a poem that specifically enunciates a skeptical point of view. The last original poem in Part One (it is followed by five translations) is "Aspecta Medusa," which Rossetti moved to that position after the volume

101

was already in proofs.[42] The poem, originally intended for a picture that was never completed, describes how Andromeda avoided looking directly at the Gorgon's head, but saw it "mirrored in the wave," and concludes with a moral:

> Let not thine eyes know
> Any forbidden thing itself, although
> It once should save as well as kill: but be
> Its shadow upon life enough for thee.
>
> [*Poems*, 100]

The lines, reminiscent of Shelley's "Preface" to *Alastor* and of his sonnet "Lift Not the Painted Veil," suggest that any attempt to see beyond the bounds of normal human perception is dangerous. Man must be content with what he can see, the reflection or the painted veil, without attempting to penetrate the mysteries of death.

The last poem of the second section, "The Sea-limits," much more clearly expresses a skepticism that now borders on solipsism. The first two stanzas of "The Sea-limits" are a greatly revised version of a poem first written in 1849, and originally called "At Boulogne. Upon the Cliffs: Noon." The revisions are characteristic—the first version had suggested the limitations of sense, but not of thought. At the horizon "Sense, without Thought, can pass / No stadium further."[43] In the 1870 version the idea that thought may reach where sense cannot has been eliminated:

> Secret continuance sublime
> Is the sea's end: our sight may pass
> No furlong further.
>
> [*Poems*, 136]

What the eyes cannot see remains secret. But the real point of "The Sea-limits" is expressed in two stanzas added at some later date (William Rossetti dates the revised poem 1849, an error that

---

[42]*Letters*, II:812. Rossetti did not fully explain his reason for moving the poem, but said only that it "seemed best as an inscription which it really was."

[43]*Letters*, I:61–62. A revised version of the poem appeared in *The Germ*, with the title "From the Cliffs: Noon."

illustrates the danger of relying on his datings, which characteristically make Rossetti appear more precocious than he was and
confuse his earlier thought with his later). The added stanzas ex-
hort the reader to "Listen alone beside the sea":

> Gather a shell from the strown beach
>> And listen at its lips: they [the sea and woods] sigh
>> The same desire and mystery,
> The echo of the whole sea's speech.
>> And all mankind is thus at heart
>> Not anything but what thou art,
> And Earth, Sea, Man, are all in each.
>
> [*Poems,* 136]

All knowledge is sensual apprehension—everything that man can
know is in the sound of the shell. The poem expresses a complete
solipsism, of course, since everything that man can know, "Earth,
Sea, Man" is not anything but what he is, and his knowledge,
gained from the shell, is only the sound of his own blood rushing in
his ears. All perception is thus reduced to what man feels upon his
pulses.

Finally, "The Monochord," the last poem of Part Three, the last
poem of the volume, expresses skepticism in a series of four unanswered and unanswerable questions. The poet cannot identify
what is "Life's self" or even distinguish between "Life or Death." A
biblical allusion in the sestet draws attention to the pillars of cloud
and fire that showed the way to God's chosen people, but only to
illustrate that in a skeptical age signs are unreadable and the way
remains lost:

> Oh! what is this that knows the road I came,
> The flame turned cloud, the cloud returned to flame
>> The lifted shifted steeps and all the way?—
>>
>> [*Poems,* 148]

The volume ends, then, with a series of questions that imply the
inscrutability of life, and with an allusion that acknowledges and
denies the old grounds of faith.

103

All of Rossetti's enormous labors in finally preparing his poems for publication in 1870, then, were aimed at obscuring his own tracks, eradicating immaturities of style and obliterating any traces of his early thought. He included a note on the title page of *Poems* that was obviously intended for the same purpose: "Many poems in this volume were written between 1847 and 1853. Others are of recent date, and a few belong to the intervening period. It has been thought unnecessary to specify the earlier work, as nothing is included which the author believes to be immature" (*Poems*, 1). Of course nothing is immature because, in fact, practically none of the poems as published can be said to belong to the earlier period. His revisions and studied arrangement had rendered the volume entirely a product of 1870. Unfortunately for Rossetti's posthumous reputation, his systematic obliteration of his footsteps has led many critics to condemn him for failure to "develop with the years."[44] Yet his successful efforts to produce a volume unified in style and sensibility is praiseworthy, however much it has muddied the waters of criticism. Rossetti would readily have agreed that what is most important is the finished work of art, not the history of its production. His revisions and careful arrangement made *Poems* a coherent, polished work that beautifully articulates the somber mood of Rossetti's middle years, his skepticism, his recognition that the primary experience of sensation is all he could be certain of, his consequent solipsism and fleshliness.

[44]Doughty, *A Victorian Romantic*, p. 475.

PART II

Limited Vision and Victorian Love Poetry (1868–1872)

4

Diminished Romanticism

THE years 1868 to 1872 were by far the most important in Rossetti's poetic career; his productions of this period define him as a poet. After years of struggling to find his own voice and style, he had finally, with the new poems of the period, and the revisions of old ones, achieved a kind of self-definition, which was also, necessarily, a kind of self-limiting. He was unquestionably at his poetic peak at this time, and wrote most of his best lyrics, including most of the sonnets of *The House of Life*. Further, as we have seen, even most of his best "early" work was so heavily revised that the best-known versions actually date from this time, and as we shall see, Rossetti wrote little of value after 1872. From 1868 to 1872, then, Rossetti, in his best and most mature style, articulated his most important and most characteristic concerns. Consequently, it is from the works of this period that what is most quintessentially Rossettian, his "Victorian Romanticism," must be defined. As becomes evident from a brief survey of the Romantic background and of the themes and images that Rossetti adopted and adapted from his Romantic predecessors, his Victorian rationalism, skepticism, and materialism forced him to limit his Romantic vision. Even at his most confident he continually restrained his imagination, refusing to place more than a limited faith in its productions.

Certainly, Rossetti's limited vision won almost unlimited praise among his artistic coterie. When he finally produced his first volume of original poetry, *Poems*, in 1870, it was greeted with loud and enthusiastic adulation in the press. As is well known, however, Rossetti had rigged the critical jury by providing advance copies of his book to friends and admirers who were certain both to praise him and to find prominent places for their praise. Rossetti has been both blamed and excused for his tactics, but what is most remarkable about his arrangements is that he was able to make them—that he was able to influence so many poets and critics to sing his praises. Such men as Swinburne, Morris (though somewhat grudgingly), the blind poet Philip Bourke Marston, Thomas Gordon Hake, and Sidney Colvin were all prepared to eulogize him and, more remarkable still, to do so sincerely. Swinburne actually had to be restrained from excessive and possibly embarrassing praise—though his review shows little enough restraint. The response to Rossetti's call was so prompt, in fact, that at least one sympathetic reviewer could not find an outlet for his enthusiasm. Shortly after the publication, George Meredith wrote to Rossetti saying that he would have liked to lavish praise upon the volume, but had been beaten to it. He gave some idea of what he might have said when he told Rossetti, "You are our Master, of all of us," and observed that Swinburne "threw flowers on you in the *Fortnightly:* not one was undeserved. After first finishing this book my voice would have been as unrestrained, less eloquent."[1]

Swinburne's was by far the most eloquent and enthusiastic of these friendly reviews. He did indeed throw flowers on Rossetti, comparing him favorably, in some respects at least, with Milton and Shakespeare and declaring him the foremost of living poets. But for all his extravagance, Swinburne did isolate the characteristics of Rossetti's poetry that remain at the center of critical discus-

[1]For an account of Rossetti's orchestration of praise, see Oswald Doughty, *A Victorian Romantic: Dante Gabriel Rossetti* (London: Frederick Muller, 1949), pp. 442–448. For Meredith's comment, see *The Collected Letters of George Meredith*, ed. C. L. Cline (London: Oxford University Press, 1970), I: 418.

sions of Rossetti today. He praised his friend for lucidity while anticipating charges of obscurity, and for intense focus and "ardent harmony" while anticipating charges of a lack of variety, but most emphatically he repeatedly, even redundantly, praised Rossetti for his combination of perfect aesthetic form with his celebration of a sacramental vision of Love, "his eucharistic presence, . . . his utter union in flesh and spirit." Swinburne's description of Rossetti's sonnets seems even to emulate the effects of the master by uniting ideas of form and "fleshliness": "No nakedness could be more harmonious, more consummate in its fleshly sculpture, than the imperial array and ornament of this august poetry."[2] All of his evident attempts to anticipate and disarm hostile criticism, unfortunately, were nullified by this emphasis, which may have armed Robert Buchanan, the poet-critic-moralist Rossetti most feared, with the word "fleshly" and the title of his notorious attack, "The Fleshly School of Poetry." Buchanan, of course, needed no help from Swinburne, but he does seem to have attacked Rossetti precisely where Swinburne praised him. He accused him of obscurity, narrowness of range, confusion about the distinction between soul and body rather than a sacramental vision and, above all, of sheer, beastly fleshliness. Whatever his subject, said Buchanan, Rossetti "is fleshly all over, from the roots of his hair to the tips of his toes; never a true lover merging his identity into that of the beloved one; never spiritual, never tender; always self-conscious and aesthetic."[3] Buchanan was as willing as Swinburne to grant Rossetti's fusion of form and content, his "fleshy sculpture"; he accused Rossetti of beastliness both because he was "fleshly" and because he was "aesthetic." Buchanan's outspoken attack against aesthetic fleshliness caused a furor by raising many of the issues underlying the mid-Victorian fear of art—along with Whistler's lawsuit against Ruskin, it marks one of the last great battles in the West between those who believed in the autonomy of art and those who believed that art

---

[2]"The Poems of Dante Gabriel Rossetti," in *The Complete Works of Algernon Charles Swinburne,* ed. Edmund Gosse and Thomas James Wise, 20 vols. (London: Heinemann, 1925–1927), 15: 6, 4, 9, 7.

[3]Robert Buchanan, *The Fleshly School of Poetry and Other Phenomena of the Day* (London: Strahan, 1872), p. 45.

should be a handmaiden to morality.[4] Perhaps Buchanan could have found considerable support in addition to the private support he claimed from Browning and Tennyson, but his attack was too outspoken, was, in fact, scurrilously *ad hominem,* and few were willing to be publicly associated with such tactics. Buchanan was ridiculed and ultimately retracted his position to join the chorus of praise for Rossetti. Art, it seems, had won.

But in the long run, Rossetti, perhaps, had not. Rossetti's most recent critics have more often than not agreed with Buchanan's, rather than Swinburne's, estimate of Rossetti's treatment of love. Certainly Buchanan was right in insisting that Rossetti's poetry is overtly and explicitly concerned with sexual love, since many of the sonnets are about kisses, embraces, or the repletion that follows sexual intercourse. And many recent critics have agreed with him that Rossetti's description of love is merely confused when it aspires to be sacramental. Masao Miyoshi, for example, has written that in "the Rossettian mana of words, the act of love is an instant sacra- ment, without benefit of any of the richer metaphysical sanctions utilized, for example, in Donne's sonnets."[5] Graham Hough has succinctly stated what he sees as the basis of Rossetti's confusion:

> Perpetually tormented by the irreconcilability of the unsensual love he had idealized and the love of the senses, he tries to identify them. Knowing that Dante's ideal love became in some way identified with the highest spiritual values, but blankly unaware of the austere scho- lastic method, the exact analysis and definition by which the trans- formation was accomplished, he simply turns his own confused and all too human conception of love into the highest value, and calls it God.[6]

Though the moral outrage of Buchanan is gone, the objection that Rossetti failed to achieve a sacramental vision remains, as does the

[4]See Jerome Hamilton Buckley's chapter "The Fear of Art," pp. 161–184 in his *The Victorian Temper: A Study in Literary Culture* (New York: Random House, 1964).

[5]Masao Miyoshi, *The Divided Self: A Perspective on the Literature of the Victorians* (New York: New York University Press, 1969), p. 254.

[6]Graham Hough, *The Last Romantics* (1947; rpt. London: Methuen, 1961), p. 80.

claim that he failed to take seriously the Christian symbolism he borrowed from Dante and the *stilnovisti*. But although these assertions are true, they are not very relevant as grounds for critical judgment. In the first place, Rossetti could argue, with Blake, Shelley, Swinburne, and many others, that it is impossible to be "too human" and that the human *is* the highest value. Rossetti was not only an agnostic, but by 1870 he had been taking pains to eliminate everything in his work that might even suggest that he was a believer. His agnosticism was the source of his artistic difficulties, it is true, but only because it was his artistic challenge. It is also true that he could not achieve a Dantean apotheosis of love, but not because he was "blankly unaware of the austere scholastic method"—he was, after all, raised in a household where Dante's scholasticism was under constant scrutiny. He was, however, indifferent to such austere scholasticism, because he did not believe in Dante's metaphysics, but only in Dante's art.[7] He criticized a poem by Guido Cavalcanti because it was too much concerned with "metaphysical jargon" and so "beside the purpose of poetry" (*Works*, 302). He imitated the forms of these poets, to some extent, and some of their imagery to a considerable extent, but he was fully aware that love, in his poetry, could not lead to the consummation that it did in the Christianity of the Italian thirteenth century. Such poets as Fra Guittone d'Arezzo could conclude a sonnet to their beloved with an invocation to the Blessed Virgin; the poem of love could become a prayer that "earthly Love" be replaced by "that holy love / Which leads back to its origin" just "As nail from out a plank is struck by nail."[8] But Rossetti, who could feel the same passion of love, could not replace "earthly Love" and did not want to. As Swinburne was the first to observe, Rossetti was not attracted to Christian doctrine or faith, but only to "Christian

[7]If Rossetti ever did forget Dante's scholasticism, he was likely to be quickly reminded of it, as by a letter from Thomas Keightley, praising him for his translations but adding, "But, you degenerate, you seem to regard the *Vita Nuova* as a real autobiography! Now I not only think but am certain that your father actually demonstrated to the contrary. To my mind Beatrice, Laura, Mandilla and all the rest of the bevy are as ideal as Queen Mab" (Keightley's letter, dated December 25, 1861, is in the Janet Camp Troxell Collection at Princeton University).

[8]"Sonnet: To the Blessed Virgin Mary," Rossetti's translation, *Works*, pp. 452–453.

forms and images . . . the mythologic side of the creed. It is from the sandbanks of tradition and poetry that the sacred sirens sing to this seafarer."[9] It is important to remember that when Rossetti, an agnostic, speaks of God in his poetry, he does not mean or intend to mean what Dante meant—any more than Swinburne, an atheist, means that the "eucharistic presence" of love brings Christ into men's lives. As his revisions repeatedly indicate, such words as God and soul were interchangeable for Rossetti with words like Truth, and Love, and mind.

Rossetti's use of Christian forms without Christian faith does not indicate, however, that his imagery and diction are merely decorative. Rather the forms indicate a psychological need to reach for something that exceeds his grasp; just as the Christian reaches to the infinite and eternal God, so the Rossettian lover reaches for some infinite and eternal certainty that, for lack of a better name, he may call God. This aspiration, this seeking for the infinite, is neither particularly Dantean nor Christian, but is universal and takes different forms in different times and different cultures. Despite Rossetti's pose of being not at home in the nineteenth century, and despite his occasional medievalism, his most serious poetry is very much a product of his age.

The various labels that have been attached to Rossetti indicate that, despite the superficial medievalism, he has always been regarded as a belated Romantic. He has been variously described as a Victorian Romantic, one of the Last Romantics, and a failed Romantic, presumably because he is perceived as carrying on, or attempting to carry on, the Romantic tradition of his great predecessors.[10] The ways in which Rossetti followed in the wake of Keats have been well studied, particularly by George Ford, but Ford's comment on Rossetti's debts to the other Romantic poets may

[9]Swinburne, p. 21.

[10]The phrase "Victorian Romantic" was applied to Rossetti by T. Earle Welby in *The Victorian Romantics* (London: Gerald Howe, 1929) and later became well known through the title of Oswald Doughty's *A Victorian Romantic: Dante Gabriel Rossetti*. Graham Hough's *The Last Romantics* includes a discussion of Rossetti. Rossetti has been described as a failed Romantic by Stephen J. Spector in "Love, Unity, and Desire in the Poetry of Dante Gabriel Rossetti," *English Literary History*, 38 (1971), 432–458.

make us wonder if the labels that have been attached to Rossetti are appropriate; Ford asserts that except for Keats and "parts of Coleridge," Rossetti "has little in common" with the Romantic poets: "he reacted against Wordsworth and Shelley, and even Byron was not in his line."[11] And in fact, Rossetti completely disassociated himself from Wordsworth, whom he did not like ("He's good, you know, but unbearable"), praised Coleridge only for "Six years from sixty saved," outgrew a youthful passion for Byron, and expressed gratification that Shelley died young and so ceased to hatch "yearly universes."[12] But whether or not Shelley directly influenced him, Rossetti's poetry shows far more striking analogues in theme and imagery with Shelley than with Keats or any of the other Romantic poets. His distaste for Shelley's "yearly universes" indicates not that he disliked Shelley—in fact he revered him—but only that he was exasperated by Shelley's vastness of scope. If the phrases "Victorian Romantic," "Last Romantics" and "failed Romantic" mean anything, they must mean that Rossetti was what James Richardson, describing the poetry of Thomas Hardy, called a diminished Romantic: "though Hardy has much in common with his Romantic forebears and though he admired them past idolatry, he was unable and unwilling to repeat their performance. He felt dwarfed by them, but he felt even more strongly the necessity of his diminution, perceiving that their styles, aspirations and modes of thought were, for him, not only impossible but also inappropriate, and perhaps even embarrassing."[13] Rossetti, an agnostic in an increasingly skeptical age, could not, like Shelley, poetically embrace cosmic themes. Rather, he limited himself, for the most part, to the diminished theme of love, but within this sphere his parallels in theme and imagery with Shelley are remarkable.

[11]George Ford, *Keats and the Victorians* (New Haven: Yale University Press, 1944), p. 142.

[12]The comment on Wordsworth is in *Letters*, I:361. That on Shelley is recorded by T. Hall Caine, *Recollections of Dante Gabriel Rossetti* (London: Elliot Stock, 1882), p. 170. On another occasion, however, Rossetti told Caine that Shelley was, with Shakespeare and Coleridge, one of the three "Greatest English imaginations" (p. 148).

[13]James Richardson, *Thomas Hardy: The Poetry of Necessity* (Chicago: University of Chicago Press, 1977), pp. 1–2.

All the Romantic poets were concerned with the disparity between man's infinite aspirations and his limited capacities, with the
dilemma that man is, as Byron said, "Half dust, half deity, alike
unfit / To sink or soar." The poet of love is almost necessarily concerned also with what Browning, in one of the great love poems of
English literature, called the "infinite passion, and the pain / Of
finite hearts that yearn." The universal dilemma of the lover was
economically described by Sir Thomas Browne: "United souls are
not satisfied with imbraces, but desire to be truly each other; which
being impossible, their desires are infinite."[14] In one of the most
penetrating critical studies to date of Rossetti's poetry, Stephen
Spector has argued that Rossetti is concerned with the theme of
love in just this way: "The lover's desire for unity with his beloved
is best understood as the most important manifestation of man's
overarching desire to be united with something outside of himself,
especially God. Love is not generated by regard for another person,
but by the universal desire to heal the wound of existence."[15]
Spector, however, regards Rossetti as a failed Romantic, since he
did not fully achieve the "creative act of the Romantic Imagination" that ends in fusing the subjective and objective worlds,[16] self
and other, in a union that gives meaning both to the sense of self by
locating it in a larger context, and to the objective world by hu-
manizing it. Through an examination of two of Rossetti's most
characteristic images, the mirror and the horizon line, he shows
that Rossetti was never able to escape from "the prison of subjectivism," that his love was ultimately narcissistic since his "beloved
never exists as another consciousness" but is "only a mirror for the
lover." He concludes that Rossetti's combination of narcissism and
agnosticism condemns him to despair: "Without God the self needs
some ground of value outside itself in order to be sustained, and by
denying the alterity of his beloved, by using her merely to reflect
himself, the lover destroys his own best hope for salvation."[17] Spector's argument sounds ominously like Buchanan's condemnation of
Rossetti and the rest of "The Fleshly School of Poetry" on the

[14]*Manfred*, I.ii, 40–41; "Two in the Campagna," 11. 59–60; *Religio Medici*, II:6.
[15]Spector, "Love, Unity, and Desire," p. 438.
[16]Ibid., p. 432.
[17]Ibid., p. 458.

grounds that poetry "must deal with great issues, not with the 'damnable face-making' of Narcissus in a mirror,"[18] but it is, nevertheless, essentially correct, except that Rossetti does achieve a certain success and that a kind of narcissism, purged of its pejorative connotations, is, as a comparison with Shelley will illustrate, a necessary characteristic of diminished—not failed—Romanticism. In fact a brief survey of the work of his Romantic predecessors reveals the historical necessity for Rossetti's diminution into a kind of imaginative narcissism.

The creative act of Wordsworth and Coleridge was ideally, as Coleridge described it, "a repetition in the finite mind of the eternal act of creation in the infinite I AM."[19] Coleridge's Christian faith sanctioned his assertion that the voice of man, at its clearest and highest pitch, literally reverberates in the divine Logos, that the harmony of man's song and God's was a fusion of the individual mind in the One Mind. But without the sanction of faith, Byron, Shelley, and Keats, all skeptics, could not unite with God by proclaiming their own identities. The problem for the belated Romantic was that if he climbed to the mountain top and cried, "I am," the only echo he heard was the one Narcissus rejected. Rather than joining in the universal harmony of God, Nature, and Man, he was singing a solo in a voice that asserted its own identity but found no replies. Byron, Shelley, and Keats all anticipated Rossetti by losing faith in the attempts of their predecessors to fuse the self with the soul of all and so liberate themselves from the burden of isolation. They did not, however, withdraw from the attempt to unite their self-consciousnesses with some external object that would both strengthen their conviction, "I AM," and allow them to escape, at least in some small measure, from solipsism. Their aspirations remained as high as Wordsworth's and Coleridge's, but their expectations diminished. The history of Romanticism is largely a history of retreat from unattainable aspirations and of consequently limited scope for the imagination. The Romantic reliance on the sense of self, Wordsworth's "egotistical sublime" and Coleridge's "I AM," becomes increasingly centered in the self alone, without transcen-

---

[18]Buchanan, p. 90.
[19]*Biographia Literaria*, Chapter XIII.

dent sanctions. It becomes, in fact, a justifiable imaginative narcissism.

One of the reasons for Rossetti's admiration and emulation of Dante may well have been that in an agnostic age even Dante—a kind of diminished Dante—could be read as a narcissistic poet. Paul Valéry's *Narcissus Cantata*, for example, has been read as a Dantean work: "Narcissus' contemplation of his own reflection in the pool is analogous to the end of philosophy as Dante describes it: 'The philosophizing soul not only contemplates the truth, but also contemplates its own contemplation and the beauty thereof, turning upon itself and enamoring itself of itself by reason of the beauty of its direct contemplation.'"[20] The agnostic cannot, of course, be certain that he is contemplating truth (hence his diminishment), but he can become enamored of his own contemplation and assert that "Beauty is Truth"—or the closest he can come to it.

The extent to which the Romantic legacy inherited by Rossetti and other "Victorian Romantics" led to contemplation of one's own contemplation can best be appreciated by examining the Romantic uses of one of the images Spector isolated as peculiarly Rossettian—that of the mirror, or more generally, of the reflecting surface. As Romantic poetry became more and more concerned, in the second generation, with the theme of love, the mirror imagery came more and more to anticipate Rossetti's use of it. And Rossetti's narcissistic preoccupation with the theme of love, moreover, both partakes of the Romantic tradition and modulates into more specifically Victorian concerns. Most particularly, Rossetti's conception of love, as expressed in his imagery, epitomizes some of the ways in which the cultural continuity of the nineteenth century manifested itself, and consequently provides an approach to interpreting that seemingly oxymoronic phrase, "Victorian Romanticism."

More often than not, generalizations about Romanticism tend to be generalizations about Wordsworth's poetic achievements and Coleridge's poetic theories. Certainly it is usually against the mag-

---

[20]Francis Fergusson, introduction to Paul Valéry, *Plays*, trans. David Paul and Robert Fitzgerald (New York: Pantheon, 1960), pp. xii–xiv. See also Donald Stuart, "Bitter Fantasy: Narcissus in Dante Gabriel Rossetti's Lyrics," *Victorians Institute Journal*, 2 (1973), 29.

nitude of Wordsworth's vision that Rossetti has often been judged as falling short of the Romantic ideal—Buchanan's attack, for example, asserts that Wordsworth is the savior of the English poetic tradition and pillories Rossetti for, among other things, the relative pettiness of his concerns. Spector's argument that the characteristic Romantic act of creation bridges the "gap between the subjective and objective worlds" accurately defines the frequent achievement of Wordsworth and the occasional achievement of Coleridge, but it defines only the aspirations of Byron, Shelley, and Keats. To place Rossetti firmly in the tradition of these latter Romantics, in fact, we need only compare Spector's description of Rossetti's failed aspirations with Keats's description of his own in the "Ode to a Nightingale," his greatest attempt to achieve a union of self and other. Spector's comment that in Rossetti's verse "the lover's desire for unity is often expressed as if it were a desire for death" is clearly paralleled by Keats's "many a time / I have been half in love with easeful Death," and his observation that Rossetti never achieves the Romantic escape from self-consciousness is paralleled by Keats's forlorn return to his "sole self" near the end of the ode.

The parallels are not merely fortuitous, but reflect a necessary diminishment from the bardic Wordsworthian stance, not only for Rossetti, but for Keats, as his struggles to cope with the anxieties of Wordsworthian influence illustrate. The record of that struggle wonderfully demonstrates the dilemma of all post-Wordsworthian Romantics. In February 1818, Keats was striving to escape from the shadow of Wordsworth by reducing the size of the shadow, by attempting to regard Wordsworth himself as a diminished poet. Comparing Wordsworth and other moderns to the Elizabethans, who were "Emperors of vast provinces," he complained that "Each of the moderns like an Elector of Hanover governs his petty state, & knows how many straws are swept daily from the Causeways in all his dominions & has a continual itching that all the Housewives should have their coppers well scoured." He went on to ask "Why should we be owls, when we can be Eagles?"[21] Exactly four months later Keats had matured sufficiently to realize that despite his di-

[21]*The Letters of John Keats, 1814–1821*, ed. Hyder Edward Rollins, 2 vols. (Cambridge: Harvard University Press, 1958), I:224.

117

minished province, Wordsworth was in fact an eagle, whether "in his nest, or on the wing." His changed assessment of Wordsworth had resulted from a realization that as the "grand march of intellect" expands the realms of human thought, the possibility of governing vast provinces is reduced, and even the "mightiest Minds" are subdued to "the service of the time being."[22] The great poets of the future, Keats's comments imply, will be those who watch the straws on their causeways most carefully.

Keats suggests, in other words, that the "grand march of intellect" that has diminished Wordsworth's province will continue to diminish the provinces of succeeding poets. The process of diminishment can be followed in the grand march through the Romantic period. What Spector describes as characteristic Romanticism is actually only fully realized in what may be called the undiminished poetry of Wordsworth and Coleridge during their mutual great decade. During this period Wordsworth's high argument and the main region of his song was "the mind of man" and its wedding to "this goodly universe."[23] His theme was love, but "intellectual Love," synonymous with the Imagination that binds not man and woman, but man and nature:

> Imagination having been our theme,
> So also hath that intellectual Love,
> For they are each in each, and cannot stand
> Dividually.

Despite his "egotistical sublime," Wordsworth was assuredly not a narcissistic poet, but his insistence on the "auxiliar light" that impresses the forms of imagination on nature does indicate that, to an extent, he sought in nature the mirror of his own mind. On the top of Mount Snowdon he received the revelation that the "power" nature "exhibits" is "the express / Resemblance" of the imagination in "higher minds." And further, he learned that "higher minds"

> from their native selves can send abroad
> Kindred mutations; for themselves create

[22]Ibid., p. 280.
[23]"Prospectus" to *The Excursion*, ll. 40–41, 53.

118

A like existence; and whene'er it dawns
Created for them, catch it, or are caught
By its inevitable mastery.

Wordsworth was neither solipsistic nor narcissistic, since he recognized a power in nature that resembled mind and transcended it. His pantheistic sanction enabled him to see the mirror image of his "I Am" as a reverberation of a larger "I AM," and so confirmed his sense of self and gave it value. From this intercourse with nature, he asserted, higher minds gain the "highest bliss / That flesh can know . . . the consciousness / Of Whom they are." But without the leap of faith to pantheism or something very much like it, Wordsworth's consciousness would be only consciousness of the "sole self"—and the leap of faith became all but impossible for later poets. Wordsworth's insistence on the authority of the individual imagination, moreover, could occasionally draw him perilously close to the isolation of complete subjectivity, since "intellectual Love" is found only in "the recesses of thy nature, far / From any reach of outward fellowship." In later poets this realization led, not unnaturally, to fears of solipsism and the absorbed introspection represented by the symbol of Narcissus. Characteristically, when Wordsworth looked into the reflecting surface of water, he saw the "beauteous sights" in the stream's bed as well as the reflection, and the reflection, mostly of "rocks and sky, / Mountains and clouds," was only occasionally "crossed by gleam / Of his own image."[24] Later poets would find the waters darker, their own reflections more prominent.

From the start the distinction between egocentric poetry and narcissism was less clearly marked in Coleridge than in Wordsworth. His description, in 1801, of a way to escape the domination of the self provides a curious gloss on one of Wordsworth's poetic descriptions, in "Tintern Abbey," of "Romantic creation":

—and the deep power of Joy
We see into the *Life* of Things—

[24]*The Prelude*, Book 14, ll. 207–210, 88–90, 93–97, 113–115, 216–217; Book 4, ll. 256–270.

119

i.e.—By deep feeling we make our *Ideas dim*—& this is what we mean
by our Life—ourselves. I think of the Wall—it is before me, a distinct
Image—here. I necessarily think of the *Idea* & the Thinking I as two
distinct & opposite Things. Now let me think of *myself*—of the
thinking Being—the Idea becomes dim whatever it be—so dim that I
know not what it is—but the Feeling is deep & steady—and this I call
I ~~the~~ [sic] identifying the Percipient & the Perceived—[25]

More clearly than Wordsworth, Coleridge is contemplating his own
contemplation. In her fine essay "Reflections in a Coleridge Mirror: Some Images in His Poems," Kathleen Coburn has traced
Coleridge's uses of the imagery of reflection in his prose and poetry.
Her just and perceptive argument, which places Coleridge firmly in
the tradition I have been sketchily tracing, asserts that as Coleridge's "larger constructive poetic drives disappeared," he became
increasingly concerned with finding a self-image that would be
connected, like Wordsworth's, to some vital source of being. The
image of the mirror became more and more ambivalent for him—
the mirror does, argues Coburn, reflect "the image of an inward
self," but it "also distances the self from itself. The intervention of
a reflecting surface . . . asserts the essential severance of the self
from the other, from the image even."[26] Coburn's reading of Coleridge, which sounds very much like Spector's reading of Rossetti,
suggests both that the failure to identify fully the percipient and the
perceived may be inevitable, and that the attempt to do so by
studying one's own image in the mirror is, however desperate,
legitimate and meaningful. Coleridge cannot be regarded as a diminished poet in the same sense as Rossetti, since the glass he
looked in was the universe itself, not simply a mirror, or a reflecting
stream, or a lover's eyes, but his failure on a grand scale does justify
the attempts of later poets to reduce the scale.

The second generation of Romantic poets did, in certain respects, and in certain moods, attempt just such a reduction in scale,

[25]Quoted in Kathleeen Coburn, "Reflections in a Coleridge Mirror: Some Images in His Poems," in *From Sensibility to Romanticism: Essays Presented to Frederick
A. Pottle*, ed. Frederick W. Hilles and Harold Bloom (New York: Oxford University Press, 1965), pp. 421–422.
[26]Ibid., pp. 415, 433.

120

as the efforts of Keats to free himself from the anxiety of Wordsworth's influence clearly illustrate. One consequence of the realization that imagination has less scope than Wordsworth had hoped
was that the object of Romantic imagination changed, or diminished, from "the vast empire" of nature and the universal all to the
more manageable province of human love, man's love for woman.
This shift, which has obvious implications for any understanding of
Rossetti's love poetry, is evident in Keats's work from the beginning
to the end of his short career. The hero of *Endymion* seeks to satisfy
his vague Romantic longings by union with a dream vision of a very
human—all too human, as some would have it—goddess. His first
waking vision of his ideal is seen as a reflection in a "clear well,"[27]
significantly like the vision of Narcissus. In the end Endymion finds
happiness only after the goddess descends from the empyrean and
takes the identity of a fully human, suffering and sorrowful Indian
maiden. In the process of writing the poem, or perhaps earlier,
Keats had learned that man's desires, however vast, must find satisfaction in a limited object of love. His romances, "Isabella," "The
Eve of St. Agnes," and "Lamia," have frequently been described as
escapist poetry, but they reflect his realization that the proper object of man's desires should not be infinite but warm, palpable, and
attainable. When he tried, in *Hyperion* and *The Fall of Hyperion,* to
write on a larger scale, he was stymied by his inability to find his
own voice rather than echoing the voices of earlier epic poets—he
rejected *Hyperion* because it was too Miltonic and, had he lived, he
might have come to regard *The Fall of Hyperion* as too Dantean. In
any case, his finest work, including the great odes, addresses itself
to limited objects and is concerned more to show the limits of the
fancy, which "cannot cheat so well / As she is fam'd to do,"[28] than
to exalt a visionary imagination. His poetry is always sensual, not
transcendent: the sacramental act of Porphyro, an "eremite," is
sexual union with Madeline, his "heaven."[29]

As George Ford has persuasively argued, Keats's sensual love
poetry opened new possibilities for Victorian poets, possibilities

---

[27]*Endymion,* I, 896.
[28]"Ode to a Nightingale," ll. 73–74.
[29]"The Eve of St. Agnes," l. 276.

that Rossetti fully exploited. Rossetti's treatment of love and his freedom to indulge in sensual description certainly owe much to the precedent of Keats, but his characteristically self-absorbed approach to ideal love has more in common with the work of Byron, and especially of Shelley. Like Keats, though more satirically, Byron reacted against the transcendental metaphysics of Wordsworth and Coleridge. In one of the funniest passages of *Don Juan*, Byron wittily described precisely the shift of imaginative sympathy that I have been attempting to sketch. Recounting Juan's perplexed responses to Donna Julia, Byron first traces Juan's growth through Wordsworthianism—under the auspices of nature Juan thought the kinds of "unutterable things" that poets use as "materials for their books" even though "like Wordsworth" they may "prove unintelligible." After his Wordsworthian "self-communion with his own high soul," Juan went into a Coleridgean phase:

> he did the best he could
> With things not very subject to control,
> And turned, without perceiving his condition,
> Like Coleridge, into a metaphysician.

The next two stanzas are worth quoting entirely, both for their quality and for their pertinence:

> He thought about himself, and the whole earth
> Of man the wonderful, and of the stars,
> And how the deuce they ever could have birth;
> And then he thought of earthquakes, and of wars,
> How many miles the moon might have in girth,
> Of air-balloons, and of the many bars
> To perfect knowledge of the boundless skies;—
> And then he thought of Donna Julia's eyes.

> In thoughts like these true Wisdom may discern
> Longings sublime and aspirations high,
> Which some are born with, but the most part learn
> To plague themselves withal, they know not why:
> 'T was strange that one so young should thus concern
> His brain about the action of the sky;

122

If *you* think 't was Philosophy that this did,
I can't help thinking puberty assisted.[30]

Byron's wit should not be allowed to obscure the serious import of the passage. The lines perfectly illustrate his considered response to the themes of Wordsworth and Coleridge—their concerns are lofty, but there is too much to know for man to embrace it all without becoming divorced from the more immediate concerns of his nature. Juan's fully human impulse is not to possess the all, not to "possess all things with intensest love," but only to possess Donna Julia. Juan matures and grows away from what Coleridge himself described as "vain Philosophy's aye-babbling spring."[31] It is not, I think, stretching the point too far to suggest that just as "a deep distress . . . humanised [Wordsworth's] Soul" in "Elegiac Stanzas,"[32] so a deep love has humanized Juan's. Byron is perhaps unjust to Wordsworth and Coleridge, who sought always to be true to their immediate experiences, but as Wordsworth's constant evocation of his childhood indicates, the experiences they celebrated were not those of full maturity. The most honest account of man's true nature, Byron suggests, must stem from an understanding of his most primitive self, and his most primitive desires.

The note of despair that characterizes Byron's more "serious" poetry results from his realization, however, that even sexual love is not simple, and is not enough. He fully realized, and fully felt, that something in man's nature aspires to embrace the infinite, but unlike Wordsworth and Coleridge, he realized the futility of that aspiration from the start. In *Manfred* he lamented the sad fact that man is "Half dust, half deity, alike unfit / To sink or soar." Manfred, despite his ability to communicate with the supernatural, cannot escape from his tormented, divided self through philosophy or magic. His one hope—and even that is a forlorn hope—is through love, love which, as Spector observed, "is not generated by regard for another person, but by the universal desire to heal the wound of existence." And Manfred's love exhibits precisely the

---

[30]Canto I, stanzas XC-XCIII.
[31]"The Eolian Harp," l. 57.
[32]"Elegiac Stanzas," l. 36.

characteristics that Spector identifies as Rossettian. Whether or not Manfred's passion for Astarte is incestuous, as Byron broadly hints, it is certainly narcissistic. Like Rossetti's lovers, Manfred seems to see in Astarte only an idealized image of himself:

> She was like me in lineaments; her eyes;
> Her hair, her features, all, to the very tone
> Even of her voice, they said, were like to mine;
> But softened all, and tempered into beauty . . .
>
> . . . . .
> Her faults were mine—her virtues were her own—[33]

And when the Phantom of Astarte appears to him, she is able only to confirm his own identity, twice repeating his name: "Manfred!" Also like Rossettian love, Manfred's leads only to death, as is clearly implied both by his seeking Astarte in the realms of death and by his own death at the end of the drama.

Byron's treatment of the theme of love suggests the dilemma that a late Romantic might face; Shelley's treatment of the theme, both in his poetry and his prose, suggests that it is a dilemma that a late Romantic *must* face, and also suggests why. Like Byron, Shelley was obsessed with the idea of incestuous love, but for Shelley the idea is less involved with guilt, and more explicitly related to a search for spiritual wholeness, a search for some way to unite the normally isolated self with external spiritual values. As Earl Wasserman has said, in a comment that applies to both Byron and Shelley, the "incestuous desire of brother and sister motivated by love, though 'incorrect,' expresses the desire of the self for union with its own perfection."[34] In *Alastor*, his first fully mature expression of his deepest poetic impulses, Shelley described the quest of the visionary Romantic as just such a desire for union with his own perfection. The vision that appears to the visionary in an erotic dream is "Herself a poet" who reflects all of his own best and highest

---

[33]*Manfred*, II.iii. 106–109, 117.

[34]Earl Wasserman, *Shelley: A Critical Reading* (Baltimore: Johns Hopkins University Press, 1971), p. 85.

themes, addressing him with a voice, "like the voice of his own soul." The visionary seeks his ideal, "Vision and Love," by retracing the stream of his own life, following the path marked by the reflections of his own searching eyes in the darkness of the stream. Shelley, like Byron, was aware that the Wordsworthian quest for union with otherness was essentially regressive because it depended on "Recollections of Early Childhood"; *Alastor* self-consciously demonstrates Shelley's conviction that such a quest could not succeed. The visionary is, like Wordsworth in the "Immortality Ode," "Obedient to the light / That shone within his soul," but Shelley's despair in *Alastor,* his insistence that the visionary light prompts only a restless longing that ends in death, reveals his awareness that the Wordsworthian attempt to escape from the prison of selfhood is itself solipsistic: since the image he seeks is the image he projects, it must always remain just out of reach. Shelley's symbol for the dilemma—a symbol taken up and modified by Rossetti—is the pose of Narcissus:

> Hither the Poet came. His eyes beheld
> Their own wan light through the reflected lines
> Of his thin hair, distinct in the dark depth
> Of that still fountain; as the human heart,
> Gazing in dreams over the gloomy grave,
> Sees its own treacherous likeness there.[35]

The tantalizing projection is before him constantly, but the attempt to unite with it would result in death by drowning—or, in larger terms, absorption in the universal all. In "A Slumber Did My Spirit Seal" Wordsworth was consoled by the dead Lucy's fusion with the life of nature:

> No motion has she now, no force;
>   She neither hears nor sees;
> Rolled round in earth's diurnal course,
>   With rocks, and stones, and trees.

[35]*Alastor,* ll. 161, 153, 367, 491–42, 469–474.

Describing the death of the Poet, Shelley rejected both this consolation and the great Wordsworthian and Coleridgean image of
man's harmony with the breath and life of nature, the eolian harp:

> No sense, no motion, no divinity—
> A fragile lute, on whose harmonious strings
> The breath of heaven did wander—a bright stream
> Once fed with many-voiced waves—a dream
> Of youth, which night and time have quenched for ever.
> Still, dark, and dry, and unremembered now.[36]

Like Keats and Byron, Shelley, with the example of Wordsworth's
and Coleridge's failure to maintain the vision before him, was unable to believe in the possibility of meaningful escape from the self.

Shelley's characterization of the Romantic vision as a woman
who is also a projected ideal self, a characterization that epitomizes
the diminution of the late Romantic, is consistent throughout his
work. And his description of the quest as an erotic longing shows
not only a diminution from the cosmic union of Wordsworth and
Coleridge, but also from the imaginative vision of Blake, who, in
"The Crystal Cabinet," implied that the erotic vision that may lead
to momentary satisfaction and even to a hint of a greater vision is,
in fact, delusive. Once entrapped in the erotic vision, as Blake saw
it, the only way out is not to higher vision, but back to a natural,
primitive state.

Shelley's clearest poetic treatment of the theme of visionary erot-
icism is, of course, *Epipsychidion,* a poem in which he attempted,
and failed, to unite himself with his idealized epipsyche—the soul
within his soul. But his most direct discussion of the problem is the
short essay "On Love." Shelley's definition of love immediately
identifies it as both man's best means of escape from himself, and as
a necessarily limited means: "It is that powerful attraction towards
all that we conceive or fear or hope beyond ourselves when we find
within our own thoughts the chasm of an insufficient void and seek
to awaken in all things that are, a community with what we experience within ourselves." Our longing for communion, our "fear or

[36]*Alastor,* ll. 666–671.

hope beyond ourselves," is limited because our fears and hopes are limited to "what we experience within ourselves." Our aspirations are necessarily constrained to a kind of intellectual narcissism, a "thirst" after our own "likeness," as is shown in Shelley's choice of images to illustrate the object of man's desires: "Not only the *portrait* of our external being, but an assemblage of the minutest particulars of which our nature is composed: a *mirror* whose surface reflects only the forms of purity and brightness. . . ."[37] The images I have emphasized bring us back, at last, to Rossetti, since they are preeminently Rossettian images for the object of his Romantic longing. Within the larger context of Romantic diminishment, within the narrowed province of imagination implied by his continual return to the imagery of portraits, mirrors, the well of Narcissus, and other reflecting surfaces, Rossetti—his achievement and his place in the poetic tradition—can be better appreciated.

[37]"On Love," in *Shelley's Works in Verse and Prose*, ed. Harry Buxton Forman, 8 vols. (London: Reeves and Turner, 1880), 6:267–269.

5

Romantic Reflections

ROSSETTI's poetry was, much more often than not, love poetry, but it was rarely, if ever, only about love—love itself is a metaphor for the condition of desiring. Whatever autobiographical elements may be found in Rossetti's poetry, the love he described is never simply the love of Gabriel Rossetti for Lizzie Siddal, or for Fanny Cornforth, or for Jane Morris; rather it is, like the love Shelley described, a love for an ideal of perfection. The distinction between ideal love and actual love has not always been clear to Rossetti's readers. *The House of Life,* for example, has been frequently described as a House of Love, but it has also been described as an elegy. Both descriptions are right, but the more perceptive interpretation, which recognizes the metaphoric significance of love, places the poem in the tradition of *In Memoriam,* a poem that seeks answers to the weighty Victorian questions about the meaning of life and death in a world rapidly losing its traditional assumptions and values.[1] Both poems are diminished, without faith, though *In Memoriam* ends optimistically after the mystical experience of section 95; the very form of both poems, a series

---

[1]See William E. Fredeman, "Rossetti's 'In Memoriam': An Elegiac Reading of *The House of Life,*" *Bulletin of the John Rylands Library,* 47 (1965), 298–341.

of lyrics, indicates the refusal of the poets to attempt sustained discourse on high topics. Kathleen Coburn has said that Coleridge never achieved the poetic or philosophical goal that he sought through a metaphysical system, but reached it only by occasional brilliant *aperçus;* Tennyson and Rossetti, in their greatest poems, were willing to content themselves with the *aperçus,* without striving for a coherent system. But *The House of Life* is more limited in scope and range than *In Memoriam.* Though love is a metaphor for larger concerns, it is an obsessive one—in this sense *The House of Life* does remain a House of Love.

Most studies of *The House of Life* have been concerned either with identifying autobiographical referents or with questions about the poem's structure, so the imagery has been largely neglected. Such neglect is particularly unfortunate since, as Cecil Lang has observed, for Rossetti "the images are the poetry instead of the vehicle of a poetic effect." However much Rossetti's outward concerns changed over the course of his poetic career, however much the manifestations of his sensibility changed, his sensibility itself did not. Lang has made the point beautifully:

> The lovers who, hand in hand, bathe in God's sight in "The Blessed Damozel" have become, in "The One Hope," "vain desire" and vain regret, "going hand in hand to death." The falling autumn leaves of "The Blessed Damozel," which energize and particularize the scene with such precision and originality, are, as dropping rose petals, actually woven into the very integrity of the fabric of "Willowwood," and, as the hyacinthine petals of "The One Hope" scriptured with "Ai, Ai," are as complex and condensed as any symbol in Blake or Shelley. The "deep wells of light" of "The Blessed Damozel" are darkened to the "woodside well" of "Willowwood" and are mocked by the "sunk stream" and "Sweet life-fountain" of "The One Hope," as the mound of tree and earth on which the earth-bound lover leans his head in "The Blessed Damozel"—implied in the poem, explicit in the painting—becomes the grim pillow of "Willowwood," the "bitter banks" wan with that most hallucinogenic of surrealistic flora, the "tear-spurge."[2]

[2]Cecil Lang, *Introduction to the Pre-Raphaelites and Their Circle* (Chicago: The University of Chicago Press, 1975), p. xxix.

Consequently Rossetti's ways of seeing and knowing, of coming to terms with his problems, can be understood by studying the images that obsessed him throughout his career. The most important of these images is certainly the mirror, the reflecting surface.

Rossetti's symbolic use of the mirror is present in even his earliest poems. The enigmatic little poem "The Mirror" was written in 1850 and sent to William with the query, "Can you explain the following?"

> She knew it not,—most perfect pain
>   To learn; and this she knew not. Strife
>   For me, calm hers, as from the first.
>   'Twas but another bubble burst
>   Upon the curdling draught of life;—
> My silent patience mine again.
>
> As who, of forms that crowd unknown
>   Within a dusky mirror's shade,
>   Deems such an one himself, and makes
>   Some sign, but, when that image shakes
>   No whit, he finds his thought betrayed,
> And must seek elsewhere for his own.[3]

The obscurity of this poem results from Rossetti's frequent fault of excessive condensation, which often leads to tortured syntax, but as is common in Rossetti, the failure of syntax forces the reader to concentrate on the images. The first stanza of the poem evidently describes a lover's failure to communicate his love to a woman—the image of the "bubble burst / Upon the curdling draught of life" is more confusing than illuminating, but implies a buried metaphor of the stream of life. The bubble that rises to the surface of the waters of life later becomes an important symbol in Rossetti's poetry and is used frequently, as here, to suggest the struggle of what Matthew Arnold, in a similar image, called the "buried life" to come to the surface. The bursting suggests the inevitable fate of such impulses. The imagery in the second stanza is more fully developed, and more suggestive. The lover is compared to a man who, like Shelley, tries

[3]*Letters*, I:92–93.

to find himself reflected in a mirror—the beloved—that will in some way complete his existence. But the mirror is crowded with forms, and the attempt to find his own likeness fails. In "On Love" Shelley described his motivation to seek his own likeness in terms that closely resemble the difficulties of Rossetti's lover: "I see that in some external attributes they resemble me, but when misled by that appearance I have thought to appeal to something in common and unburden my inmost soul to them, I have found my language misunderstood like one in a distant and savage land."[4] Rossetti's simile vividly evokes the same terrifying idea of utter isolation and diminishment in a crowd of humanity—a diminishment so complete that he is unable to find his own image. The failure of love, then, is a failure to project one's identity on some external object, a failure, that is, to escape from the self. The final line of the poem, however, sets limits to Rossetti's pessimism—though his "thought" has been betrayed by his mistaken belief that he had found his own image, he will not give up but will "seek elsewhere for his own."

Rossetti used a similar image for a similar purpose in the previously quoted sonnet "The Landmark." The octave suggests the same failure of recognition as in "The Mirror":

> Was *that* the landmark? What,—the foolish well
>   Whose wave, low down, I did not stoop to drink,
>   But sat and flung the pebbles from its brink
> In sport to send its imaged skies pell-mell,
> (And mine own image, had I noted well!)—
>   Was that my point of turning?—I had thought
>   The stations of my course should rise unsought,
> As altar-stone or ensigned citadel.
>
> [*Poems*, 119]

The trivial acts that disturb the surface of a man's life, Rossetti suggests, prevent him from finding his true self and his true course. The religious imagery—the altar-stone and the pun on the stations of the cross—obliquely suggests the difficulty faced by the belated poet, or by anyone living in an agnostic age for whom "The world is

---

[4]"On Love," in *Shelley's Works in Verse and Prose*, ed. Harry Buxton Forman, 8 vols. (London: Reeves and Turner, 1880), 6:267.

too much with us." In an age when revelation dictated the stations of one's course the landmarks were self-evident, but as life becomes more complex—and more busy—one must look more carefully for meaning. But Rossetti is more specifically, and more strikingly, thinking of his own image mirrored in the waters; his astonished realization of the significance of that image reveals both wonder at its seeming triviality and gratification that at least something exists to mark his path. Like Shelley, he is willing to accept even the limited revelation provided by his own reflection, so in the sestet he rejoices that though "the path is missed," he may "thank God, hastening, / That the same goal is still on the same track."

The image of the self reflected in water is, as in Shelley's *Alastor*, highly ambivalent. On the one hand, it does suggest an idealized projection, since the undisturbed surface of the water holds the image of man, the skies, and the water itself in placid harmony, but on the other hand the image must always be out of reach—if the narrator were to "stoop to drink," he would be, in effect, kissing his own image, but he would also send the imaged skies and his own image pell-mell. The ambivalence of this image is typical of Rossetti's peculiar combination of acknowledged failure to find spiritual value and his hope of eventual success if he stubbornly continues to seek his own idealized self. Most frequently he tries to find value not merely in a reflecting pond or a mirror but, like Shelley, in the projected image of an ideal love. But because the lover expects to find a reflection of his own inmost nature in the beloved, the imagery of reflection persists—and continues to have the same ambivalence, as is implied by such titles from *The House of Life* as "Through Death to Love," "Death-in-Love," "Love's Fatality" and "Stillborn Love." Throughout these sonnets, as in "Her Love" where the imagery of reflection is used positively and simply, the symbol takes on increased significance.

> Passion in her is
> A glass facing his fire, where the bright bliss
> Is mirrored, and the heat returned.
> [*Poems*, 227]

What had been a simile in "The Mirror" has become a metaphor—glass, love, and, implicitly, the beloved are now fully identified. Rossetti's use of the beloved, beautiful woman as a symbol for his own soul—a symbol developed at length in the prose tale "Hand and Soul"—has been often noted, but here, and frequently in his poetry, the dominant symbols for the soul meet. The close parallel with Shelley's, however, has not been observed and it is partly for this reason that Rossetti's "failure" as a Romantic has been too often exaggerated.

In "The Dark Glass" the fused images raise unsettling questions. The title signifies the mysteries of life and birth, which our senses cannot penetrate. Like the Poet of *Alastor*, Rossetti's lover wonders if it is possible to see through the opacity of death and the grave to some meaning that transcends it. The octave ends with a question:

> And shall my sense pierce love,—the last relay
> And ultimate outpost of eternity?
> [*Poems*, 222]

The speaker seemingly resolves the problem just as Don Juan had, by dismissing the unanswerable question, gazing on his beloved's eyes, and depending on his "primordial" instincts:

> Yet through thine eyes [Love] grants me clearest call
> And veriest touch of powers primordial
> That any hour-girt life may understand.
> [*Poems*, 222]

The Byronic solution can only be momentarily satisfying, however, for the questions left unanswered by the dark glass will continue to torment the poet—something in man's nature, as all the Romantics recognized, prevents him from complacently accepting his mortality, his "hour-girt life," and compels him to look for larger answers in the dark glass. Though Rossetti is, perhaps, asking too much of his reader to follow him, to recognize the significance of his undeveloped image, he is not merely resting content with sublunary passion—here, as nearly always, the woman represents *both* a physical reality of the flesh, and the soul or epipsyche; and love stands for the desire to defeat the terrors of mortality.

Elsewhere Rossetti finds a significance in love that does not seem so lightly to set aside the pains of mortality. In "Through Death to

133

Love" he boldly sets forth a series of similes that evoke the terrors of intimations of mortality, a series culminating in a reminiscence of the treacherous reflecting pools of *Alastor*:

> within some glass dimmed by our breath,
> Our hearts discern wild images of Death,
> Shadows and shoals that edge eternity.
>
> [*Poems*, 224]

The consolation for mortality, he suggests in the sestet, is love: "Howbeit athwart Death's imminent shade doth soar / One Power," the power of love. The consolation does not at first appear to be earned—it is merely asserted by the off-hand rhetorical about-face "Howbeit." But the idea that love soars athwart, and consequently covers the dark glass is, nevertheless, Rossetti's saving vision. The word "Through" in the title is misleading since his solace is found not through the glass, but on its surface. Paradoxically the love that covers the dark glass does not further darken it, but casts light on it. M. H. Abrams, in his famous study of Romantic aesthetics, has shown that the proper emblem of the eighteenth-century creative imagination is the mirror that reflects the objective truth of the material world; that of the nineteenth century is the lamp of mind that floods the world with the light of subjective perception.[5] The proper emblem of Rossetti's imagination, a striking combination of these, is the mirror made when the light of love cast on the dark window looking out on eternity transforms it to a reflecting surface. This image, which wonderfully and economically makes the most of the agnostic poet's inability to cast his imagination beyond the grave, mitigates the terror implicit in Shelley's image of the reflecting surface of death by fusing the mirror of fatal self-reflection with the mirror of ideal love described in "On Love." The image, implicit in "The Dark Glass" and "Through Death to Love," is more explicit in a number of other sonnets of *The House of Life*.

In "Severed Selves" the image is used to provide hope that the division of soul caused by parted love may be healed. The octave describes both the pain of separation and the hope of love:

[5]M. H. Abrams, *The Mirror and the Lamp* (New York: Norton, 1958).

Two separate divided silences,
  Which, brought together, would find loving voice;
  Two glances which together would rejoice
In love, now lost like stars beyond dark trees;
Two hands apart whose touch alone gives ease;
  Two bosoms which, heart-shrined with mutual flame,
  Would, meeting in one clasp, be made the same;
Two souls, the shores wave-mocked of sundering seas:—
           [*Poems*, 223]

These lines emphasize not only the spiritual isolation of the divided lovers but also their incompleteness—they are voiceless (and so unable to achieve spiritual "harmony") and even, as in "The Mirror," imageless—their glances are "lost like stars beyond dark trees." According to Paull F. Baum, the circumstances that have divided the two lovers are "not even hinted at," and he suggests that if we knew the "personal history" behind it, the poem might "receive an added poignancy."[6] Baum may be right in some respects, but the lack of circumstantial detail makes the poem all the more suggestive. Because the beloved remains generalized, she can be seen not as any specific woman, but as the very idea of love itself. The separation of the lovers, then, suggests the divided soul of the speaker who seeks completion, wholeness. Further, the vast abyss between the severed selves does "hint at" the nature of the separation, since the final line of the octave puts the lovers in two wholly different realms, separated, seemingly irrevocably, by "sundering seas." The implication that they are separated by death is reinforced by the imagery of the sestet:

Such are we now. Ah! may our hope forecast
  Indeed one hour again, when on this stream
  Of darkened love once more the light shall gleam?—
An hour how slow to come, how quickly past,—
Which blooms and fades, and only leaves at last,
  Faint as shed flowers, the attenuated dream.

[6]*The House of Life: A Sonnet-Sequence*, ed. Paull Franklin Baum (Cambridge: Harvard University Press, 1928), p. 122.

The hope that "on this stream / Of darkened love once more the light shall gleam" is thoroughly enigmatic unless it is understood as a continuation of the imagery we have been tracing. The light thrown on the darkened stream transforms it to a reflecting surface in which the lover can perceive his projected ideal image, a reflection of the soul within his soul. The consolation is not great even if the hope is fulfilled—he perceives, at best, only an "attenuated dream"—but it would, nevertheless, imply the possibility of healing the soul's division by at least confirming that there *is* a soul within the soul.

The implication that the beloved has passed beyond the boundary of life suggests that the lover's hope of reunion with her, and with his own soul, is a hope that reaches beyond death. Like Shelley's Poet, Rossetti desperately hoped that the vision of love projected on the waters of death would lead to union with the soul's ideal, that it would indeed be a passage "Through Death to Love." Unlike the Poet, however, he forced himself to be satisfied with the hope itself—with "only the one Hope's one name . . . / Not less nor more, but even that word alone" (*Poems*, 128). Rossetti's most extensive attempt to find saving significance in the imagery used in "Severed Selves" is the moving, but often confused and confusing, "The Stream's Secret," a poem that Stuart has described as "a formal meditation upon the myth of Narcissus."[7] The stream in the title is, much more clearly than in "Severed Selves," a symbol for the passage of time and the passage of life into death; its secret is whether or not love persists through death. The poem describes a lover, whose beloved has evidently died, in a rapt if one-sided communication with the stream that he hopes will convey some

[7]Donald Stuart, "Bitter Fantasy: Narcissus in Dante Gabriel Rossetti's Lyrics," *Victorians Institute Journal*, 2 (1973), 27. As his use of the phrase "formal meditation" implies, Stuart is concerned more with the meditative structure of the poem than with the ways in which the imagery works. His article shows Rossetti's place in the tradition of Romantic narcissism but emphasizes his debt to the meditative patterns of the *stilnovisti*. I do not entirely agree either with his emphasis on Rossetti's formal metaphysical treatment of the myth of Narcissus or with his reading of "The Stream's Secret," a reading that sees the symbolism as part of a successful "allegorical meditation" (p. 34). As my reading of the poem will emphasize, I do not think the images are sufficiently controlled to articulate the poet's deepest concerns.

136

news "of her," presumably from beyond the grave. Specifically, he hopes that Love, stronger than Death, has "leaned low / This hour beside thy far well-head," has spoken a message that the "whispering" of the water dimly echoes further downstream, where he himself leans low, listening (*Poems*, 88). The whispering of the stream suggests both the possibility, or at least hope, of revelation and the difficulty of comprehending it. The movement of water, the passage of time, both stimulates and stymies the lover's hope, so that the stream

> dost ill expound the words of love,
> Even as thine eddy's rippling race
> Would blur the perfect image of his face
> [*Poems*, 89]

even, perhaps, as his "own image, had he noted well." As in Rossetti's many poems of self-rebuke, the reflection in the waters is analogous to the speaker's internal act of troubled reflection, of his contemplation of his past in the dim glass of memory. Because his past is not guiltless, the stream first summons up the *döppelganger* figures of "dead hours," the "ghosts" of what Rossetti called, in "Lost Days," his murdered selves. In both "The Stream's Secret" and *The House of Life*, this guilt must surface and be purged before the vision of love can be achieved. Once cleansed of guilt, the lover can dare to hope that the stream will reflect, in Shelley's phrase, only his "forms of purity and brightness." When this occurs, the severed self may achieve completion and unity:

> Each on the other gazing shall but see
> A self that has no need to speak:
> All things unsought, yet nothing more to seek,—
> One love in unity.
> [*Poems*, 92]

The gnomic tone of the third line which seems more "bookish" than convinced, betrays the uncertainty of Rossetti's aspirations. Later in the poem the image is developed more fully and more

137

convincingly, as the speaker envisions a future hour when in the stream's

> mirror shown
> The twofold image softly lies,
> Until we kiss, and each in other's eyes
> Is imaged all alone.
> [*Poems,* 94]

Here Rossetti has depended solely on the force of the imagery, without attempting to draw mystic conclusions—the greater impact of the lines reveals just how heavily he did depend on the imaginative vision, without being fully able to conceptualize or articulate its meaning. He envisions paradisal joy glutted with reciprocal reflections—a union of self with the soul envisioned both as the beloved woman, and as the reflected image. The four stanzas that conclude the poem, however, reveal Rossetti's inability fully to realize the vision in this poem. They are worth quoting entire because they epitomize the desperate plight of the poet who seeks joy in this world, fails to find it, and then seeks for it in an afterlife that he cannot bring himself to believe in.

> Ah! by a colder wave
> On deathlier airs the hour must come
> Which to thy heart, my love, shall call me home.
> Between the lips of the low cave
> Against that night the lapping waters lave,
> And the dark lips are dumb.
>
> But there Love's self doth stand,
> And with Life's weary wings far-flown,
> And with Death's eyes that make the water moan,
> Gathers the water in his hand:
> And they that drink know nought of sky or land
> But only love alone.
>
> O soul-sequestered face
> Far off,—O were that night but now!
> So even beside that stream even I and thou
> Through thirsting lips should draw Love's grace,

> And in the zone of that supreme embrace
> Bind aching breast and brow.
>
> Oh water whispering
> Still through the dark into mine ears,—
> As with mine eyes, is it not now with hers?—
> Mine eyes that add to thy cold spring,
> Wan water, wandering water weltering,
> This hidden tide of tears.
>
> [*Poems*, 94–95]

Rossetti's concern to show that union can only occur after death is made clear by his choice of the clumsy word "deathlier," a word he did not like, but defended, saying he could find nothing else "so clearly introducing the idea of a *spiritual* locality differing from the *actual* stream-side."[8] His sacrifice of poetic beauty for clarity of meaning, unusual in his work, reveals his own awareness that his spiritual vision, but dimly perceived, is still more obscurely set forth.

The "spiritual locality" Rossetti describes when he looks through death to love, though confusing, is lent a certain evocative power by the imagery of reflection, especially if considered in the context of similar imagery and a similar—but ultimately very different— vision of heaven. The lover of "The Blessed Damozel" also envisioned an afterlife of union with his beloved, but in this case the vision was clear and unambiguously reassuring. Strengthened by his Christian faith—not Rossetti's, but one adopted for the poem—the lover will, after death, descend rapturously "To the deep wells of light;/ . . . as to a stream,/ And bathe there in God's sight" (*Poems*, 5). The vision of orthodox faith is easy, both emotionally and poetically, because it is, in effect, a stock vision. The saving vision of "The Stream's Secret" is far more difficult, both because it much more sincerely copes with Rossetti's doubts, and because it is generated from within, from Rossetti's deepest fears, and hard-won hopes. The waters of "The Stream's Secret" are not bathed in God's light and cherished in God's sight; they are dark and dumb,

---

[8]*Letters*, II:871, Rossetti's emphases.

watched over by "Death's eyes," which make them moan. The confluence of Death's eyes, the lover's eyes, and his envisioned beloved's eyes suggests again the image of reflection, but now, despite the lover's ardent hopes, his eyes reflect not a living soul, but death. The cold, wan water, the question of the last stanza, and the final "tide of tears" all indicate that the pain of skepticism triumphs in the end. The tone of the poem finally expresses a hope not for eternal love, but for death.

Rossetti's hope seems scarcely a hope at all, but it does, barely, skirt despair. The image of his "hidden tide of tears" does suggest to him that his beloved may also have contributed a hidden tide and that at least union in the wandering waters of death may be possible. Further, Death is, at least partially, composed of Love, so absorption into the waters may be an absorption into Love. The speaker's very desire for the beloved and death becomes, paradoxically, his consolation. His death-wish, his thirst for the waters, seems to suggest that the waters are desirable. Early in the poem he had asked to "Slake in one kiss the thirst of memory" (*Poems*, 89), and now, at the end, he describes that kiss:

> And they that drink know nought of sky or land
> But only love alone.

Because Love, Life, and Death become one in the image of the water, Rossetti is, like Keats, half in love with easeful death. But at this point the "picture" becomes almost hopelessly confused—we may well fail to conjure up any picture at all of the mysterious personified Love–Life–Death and we certainly cannot easily conceptualize its significance. The metaphors have led to a conceptual impasse—because memory and grief are one for the lover, the "thirst of memory" is the "thirst of grief," a thirst for death to end grief. But grief and memory are also the preservers of the beloved, so must not be ended. If the lover, like the lover of "The Blessed Damozel," could be sure of an afterlife, he could die, but because the only intimation of an afterlife is memory, in which the ideal love is still preserved despite the stream's flow and the passage of time, he cannot. Swinburne once argued, in a wholly different

140

context, that without the "gradation of correlative parts and significance of corresponsive details . . . the whole aerial and tremulous fabric of symbolism must decompose into . . . formless and
fruitless chaos. Even allegory or prophecy must live and work by
rule as well as by rapture; transparent it need not be, but it must be
translucent."[9] The problem with "The Stream's Secret" is that the
"significance of corresponsive details" breaks down in the ending;
Rossetti, trying to make the symbolic stream stand for too many
things, has lost track of the tenor of his metaphor. The lover gazing
into the stream of his life had been gazing into his own memory—
but when Rossetti projects the stream into the future, memory, the
tenor of the metaphor of reflection, necessarily leaves the vehicle.
The poetic difficulty corresponds to the conceptual one—the
speaker can only base his hopes on experiences, and to examine his
experience he must necessarily look to the past, not to the future,
and he can only form images from what he can see, in the mortal
world, by the "actual stream-side." The poem's melancholy ending
is partly due to the disparity between tenor and vehicle—the stream
must necessarily flow on to an imageless future, but the memory,
more consolingly, can draw images from a past in which the ideal
love still exists and ideal union can still be envisioned.

Rossetti's inability either to conceptualize or to portray the "*spiritual* location," then, is an index of his agnostic dilemma—it is
significant that the most moving image of the passage, the final
picture of the weeping lover, takes place by the "*actual* stream-
side." Rossetti's difficulties with the conclusion to "The Stream's
Secret" illustrate, among other things, why he was necessarily a
diminished Romantic. His skepticism, to put it simply, prevented
him from a full commitment to the unseen—and despite his occasional large mystical gestures, Rossetti, a painter as well as a poet,
based his best work on literal, not prophetic, vision. Consequently
he depends heavily, almost exclusively, on images that can be
sensually apprehended—like the imagist poets of our century, to
whom he has been compared, Rossetti works best with limited,

---

[9]"Simeon Solomon's 'Vision of Love' and Other Studies," in *The Complete
Works of Algernon Charles Swinburne*, ed. Edmund Gosse and Thomas James Wise,
20 vols. (London: Heinemann, 1925–1927), 15:446.

definite images.[10] For this reason, perhaps, he is at his best in short poems, and especially in sonnets, where he can develop an image fully without feeling compelled to philosophize upon its significance. He is rather like a hypothetically diminished Wordsworth, whose *Prelude* would consist solely of "spots of time."

In many of the best sonnets of *The House of Life,* Rossetti uses the same imagery as in "The Stream's Secret," but less ambitiously and more successfully. In "Life the Beloved," for example, he wrestles with his ambivalence about whether life is worth living, arguing that though it scarcely seems to be, yet life "Glows with fresh flowers for hope to glorify." His most forceful simile to justify this hope is significant:

> As thy love's death-bound features never dead
> To memory's glass return, but contravene
> Frail fugitive days, and alway keep, I ween,
> Than all new life a livelier lovelihead:—
>
> [*Poems,* 235]

The implication is that past passion, past love, provides the consolation of memory and the hope of eventual redemption. Memory proves that time does not obliterate love, and suggests that death will not obliterate it—the image economically sets forth a good part of the meaning that the tortured imagery of "The Stream's Secret" has only obscurely hinted at. And the economy results, of course, not only in greater clarity, but in more immediate poetic impact.

Many of Rossetti's other sonnets, closer in tone to the despair of "The Stream's Secret," suggest more clearly what the reader only feels in the longer poem's desperate attempt to base a hope on the obsessive imagery of reflection—that the hope of redemption is a willed hope, possible only when the light of love and hope is strong enough to cast a reflection, and when the reflecting surface is not too far distorted by the strong current of guilt or the tears of grief. In moments of despair Rossetti used the same image as in "The Mir-

---

[10]See Richard L. Stein, *The Ritual of Interpretation: The Fine Arts as Literature in Ruskin, Rossetti, and Pater* (Cambridge: Harvard University Press, 1975), pp. 203–204.

ror," the failure to find reflection, to describe hopelessness. The image, implicit in "Death-in-Love," "Without Her," "Farewell to the Glen," and "Lost Days," is forcefully explicit in one of Rossetti's most famous sonnets, "A Superscription":

> Look in my face; my name is Might-have-been;
>   I am also called No-more, Too-late, Farewell;
>   Unto thine ear I hold the dead-sea shell
> Cast up thy Life's foam-fretted feet between;
> Unto thine eyes the glass where that is seen
>   Which had Life's form and Love's, but by my spell
>   Is now a shaken shadow intolerable,
> Of ultimate things unuttered the frail screen.
>
>   [*Poems,* 126]

Paull F. Baum's gloss on the relevant image is, I think, correct: "Unto thine eyes I (thy dead and wasted life) hold the mirror which reveals the life and love that once were thine, but are now through thine own fault an intolerable shadow, shaken and broken, a mere screen between life and ultimate death and punishment."[11] The octave describes, in other words, the speaker's failure to achieve salvation through self-realization in life and love. The glass, with the light of self-love (that is, love for the ideal part of the self) thrown upon it, is a "dark glass," a window looking out upon the terrors of death.

But—a significant point—the glass is not wholly darkened, the mystery not wholly penetrated. The glass now reflects only a "shaken shadow," but that is still something. To complicate the image further, the self is not only reflected in the glass, but is, itself, a "frail screen" on which are cast the ultimate, unutterable terrors of the dark glass. The image suggests a reciprocal reflection that merges the slight image still projected by the self and the dark shadow cast upon it by despair. To return to my earlier image for Rossetti's imagination—it is as if the light cast upon the window were sufficiently strong to make it a mirror, but sufficiently dim to allow external images to be seen. Under such conditions the win-

---

[11]Baum, *House of Life,* p. 218.

dow's surface becomes a screen fusing the observer within, casting his wan light of vision, with the unutterable fears without. The image, then, suggests entrapment on the narrow surface between hope and despair; the reflected soul, the hope of eternity, is still present, but compassed round with temptations to hopelessness. The speaker, tormented by despair, holds it literally at arm's length, on the surface of the glass. The image is essentially the same as "Through Death to Love," in which Love is thrown "athwart Death's imminent shade," except that here the speaker, forlorn, cannot summon up sufficient light of love. The glass, in fact, is a kind of light meter measuring the brightness—or darkness—of the poet's inner light of hope and love.

Rossetti's most compelling and successful use of all these symbols is in the deeply moving poem "Willowwood," a single poem consisting of four linked sonnets. The octave of the first of these sonnets presents a situation nearly identical to that described in "The Stream's Secret":

> I sat with Love upon a woodside well,
>   Leaning across the water, I and he;
>   Nor ever did he speak nor looked at me,
> But touched his lute wherein was audible
> The certain secret thing he had to tell:
>   Only our mirrored eyes met silently
>   In the low wave; and that sound came to be
> The passionate voice I knew; and my tears fell.
>
> [*Poems*, 116]

The crucial difference in the setting is that the speaker is no longer downstream, but is at the well-head with Love and consequently the secret, "The certain secret thing he had to tell" is audible. Further, in "The Stream's Secret" the hoped-for vision was of the lover and beloved and of their mutual reflection in the water, but here the lover, Love, and the beloved have been identified, as the image of the final three lines subtly suggests, since the "mirrored eyes" apparently are the observer's own. The concrete imagery of the symbolism, in other words, suggests internal reflection rather than an *actual* future meeting with the beloved at a "*spiritual* loca-

144

tion." In the longer poem Rossetti tries to stretch his poetic vision beyond his physical vision; here he concentrates on the psychological truth of actual perception. And because he is able to make the most of the present moment, the tears of grief no longer suggest despair but lead to union with the beloved:

> And at their fall, his eyes beneath grew hers;
> And with his foot and with his wing-feathers
>> He swept the spring that watered my heart's drouth.
> Then the dark ripples spread to waving hair,
> And as I stooped, her own lips rising there
>> Bubbled with brimming kisses at my mouth.

Grief, which holds the beloved in memory, leads to a vision of fulfilled love. And the image leading to fulfilled love, "his eyes beneath grew hers," is precisely the image of "On Love," for the reflected eyes of love, "his eyes," are necessarily the speaker's own, and so, of course, are the eyes of the beloved. Rossetti has fully united the ideal love that enables him to escape spiritual self-imprisonment with the actual mortal love preserved in grief. Grief is transformed to hope. But the symbolism is still more complex, for it merges the image of the reflecting surface with the image, which we first encountered in "The Mirror," of the inner self, the soul within the soul, rising in bubbles to the surface of conscious awareness. In the sonnet's closing lines the lover is literally and metaphorically slaking both the thirst of grief and memory, and the thirst that, as Shelley said, we all have for our own likeness, our own epipsyche, "from the instant that we live and move." In spite of these cheering implications, however, the image is highly ambivalent, for it both begins and ends with a distortion of the water's surface, a distortion suggesting that grief is modulated to hope only by the speaker's willingness to tamper with the evidence of experience. And it is further disturbing because necessarily evanescent—the rippling waters create an optical illusion that, by its very nature, can only be momentary. As in "The Stream's Secret," the "eddy's rippling race" must soon "blur the perfect image of [Love's] face."

The second and third sonnets in the series develop these pessi-

145

mistic implications. Love's song is perplexing because "Meshed with half-remembrance" (*Poems*, 117), and therefore with distorted remembrance. Again as in "The Stream's Secret," love and memory summon up not living moments of rapturous union, but the "mournful forms" of the lover's and beloved's past selves, forms that stand aloof and voiceless, unable to utter a consoling "secret," unable to translate memory into hope. Love's song implies the futility of hoping that the union perceived in the first sonnet will ever be repeated—the "mournful forms" have lost their "last hopes," though they "in vain have wooed," "in vain invite" one more kiss, they will not again "see the light" of the surface, but will ever remain sundered and alone in the depths, suffering a "fathom-depth of soul-struck widowhood." The conclusion of Love's song strongly suggests a desire for death and oblivion, though it would obliterate even the memory of the beloved:

> Alas! if ever such a pillow could
> > Steep deep the soul in sleep till she were dead,—
> Better all life forget her than this thing,
> That Willowwood should hold her wandering!

The grief of memory, it seems, has triumphed over the hope of memory.

The second quatrain of the last sonnet describes the fear implicit in *Alastor*, the fear that plunging beneath the surface, reaching through death to the image of love, would result only in drowning:

> . . . when the song died did the kiss unclose;
> > And her face fell back drowned, and was as grey
> > As its grey eyes; and if it ever may
> Meet mine again I know not if Love knows.
> > > > > [*Poems*, 117]

But in spite of all, the sestet that closes the sonnet, and the "Willowwood" series, clings to hope:

> Only I know that I leaned low and drank
> A long draught from the water where she sank,
> > Her breath and all her tears and all her soul:

146

And as I leaned, I know I felt Love's face
Pressed on my neck with moan of pity and grace,
Till both our heads were in his aureole.
[*Poems*, 118]

Seemingly the hopeful tone is based on a desperate clinging to one isolated experience, but the sonnet and the series subtly imply a far richer hope. He is clinging not to actual experience but to an emblem of hope created by artifice—Love, stirring the waters to produce the beloved's image and playing his lute to produce her voice, is creating both a picture and a song, a painting and a poem. The kiss lasted as long as Love sang, and only ended "when the song died." Both the song's success and its ultimate failure are truly Orphic, drawing the beloved from death toward life. The kiss in "Willowwood," in fact, re-creates the kiss of the beloved in life, which in "The Kiss" seemed an assurance that death could not triumph over love:

For lo! even now my lady's lips did play
With these my lips such consonant interlude
As laurelled Orpheus longed for when he wooed
The half-drawn hungering face with that last lay.
[*Poems*, 106–107]

Still more striking, the speaker at the end of "Willowwood" gazes, literally with Love, into the pool of consciousness and produces, in the last line of the poem, a picture that Rossetti might have painted, a picture in any case, much like one he described in "Jenny":

Fair shines the gilded aureole
In which our highest painters place
Some living woman's simple face.
[*Poems*, 68]

The final image of "Willowwood" is an icon of hope. Art, both painting and poetry, may take the raw materials of grief and love and mould them into hope and consolation. Shelley, as ambivalent as Rossetti about looking beyond life for ultimate, unutterable

147

truths ("the deep truth is imageless"), gave warning in one power-ful sonnet to "Lift not the painted veil which those who live / Call life." More confident than Rossetti about the powers of the imag-ination, Shelley did frequently try to lift the veil; Rossetti, a more thoroughly diminished poet, left the veil down and both literally and poetically painted it. The veil, Shelley said, was woven by "Fear / And Hope,"[12] the torments of agnosticism, and these are precisely the warp and woof that Rossetti was compelled to cover with the colors of grief and love.

[12]*Prometheus Unbound,* II.iv, 115; "Lift Not the Painted Veil," ll. 1–2, 4–5.

6

"Debateable Borders" of Vision

THOUGH the symbolism of reflecting surfaces most clearly illustrates Rossetti's diminished place in the Romantic tradition, most of his other imagery is closely related to that central symbol and has much the same function. His most important imagery is actually physically diminished, spatially diminished to the flat plane or the bounding line, precisely because Rossetti could not see through walls, could not penetrate the opacity of the material world. His "fleshliness" was a result of the limits of his vision; flesh, like the dark glass turned mirror, both conceals and reveals. In "True Woman: I. Herself," for example, flesh is described as "Heaven's own screen," which hides the "soul's purest depth and loveliest glow" (*Poems*, 227). Rossetti does not deny the importance of what is veiled, but he insists on describing what is available to sense, the veil itself—"one soft bosom's swell" (*Poems*, 227). Because flesh binds man within himself, Rossetti's love poetry, which aspires to overcome the obstacles of the flesh to achieve complete union with the beloved, does so by confronting the flesh directly. Rossetti would like to overcome the isolation of the individual by complete mergence with the other, but because the impenetrability of the fleshy surface prevents such a complete merger, he settles for the point of contact, the surface formed by flesh on flesh. In "Song and Music," for example, he describes a flat plane of contact in which the senses of lover and beloved are united:

> O leave your hand where it lies cool
>   Upon the eyes whose lids are hot:
> Its rosy shade is bountiful
>   Of silence, and assuages thought.
>
> O lay your lips against your hand
>   And let me feel your breath through it,
> While through the sense your song shall fit
>   The soul to understand.
>
>   [*Poems*, 245]

Sight, touch, and hearing unite on the plane formed by hand and eye—if "soul" is to apprehend "soul" it must be "through the sense," and the union of senses can take place on the fleshly surface. The idea that lovers can achieve complete union with one another in this way runs throughout *The House of Life*, but is perhaps expressed most clearly in "Severed Selves":

> Two bosoms which, heart-shrined with mutual flame,
> Would, meeting in one clasp, be made the same.
>   [*Poems*, 223]

Here, more sensuously than in "Willowwood," the union of lover and beloved can only be on the surface.

The relation of the imagery of reflecting surfaces to that of fleshly surfaces is evident in the beautiful sonnet "The Lover's Walk," in which images of natural reflection (a "stream that draws the skies / Deep to its heart"), narcissistic reflection ("mirrored eyes in eyes"), and physical contact ("twining hedgeflowers," "hand that clings in hand," "bodies lean unto / Each other's visible sweetness") are all brought together in the closing simile:

> As the cloud-foaming firmamental blue
>   Rests on the blue line of a foamless sea.
>   [*Poems*, 214]

150

Rossetti's descriptions of sea and sky invariably merge the two, either in the reflecting surface of the water or on the line of the horizon. In either case the union, occurring on a flat surface, is the perfect analogue for the union of lovers. Stephen Spector has pointed out the attraction of such imagery for Rossetti: "The heart of the mystery is that there is no way to determine whether the horizon-line is actually the sky or the sea or a mixture of both; in other words, man does not know whether the object of his farthest sight is human or divine."[1] Nevertheless, Rossetti is not, as Buchanan asserted, confused about what is human and what is divine, what is body and what is soul. The beloved in Rossetti's poetry is a symbol of the lover's desire for escape from himself; union in the tremulous surface represented by the horizon-line is the closest the lover can come to such escape. Defending his revision of the last line of his early sonnet on Giorgione's "A Venetian Pastoral," Rossetti declared that the description of "Life touching lips with Immortality" was not "too 'ideal'" because it "gives only the momentary contact with the immortal which results from sensuous culmination and is always a half-conscious element of it."[2] The point of sensual contact seemed, to Rossetti, to intimate a point of momentary contact with the immortal. His intimations of immortality were based, in other words, on the psychological realities of sexual experience.

Rossetti's love poetry, in fact, consistently draws on images of tremulous union where divisions between separate realms are blurred. Though he has normally been either praised or blamed for attempting to identify flesh and spirit, he most commonly did not aim at a full identification of the two but only tried to discern the point at which they meet. The image of the "sky and sea-line" in "The Portrait" (*Poems*, 109) is particularly appropriate to describe this shimmering area, but many of his other images work in the same way. Sometimes the imagery directly expresses sensuous culmination, as in "tremulous kisses" ("Secret Parting"), but it is generally more effective when drawn from nature as an analogue of

---

[1]Stephen J. Spector, "Love, Unity, and Desire in the Poetry of Dante Gabriel Rossetti," *ELH: A Journal of English History*, 38 (1971), 449.

[2]*Letters*, II:727.

human experience. In "Passion and Worship," for example, the extremes of sensuous and Platonic love are merged in a metaphor of music:

> Thy mastering music walks the sunlit sea:
> But where wan water trembles in the grove
> And the wan moon is all the light thereof,
>   This harp still makes my name its voluntary.
>   [*Poems*, 109]

As in "Willowwood," bodily and spiritual love meet in the trembling surface of the water.

Because he was interested in the liminal areas where sharp distinctions such as that between matter and spirit become meaningless, Rossetti's images frequently describe the transitional points in a day or year—moments which are neither light nor dark, days which are neither of the autumn nor of the winter. Rossetti himself provides a convenient name for such moments in "Youth's Spring-Tribute":

> On these debateable borders of the year
>   Spring's foot half falters; scarce she yet may know
>   The leafless blackthorn-blossom from the snow . . .
>   [*Poems*, 215]

These "debateable borders" appear over and over again in *The House of Life*, fitting neatly into the pattern of imagery used to describe the debatable borders between matter and spirit. Both "Beauty's Pageant" and "Soul-Light" catalogue a series of such sensual and diurnal borders to find fit comparisons for the subtly shifting expressions of "moods of varying grace" that pass across the countenance of the beloved and reveal the "changeful light of infinite love," the manifestations of inner life on the fleshy screen. In "Lovesight" Rossetti uses dusk to describe the ultimate contact of love:

> . . . when in the dusk hours, (we two alone,)
>   Close-kissed and eloquent of still replies

152

Thy twilight-hidden glimmering visage lies,
And my soul only sees thy soul its own?
[*Poems,* 106]

It is not a movement from light to darkness or darkness to light that
provides a corollary for union in love, but the undefined moment
itself, the debatable border where no definition is possible. Rossetti's imagery deliberately evades rational doubts by describing a
world in which the cold light of reason has no place, in which
"objective" perception is baffled by tremulous shades and glimmering lights. His most extreme statements about the union of souls,
rather than of bodies, characteristically express the psychological
insights that result from unclear or, as in "Willowwood," distorted
perception. His most emphatic assertions resulted from what he
himself recognized to be optical illusions. For Shelley, who believed
that nothing exists but as it is perceived, the evidence of altered
perception would be sufficient as the only possible grounds for
hope, but because Rossetti believed in the reality of the material
world, such perceptions were, for him, little more than the bare
starting point for a wistful hope. In "Willowwood," of course, the
illusion is dissipated; in "Lovesight" (the title itself suggests a distortion of perception) the image is followed by a question mark.
The incapacity to make sharp distinctions leads first to psychological affirmation, but ultimately to a rational doubt about the value of
such perception.

Not surprisingly, the most dubious border of all in Rossetti's
poetry is that between life and death, that limited region between
time and eternity where "Our hearts discern wild images of
Death / Shadows and shoals that edge eternity." Rossetti's seasonal
images are almost always concerned with this shadowy area since
they are most often autumnal, concerned with the transition of
nature from life to death. The address of "Love to his singer" in
"Love's Last Gift" reveals why Rossetti is preeminently a poet of
autumn:

. . . all sweet blooms of love
To thee I gave while Spring and Summer sang;

153

> But Autumn stops to listen, with some pang
> From those worse things the wind is moaning of.
> [*Poems, 228*]

Autumn, the season both of fullest, most fruitful life, and of impending death, provides a natural analogue for Rossetti's melancholy insistence on the preservation of past love in memory as a consolation for fast-withering life. The ambivalence of the autumnal imagery corresponds to that of the *döppelgangers,* which may appear either as ghastly specters portending death or as images of the perfected soul. It is only when the poet, gazing into his memory, sees images of fulfillment that the ripe fruit of autumn supplies a cheering emblem of human life. At other times the autumnal wind that blows fitfully through *The House of Life* only brings the pang of "worse things," as in "Memorial Thresholds":

> . . . mocking winds whirl round a chaff-strown floor
> Thee and thy years and these my words and me.
> [*Poems, 233*]

But characteristically, Rossetti attempts to make the most of the portent of doom to still, at least momentarily, the winds of time and change in the epiphanic moment of the sonnet. In "Hoarded Joy" autumnal imagery is combined with the imagery of reflection to anticipate such a moment:

> let the first fruit be:
> Even as thou sayest, it is sweet and red,
> But let it ripen still. The tree's bent head
> Sees in the stream its own fecundity
> And bides the day of fulness.

If life, like the fruit tree, ripens toward some definite goal, the culmination of life may be anticipated with pleasure and reflection may be reassuring. Unfortunately the culmination is momentary and may be missed:

> Alas! our fruit hath wooed the sun
> Too long,—'tis fallen and floats adown the stream.

154

Rossetti, like Keats, knew both the "mellow fruitfulness" of autumn and its melancholy tinge of mortality; he characteristically looks at the moment of life at its fullest, even as it begins to merge with death:

> Lo, the last clusters! Pluck them every one,
>   And let us sup with summer; ere the gleam
> Of autumn set the year's pent sorrow free,
> And the woods wail like echoes from the sea.
>   [*Poems*, 123]

Perhaps because Rossetti so ardently wished for meaning in his life, he was in love with the sense of repletion, of fulfillment, that implied some kind of achievement.

Certainly all Rossetti's images of surfaces, reflections, and debatable borders explore those liminal regions of human life where physical, sensuous experience dissolves into a timeless moment of repletion in which "Life touches lips with immortality." He could best appreciate the fullness of experience only when it was past, could best appreciate the summer only when autumn arrived. In "Last Fire" he described a resplendent summer day:

> This day at least was Summer's paramour,
> Sun-coloured to the imperishable core
>   With sweet well-being of love and full heart's ease.

He can only describe it in the past tense, when, as he says, "the light sweetened as the fire took leave." That still pause when "Autumn stops to listen" and

> All care takes refuge while we sink to rest,
> And mutual dreams the bygone bliss retrieve
>   [*Poems*, 220],

is the quintessential Rossettian moment, the moment of internal reflection when all the pictures of the past are summoned to the aid of the present, the epiphanic moment when the chaos of experience becomes ordered and meaningful. Rossetti's most fleshly poetry does not describe the sensuality of sex, but the moment of repletion following the "little death" of sexual climax. "Nuptial Sleep," the sonnet Buchanan found nastiest of all, is explicitly about this moment, but the same pleasure is found in at least three sonnets— "Soul-Light," "Her Love," and even "Last Fire." Rossetti's most fleshly fleshliness is certainly, as Buchanan recognized, explicitly sexual, but it is not descriptive of the beastly, sweaty, "animal function," that Buchanan complained of; rather it describes the fully human moment of reflective, contemplative peace.

Rossetti's sonnet style was perfectly adapted to capture the still moment of repletion. His well-known comments that art is best followed "in the dozing style" and that "one may lie and symbolize till one goes to sleep, and that be a symbol too perhaps"[3] deceptively conceal the wakeful vigilance of his craftsmanship ("With me," he said much later, "sonnets mean insomnia"[4]) but they accurately describe the calm, static quality that the sonnets formally achieve. Each sonnet at least momentarily stills the winds of time and change, stills the tumult of life in the marmoreal repletion of a "moment's monument."

When he revised the last line of his sonnet on Giorgione from "Silence of heat, and solemn poetry" to "Life touching lips with Immortality," Rossetti commented that " 'Solemn poetry' belongs to the class of phrases absolutely forbidden I think *in* poetry. It is intellectually incestuous—poetry seeking to beget its emotional offspring on its own identity."[5] But because he sought to paint the veil over the dark glass, many of his poems are about poetry or painting. The figured surface of "Willowwood" modulates into images of surfaces that are more explicitly covered by conscious artistry. The last sonnet—in fact the last sestet—of *The House of Life* describes "The One Hope" Rossetti is able to solace himself with in the face of death:

> Ah! when the wan soul in that golden air
>   Between the scriptured petals softly blown
>   Peers breathless for the gift of grace unknown,—

[3]*Letters*, I:201.
[4]*Dante Gabriel Rossetti: His Family Letters, with a Memoir by William Michael Rossetti*, 2 vols. (Boston: Roberts Brothers, 1895), I:368–369.
[5]*Letters*, II:726–727.

> Ah! let none other written spell soe'er
> But only the one Hope's one name be there,—
> Not less nor more, but even that word alone.
>
> [*Poems,* 128]

Even as the "written spell" is, in general, rejected, both the description of the soul's afterlife and the final emphasis on "that word alone" suggest the saving grace of words.

Rossetti attached great importance to the symbol of the flat surface that reflects the love of the lover and embodies the creative imagination of the artist. The symbol is, of course, natural for a painter challenged by the blank canvas and a poet challenged by the blank paper, but Rossetti adapted it to represent more perfectly the needs of the introspective artist who bases his work on his own love, memory, and grief. Occasionally, as in "The Song-Throe," he is explicit about these connotations:

> By thine own tears thy song must tears beget,
> O Singer! Magic mirror thou hast none
> Except thy manifest heart.
>
> [*Poems,* 229]

And the written page, another surface, catches the reflection of the heart's mirror and reflects it to other eyes and another heart. The meeting of images on the surface of the paper, in fact, brings lover and beloved together just as the images of reflecting pools do. In "The Love Letter" the writer peers "into her breast" to seek her lover's soul and "from the sudden confluence" catches the words to cover the "Sweet fluttering sheet" of paper. Just as the external image of the mirror may represent the internal image of the "soul within the soul," so may the sheet of paper. Lover and beloved, psyche and epipsyche, meet on the "Sweet fluttering sheet" produced by a combination of intellectual effort and emotional need (*Poems,* 109–110). Even in "Venus Victrix" the most memorable image to describe the triumphant Queen of Love is actually descriptive of the surface of the poet's paper, the "poet's page gold-shadowed in thy hair" (*Poems,* 222).

Rossetti's most obvious uses of the painted surface are, of course, his many images of painting, and particularly of portraiture. In "The Portrait," a sonnet given the same name as the earlier dramatic monologue, the speaker asks of Love both the passion and the artistic control ("compassionate control") to produce by art ("Under my hand") the perfect embodiment of his beloved's soul ("Even of her inner self the perfect whole"). Because he is painting from within, the soul he paints is his own soul as well. The artist enshrines both his beloved and his inner love, his thirst for his own likeness, merging them in the perfect unity of the painted surface. The image, in other words, combines both the external and internal symbols of soul—the physically real woman and the epipsyche—in the third image, the reflecting surface. He has, in effect, perfectly fixed the otherwise evanescent image of the reflecting waters in a monument that transcends time:

> The shadowed eyes remember and foresee.
> Her face is made her shrine.
>
> [*Poems,* 109]

And it is made his shrine as well: "They that would look on her must come to me." Even when Rossetti is ostensibly describing the ideal beauty of woman, as in "Genius in Beauty," he may end up describing not the living woman, but her living portrait:

> Beauty like hers is genius. Not the call
>   Of Homer's or of Dante's heart sublime,—
>   Not Michael's hand furrowing the zones of time,—
> Is more with compassed mysteries musical;
> Nay, not in Spring's or Summer's sweet footfall
>   More gathered gifts exuberant Life bequeathes
>   Than doth this sovereign face, whose love-spell breathes
> Even from its shadowed contour on the wall.
>
> [*Poems,* 216]

The "shadowed contour" may be just the shadow cast by the beloved, as has generally been assumed, or it may be a portrait, as the octave's emphasis on timeless art suggests—in either case it is a portrait of sorts, a surface covered by genius. The sestet more

158

strongly implies, however, that the "shadowed contour" must indeed be a portrait, since it is immune to the ravages of time:

> the envenomed years, whose tooth
> Rends shallower grace with ruin void of ruth,
> Upon this beauty's power shall wreak no wrong.
> [*Poems*, 216]

The word "shallower" seems odd, since Rossetti is describing a
beauty with no physical depth whatever, but the characteristic
paradox is that he consistently saw surfaces as the most profound
symbols of emotional and psychological depths. The surface of
water, the dark glass, and even the mirror all suggest the same
paradox.

Rossetti's emphasis on the importance of the artistically covered
surface certainly does not imply that his art is superficial, or that his
attitude toward art is a shallow aestheticism that turns its back on
life and substitutes art for living. His insistence on the depths of
soul from which his art is wrought and on the depths of soul it
communicates belies such an interpretation. Rather he should be
regarded as one who attempted to fathom the mysteries of his
innermost self and to isolate what was best in him in his art—to
mold and transform the chaotic impulses of the self into order and
beauty. Many of his finest poems, moreover, reveal a deep pessimism that even art can bring such redemption. In the opening lines
of the other poem entitled "The Portrait" he draws on many of the
images discussed here to describe a painting of a dead lover:

> This is her picture as she was:
> It seems a thing to wonder on,
> As though mine image in the glass
> Should tarry when myself am gone.
> [*Poems*, 73]

Narcissistic self-projection, an image of introspection, is combined
by simile with realistic portraiture—self and other are, again,
merged on the surface of the canvas. But the poem becomes increasingly melancholy as the poet-painter questions the value of

159

memory and of art's commemoration with the same imagery used in "Willowwood," "The Stream's Secret," and "The Dark Glass." It is significant that the doubts cast on the artificial re-creation of living love are raised by a consideration not of life itself, but of other "painted surfaces" in life:

> 'Tis she: though of herself, alas!
> Less than her shadow on the grass
> Or than her image in the stream.

The idea, clearly, is that though art may memorialize life, memorials do not adequately compensate for loss. But Rossetti's choice of imagery raises the further complication that he saw not just art, but life itself as a series of surfaces to be covered or, if possible, interpreted.

Rossetti fully understood that the self is the sum not of all one's experiences, but of all one's memories—the residue of experience as it presses upon consciousness. Consequently his occasional doubts about art are generally doubts about memory, the shadows of past life, of past selves and of dead hours. The many poems in which he encounters phantom images of himself reveal these doubts, but frequently, as in "Parted Love," he explicitly describes memory, and the self, as a series of pictures:

> Memory's art
> Parades the Past before thy face, and lures
> Thy spirit to her passionate portraitures.
> [*Poems*, 115]

Similarly, in "The Soul's Sphere" he describes all man's hopes and fears, based on memory, as "the soul's sphere of infinite images" and suggests that the sum of them may be either

> Visions of golden futures: or that last
> Wild pageant of the accumulated past
> That clangs and flashes for a drowning man.
> [*Poems*, 230]

160

For the artist, the implication is plain—if his life has been well lived, the images of the past will provide golden visions for his art; if it has been lived badly, only chaotic and dispiriting pictures will be available to him. The redemption of art is a redemption dependent upon earned redemption in life. "Inclusiveness," the sonnet immediately following "The Soul's Sphere," makes this emphatically clear by describing Heaven and Hell as alternative ways of viewing a particular picture in memory:

> May not this ancient room thou sit'st in dwell
> In separate living souls for joy or pain?
> Nay, all its corners may be painted plain
> Where Heaven shows pictures of some life spent well;
> And may be stamped, a memory all in vain,
> Upon the sight of lidless eyes in Hell.
>
> [*Poems*, 118–119]

The guilt and regret that darkened Rossetti's vision of memory in many of his poems may also darken his hopes for an afterlife—as he economically said in "The Sun's Shame, II," "Inveteracy of ill portends the doom" (*Poems*, 234). Conversely, memory's visions of beauty, recollections of fulfilled life and love, may portend greater fulfillment after death, as they ultimately do at the end of "The Portrait":

> Here with her face doth memory sit
> Meanwhile, and wait the day's decline,
> Till other eyes shall look from it,
> Eyes of the spirit's Palestine,
> Even than the old gaze tenderer.
>
> [*Poems*, 75]

Rossetti's obsession with surfaces, then, is an obsession with the meaning of life itself. His obsessive use of related imagery corresponds to something fundamental in his way of seeing the world, something fundamental in his sensibility. Perhaps this sensibility could be too simply summarized by saying that he saw life with a painter's eye—despite his hope that "my poems are in no way the result of painter's tendencies—and indeed I believe no poetry could be freer than mine from the trick of what is called 'word painting.' "[6] He does not very often "paint" scenes in his poetry with the particularity and fine strokes of Tennyson, but his descriptive imagery constantly sets forth the painter's perception of light and shade on whatever he is describing. Frequently the effects of light are seen to vary depending on the passion that controls the poet's—and painter's—perception. Passion may lead to a vision of the "sunlit sea" and "Love's Worship" to a vision of "where wan water trembles in the grove / And the wan moon is all the light thereof" (*Poems*, 109) and as in "Genius in Beauty" and "The Portrait," people are constantly described in terms of reflections or shadows. Even his infrequent descriptions of nature in his letters reveal Rossetti's painter's eye, his habit of seeing the world in terms of light and shade, reflection and shadow. He describes a churchyard, islanded by floods, where "trees & hurdles & hedges stood reflected"[7] and, more striking, a seascape in which the shadows of boats are as fully material as the boats themselves: "the near boats stand together immovable, as if their shadows clogged them."[8] Still more remarkable is his description of another view of the sea in which all external reality is reduced to a flat surface: "There are dense fogs of heat here now, through which sea and sky loom as one wall, with the webbed craft creeping on it like flies, or standing there as if they would drop off dead." And again: "The thick sky has a thin red sun stuck in the middle of it like the specimen wafer outside a box of them. Even if you turned back the lid there would be nothing behind it, be sure, but a jumble of such flat dead suns."[9] All these quotations illustrate that Rossetti did habitually see the world with a painter's eye and further, that it was the eye of a painter with Rossetti's particular strengths and weaknesses: mastery of color and no sense of perspective.

But in painting as in poetry, his illumination of the surface and his disregard for physical depth do not indicate that he is, in the pejorative sense, superficial. John Dixon Hunt has suggested that in

[6]*Letters*, II:850.
[7]*Letters*, I:175.
[8]*Letters*, I:201.
[9]*Letters*, I:204, 314.

some of Rossetti's medieval paintings, such as *The Wedding of St. George and the Princess Sabra,* he engaged in "exotic effects and easy atmospherics" so that the "central event and its characters are absorbed" into the merely decorative "exotic patterns" of the clothes and upholstery.[10] Hunt suggests that Rossetti's occasional "decorative effects," in both poetry and painting, are akin to the mere decoration of William Morris's tapestries[11]—and indeed, for Rossetti, covering the surface was all-important. He could even, on occasion, describe a landscape ("Silent Noon") or "Life's retinue" ("Death-in-Love") as a tapestry. But the value he placed on surfaces suggests that they can never be, for him, merely decorative— rather they covered the abyss behind the dark glass with the projected soul of the artist. Color itself had an almost mystical significance for him, as his strictures against the painters of the "later & more Academic Italian School" indicate: "I have always thought the soul to be too visibly in a minor ratio, as compared to the body; and colour, which constitutes the pictorial atmosphere of beauty, is a sealed mystery to them."[12] It is not clear whether Rossetti is making two distinct comments here, but evidently he links the "mystery" of color with the expression—and impression—of soul. Clearly Rossetti's decorative coloring, in both arts, is not that of the mere aesthete. Matthew Arnold used the symbol of a medieval tapestry at the end of his *Tristan and Iseult* to represent the aesthetic withdrawal from life, but to Rossetti the tapestry, like all covered and covering surfaces, symbolized confrontation with life.

Jerome McGann has said that Rossetti has received short shrift from modern interpretive critics because they "seek to define their absolutes not at the surface but below it, not in the apparition but the concept. Rossetti does not fare well in such a school because he forces the reader to attend to the surface, insists that the greatest significance lies there, unburied. He does not want deep readers, which is not to say that he does not want intelligent ones."[13]

---

[10]John Dixon Hunt, *The Pre-Raphaelite Imagination, 1848–1900* (London: Routledge and Kegan Paul, 1968), p. 35.

[11]Ibid., pp. 53–54.

[12]*Letters,* III:1328.

[13]Jerome J. McGann, "Rossetti's Significant Details," *Victorian Poetry,* 7 (1969), 54.

McGann was not thinking of the specific images I have traced here but of Rossetti's imagery generally, which insists on the importance of things as directly apprehended by the senses. He argues, cogently, that Rossetti insists on the value of direct sensual apprehension because his "ideal never admits a distinction between an order called nature and one called supernature."[14] Rossetti's persistent imagery of surfaces confirms McGann's observations, I think, but only up to a point. Rossetti does insist that the ultimate truths man can apprehend are on the surfaces of things, but he is by no means certain that no supernatural realm exists, hidden and buried. He would not endorse the dramatic utterance of the speaker in the second sonnet of "The Choice" that "spirits [are] always nigh / Though screened and hid" (*Poems*, 122), but neither would he endorse the materialistic, and hedonistic, view of the first speaker in "The Choice." His, rather, is the agnostic dilemma of the third and last speaker, who knows only that ultimate truths are unknowable. Consequently he rarely tries to express ultimate truths: when he describes heaven or hell, as McGann observed, he describes them in human terms, not in mystical abstractions. More often he contents himself with a description of the surface that both conceals and reveals. At his best, as John Dixon Hunt has noted, Rossetti finds "precise cyphers" and is able to offer "some definition" of an intuited realm "by means of limited objects."[15] Like Shelley, Rossetti perceived in the surfaces of things hieroglyphs of an unapprehended reality, but unlike Shelley he lacked the imaginative confidence—or audacity—to take the stance of the prophet-bard who interprets those hieroglyphs. A diminished Romantic, Rossetti settled for setting forth the hieroglyphs themselves. He himself once described poetry as the "apparent image of unapparent realities."[16] His art approaches modern symbolism by setting forth the direct apprehensions of his sensibility and endowing them with all the intuited but undefined suggestiveness that they have had for him. His symbols of the mirror, the surfaces of water, the surfaces of

14Ibid., p. 53.
15Hunt, p. 155.
16Quoted in Robert M. Cooper, *Lost on Both Sides: Dante Gabriel Rossetti: Critic and Poet* (Athens: Ohio University Press, 1970), p. 45.

all things, wonderfully "reflect" an artistic sensibility that saw a profound but undefinable significance in all things, a sensibility that saw the surfaces of the material world both as an impenetrable barrier to the noumenous realm beyond, and as a series of symbols suggesting the nature of that realm.

7

Confidence and the
Bardic Temptation

THE reluctance to adopt the role of prophet-bard that characterized Rossetti in the 1870 *Poems* almost broke down in the
confidence-building period of celebrity that followed publication. His efforts to escape from his role as a diminished poet
after 1870 are informative, for they show the extent to which lack
of personal confidence was a less important reason for his diminishment than was his skepticism. Even though Rossetti had prear-
ranged the chorus of praise that greeted *Poems*, he was evidently
gratified by the extent of it. His letters for the two years following
publication show him constantly commenting on the reviews of his
work, especially on the unbiased praise of reviewers outside his own
clique, and even on the congratulatory letters of fellow poets. His
gratification is not, of course, surprising. Rossetti had always been
insecure as a poet—and as an artist—and had probably deferred
publication of his poems for so long because he feared adverse
criticism. And certainly he did fear adverse criticism—not only had
he "worked the oracle," but he had continually solicited the opin-
ions of his friends before venturing into print, and he had even
tested the waters by publishing selections in the *Fortnightly* and by
circulating a limited number of "trial books." The obvious implica-

tion of Rossetti's trepidation is that he lacked confidence as a poet, but with the praise heaped on him after publication he could not help but feel more secure. Consequently it is not surprising that from 1870—even from 1869, when the praise from friends actually began to flow—until just before his nervous breakdown in the summer of 1872, Rossetti wrote with greater confidence than at any time since the early 1850s, and with greater power than he was ever to show again. During this remarkably productive period, he wrote about thirty sonnets for *The House of Life,* a number of almost bardic nature poems, and his longest and most ambitious ballad, "Rose Mary."

Rossetti's sense of being a belated romantic made him in many ways a self-consciously limited poet, but his confident mood during this period evidently led him to extend himself beyond his self-imposed limits. His attempt to range beyond his normal poetic province is most immediately obvious in a number of reflective poems written in 1871, including "Sunset Wings," "Soothsay," and, by far the most ambitious and most painstakingly composed, "The Cloud Confines." Rossetti finished a first version of this poem by August 9, 1871, but was so concerned that the philosophical and moral message be made clear that he continually sought advice from friends and revised the poem for another two months. The resulting lyric, five stanzas long, may seem somewhat slight, but it represents in distilled form the most that Rossetti felt he could say about the human condition. The various versions of the last stanza, as it was written and revised over two months, show him in the process of salvaging as much faith as he possibly could from skepticism. The first four stanzas, in all versions, all devote eight lines to showing the limitations of mortal knowledge, and each concludes with the same ambiguously hopeful refrain:

> Still we say as we go—
>   'Strange to think by the way,
> Whatever there is to know,
>   That shall we know one day.'

But in the last stanza of the earliest extant version the first eight lines state the skeptical viewpoint more strongly than ever but,

167

surprisingly, the refrain is replaced by an affirmation, though a limited one:

> The sky leans dumb on the sea
>   Aweary with all its wings;
>   And oh! the song the sea sings
> Is dark everlastingly.
>   Our past is clean forgot,
>   Our present is and is not,
>   Our future's a sealed seed-plot,
> And what betwixt them are we?
> Atoms that nought can sever
>   From one world-circling will,—
> To throb at its heart for ever,
>   Yet never to know it still.[1]

The closing lines continue to affirm that man can not know the ultimate purpose of life, but they go beyond the limits of empirical knowledge to affirm the existence of a mysterious "world-circling will." Rossetti apparently found the lines too mysterious, however, since he was soon considering another closing quatrain:

> Oh never from Thee to sever
>   Who wast and shalt be and art,
> To throb at Thy heart for ever
>   Yet never to know Thy heart.

But this ending would not do either, especially since Rossetti feared that it savored of orthodoxy: "Does this not seem as if it meant a personal God? I don't think it need do so." He almost immediately rejected it, and considered a substitute for the last five lines of the original:

> And what must our birthright be?
> Oh, never from thee to sever,
>   Thou Will that shalt be and art,

[1]*Letters*, III:972.

168

> To throb at thy heart forever,
>   Yet never to know thy heart.[2]

These lines were evidently a compromise between the pantheistic "world-circling will" and the ambiguous "Thee" that might be taken as a "personal God"—Rossetti brought the "world-circling will" to life by simply capitalizing and directly addressing "Thou Will," and he eliminated any suggestion of Christian orthodoxy. Clearly his struggle with the ending of this poem was not solely for aesthetic purposes. Like many other Victorians, Rossetti was without any firm faith, and yet needed to believe in some sort of after-life—his refusal to embrace Christianity and his simultaneous desire to change "a will" to "Thou Will" poignantly represent a need to find any acceptable compromise. His explanation of the lines reveals how far out on a theoretical limb he was willing to go in order to find some hope for immortality: "I cannot suppose that any particle of life is *extinguished*, though its permanent individuality may be more than questionable. Absorption is not annihilation; and it is even a real retributive future for the special atom of life to be re-embodied (if so it were) in a world which its own ideality had helped to fashion for pain or pleasure."[3] To say the least, Rossetti seems to be clutching at straws here—simply inventing a theory that sets aside both skepticism and faith. In the end, he would not affirm even so much, and closed the poem with the refrain that had ended the first four stanzas all along:

> Still we say as we go—
>   'Strange to think by the way,
> Whatever there is to know,
>   That shall we know one day.'
>   [*Poems*, 250]

Since he had previously felt that "to wind up with the old refrain would hardly be either valuable or artistic,"[4] his final decision

---

[2]*Letters*, III:989–990.
[3]*Letters*, III:989–990.
[4]*Letters*, III:990.

represents a retreat, of a sort. As he said to his brother, he had "meant to answer the question in a way, on the theory hardly of annihilation but of absorption," but in the end he thought best to leave "the whole question open."[5]

Although "The Cloud Confines" is not one of Rossetti's best poems, and although its contemplative tone is hardly characteristic of his usual manner, the history of its composition reveals a great deal about his position as a belated Romantic poet. During a period of unusual confidence he had set out to write a definitive lyric— perhaps on the order of Tennyson's "The Higher Pantheism"— about the meaning of life. In his first attempt he produced a vaguely pantheistic idea of a "world-circling will" that was both too undefined to be definitive, and too impersonal to be consoling. His various struggles to arrive at a better answer resulted only in a rather desperate theory about the continuity of life in some form, and ultimately even that seemed too bold. For all his confidence, Rossetti was unable to affirm anything—he had no faith, and the large Romantic gesture was no longer possible. Though one senses that he badly wanted to consolidate his position as a leading poet with at least one vatic utterance, the best he could manage in a faithless age was a theory, not a conviction. Nevertheless, his struggles with "The Cloud Confines" testify to his desire to grapple with the most challenging of all issues, to the fundamental honesty that compelled him to leave the question open, and to the inevitability of his diminishment.

But though his retreat from the bardic voice may have helped to confirm Rossetti's belief that he could not become, like some of his predecessors, the emperor of a vast poetic province, it did not diminish his confidence within his own limited poetic domain. In fact, while he was pondering the questions of "The Cloud Confines," he was also beginning his most ambitious narrative, a ballad that would explore the characteristically Rossettian themes of sexual love, betrayal, guilt, and redemption through love. Rossetti must have been especially confident with this form and these themes because he had already handled both brilliantly in two of his finest poems, "Troy Town" and the splendid "Eden Bower," and he had been assured by Swinburne and other admirers that "these two songs are the masterpieces of Mr. Rossetti's magnificent lyric faculty."[6] "Rose Mary," in fact, became not only Rossetti's finest sustained treatment of these themes but also, indirectly, his closest approach to the ultimate philosophical and religious questions that he was unable to resolve in the more direct manner of "The Cloud Confines."

In "The Staff and Scrip," "Stratton Water," "Troy Town," "Eden Bower," and "Sister Helen," Rossetti had, over the years, learned to adapt the old ballad form to meet the demands of his modern concerns. In "Sister Helen," for example, he had, as Ronnalie Roper Howard has shown, adapted a complex ballad stanza that enabled him to shift the emphasis of the traditional ballad from a terse, objective account of events to a penetrating study of "the tortured mind of Helen."[7] By slowing the narrative pace of the ballad and including three dramatic characters—Helen, her little brother, and the anonymous speaker of the refrain—Rossetti was able to examine the complex and morally ambiguous relation of guilt (Helen's and her seducer's), innocence (the little brother's), and conventional morality (the refrain). But Rossetti's alteration of the traditional ballad to express his deepest concerns is even more radical in "Rose Mary" than it had been in "Sister Helen." In "Sister Helen" the story of seduction and betrayal had been quite simple and its elaboration into thirty-four stanzas (in the 1870 version) had been for the sake of dramatic and psychological complexity; in "Rose Mary" the plot is far more involved, and the ballad form is adapted to accommodate the tale's ironies, ambiguities, and subversive moral implications. A distillation of the plot suggests its complications: the heroine, Rose Mary, must look into a magic beryl to locate the enemies who lie in ambush for her lover. She seemingly succeeds, and the lover is warned, but he is murdered anyway—the beryl had lied because Rose Mary, having once slept with her lover, was not pure. Rose Mary's mother, knowing by

[6]"The Poems of Dante Gabriel Rossetti," in *The Complete Works of Algernon Charles Swinburne*, ed. Edmund Gosse and Thomas James Wise, 20 vols. (London: Heinemann, 1925–1927), 15:38.

[7]Ronnalie Roper Howard, *The Dark Glass: Vision and Technique in the Poetry of Dante Gabriel Rossetti* (Athens: Ohio University Press, 1972), p. 69.

this that her daughter had been seduced, sadly assures her that the lover had been appropriately punished by heaven. She regrets that his death prevents him from saving Rose Mary's honor, but then she learns that his death had only prevented him from soiling it further—he had been on his way to another woman. Meanwhile Rose Mary, who never learns of his lack of faith, smashes the beryl in an act that will bring her own death and, she thinks, her reunion in heaven with her lover.

The ironies and moral ambiguity of the story are obvious. Rose Mary assumes that the spirits of the beryl are evil because they have murdered her lover, but in fact they may be doing her a favor, saving her from becoming a vengeful murderess like Sister Helen and Lilith of "Eden Bower"—they kill her seducer and betrayer for her without ever forcing her to lose her innocence. And both Rose Mary and her mother assume that the lover is killed because Rose Mary had sinned, but perhaps his betrayal of her is the real cause— he is, after all, slain by the brother of his other lover. For that matter, the brother is assumed to be the villain, but in fact the lover is. In short, the tale raises more questions than it answers about the nature of sin, guilt, and retribution. "Rose Mary" does not offer any easy didactic moral, but rather, like "The Cloud Confines," points to the limited capacity of human beings to perceive the truth—even oracles deceive.

The structure of "Rose Mary" is deliberately designed to emphasize the gap between actualities and the characters' assumptions. Rossetti carried to an extreme the narrative form of many old ballads, such as "Lord Randall," in which the speaker does not immediately see the full tragic implication of a situation. In "Rose Mary" revelation of the true state of things always comes to the characters belatedly, or not at all, so almost everything they say or do is ironically undercut. Further elaborate games are played with the reader, who is allowed to sense some ironies immediately— hints are given, for example, that Rose Mary is not pure enough to see the truth in the beryl—but is informed of other matters as belatedly as are the characters—he has no way of knowing that the lover has been unfaithful until Rose Mary's mother discovers it. The complex ironic structure serves various purposes. It builds suspense, it emphasizes the naïve innocence of Rose Mary and, most important, it forces the reader to appreciate the limited capacity of mortals to see into the moral nature of the universe, since it illustrates that nothing is what it seems.

Rossetti made this point not only in the complex structure itself, but also in the passages of explicit moralizing that would be unthinkable in a traditional ballad:

> Who hath seen or what ear hath heard
> The secret things unregister'd
> Of the place where all is past and done
> And tears and laughter sound as one
> In Hell's unhallowed unison?
>
> [*Poems,* 175]

Obviously such questions raise doubts about human percipience that go well beyond accounting for Rose Mary's naïveté. The rhetorical questions, in fact, imply the skeptical argument that man's moral categories, such as the notion of Hell, are not based on the empirical evidence of eyes and ears, but are only guesses at "secret things," and consequently have no logical validity.

Rossetti pursued the theme of skepticism in another way as well. Complicating the ballad structure still further, he freighted the traditionally spare narrative with a wealth of images that go beyond mere description to take on symbolic significance. In fact, the ultimate meaning of the poem is probably to be found in a full understanding of the recurring images of sky reflected in water— one of Rossetti's favorite images to represent the tenuous contact of the spiritual and material realms. Fittingly, the image first appears in "Rose Mary" when the heroine looks into the supernatural beryl to find the hiding place of her lover's enemies:

> 'As 'twere the turning leaves of a book,
> The road runs past me as I look;
> Or it is even as though mine eye
> Should watch calm waters filled with sky
> While lights and clouds and wings went by.'
>
> [*Poems,* 154]

To anyone familiar with Rossetti, this view into the spirit world seems far too easy. At the very best Rossetti hoped that such clarity of vision might possibly be earned by "living labour," but even then only after death, and only possibly: "After death . . . will all be sky-brimmed water, or all a desert of sand?" (*Works*, 642). And in "The Cloud Confines" the image is only slightly altered as the image of reflection is synaesthetically merged with the image of song to suggest a complete lack of communication between the two realms:

> The sky leans dumb on the sea,
>   Aweary with all its wings;
>   And oh! the song the sea sings
> Is dark everlastingly.
>
> [*Poems*, 250]

The same image, of course, had been used repeatedly in "The Stream's Secret" and in *The House of Life* to describe the always difficult and ultimately futile endeavors of mortals to know the "secret things" of the spiritual realms. In "Rose Mary" as in many of Rossetti's other poems, the attempt is not only futile, but counterproductive, although it momentarily results in Rose Mary's ironic gratitude to God: "Thank God, thank God, thank God I saw!" (*Poems*, 158).

As in many of the sonnets from *The House of Life*, especially "Willowwood," the attempt to find a window into the spiritual realm symbolizes in "Rose Mary" an introspective attempt to see one's own soul—when Rose Mary falsely thinks that her soul is corrupted, the beryl is corrupted; when she destroys the beryl, she destroys herself. The image of sky-reflecting water, in fact, is used to describe not only the deceptive clarity of the beryl, but also, after Rose Mary's "sin" has been discovered, to describe the communication of human soul with soul, in the embrace of mother and daughter:

> In the hair dark-waved the face lay white
> As the moon lies in the lap of night;
> And as night through which no moon may dart

174

Lies on a pool in the woods apart,
So lay the swoon on the weary heart.
[*Poems*, 163]

Now, as in "The Cloud Confines," the sky lies dark and dumb upon the waters. The image is used yet once more, to describe Rose Mary's awakening from her swoon, and to identify, at last conclusively, the beryl with the future state:

And now in Rose Mary's lifted eye
'Twas shadow alone that made reply
To the set face of the soul's dark sky.

Yet still through her soul there wandered past
Dread phantoms borne on a wailing blast,—
Death and sorrow and sin and shame. . . .
[*Poems*, 170]

The image does not simply mean, as it may at first seem to, that no spiritual value exists in the world, that Rose Mary's soul must necessarily be dark and haunted by shadows. Rather, her spirit has been darkened by her sense of guilt, her belief that her "sin" caused the death of her lover. Her acceptance of the doctrine that love is sin robs her of her love and of her very soul. In "Through Death to Love," a sonnet written in the month Rossetti began "Rose Mary," August 1871, a startlingly apt image describes man's spiritual state without love:

within some glass dimmed by our breath,
Our hearts discern wild images of Death,
Shadows and shoals that edge eternity.
[*Poems*, 224]

But, as the sonnet later makes clear, with love man discerns a hope that transcends death—love itself. Similarly, "Rose Mary" does not end with a pessimistic view of the soul. Rather, Rose Mary awakens from her swoon and sets out to destroy the symbol of a life-denying, love-denying religion, the beryl which, as David Sonstroem has pointed out, is her "enemy, because it, or the evil spirits that

175

inhabit it, insist upon the sinfulness of acts of love, and punish them."[8]

Clearly the narrative and the shift in the significance of the imagery combine to assert the Blakean doctrine that the Christian system, a religion of chastity, is antagonistic to what is fully human and is, in fact, evil and repressive. Rossetti even, like Blake, exploits and parodies Christian typology. The beryl, like the holy of holies, is kept hidden away on an altar, behind a veil adorned with cherubim. In accord with tradition, the apocalyptic moment is expected to come when the veil of the temple is rent and the holy of holies is exposed to view, but when Rose Mary lifts the altar-veil to expose the ultimate mystery of her religion, she is confronted with a satanic rather than heavenly revelation:

> The altar stood from its curved recess
> In a coiling serpent's life-likeness:
> Even such a serpent evermore
> Lies deep asleep at the world's dark core
> Till the last Voice shake the sea and shore.
>
> [*Poems*, 172]

The beryl itself, in what must be a deliberate parody, like Blake's "covering cherub," of the Old Testament cherubim, is nestled "'Twixt wings of a sculptured beast unknown" (*Poems*, 172). Rose Mary, ironically, does not realize that she has exposed not just a perversion of religion, but the religion of mystery and chastity itself. When she destroys the stone, however, "The veil [is] rent from the riven dome" (*Poems*, 175) and in a true judgment, her soul encounters not a repressive, Urizenic God of retribution, but a Rossettian God of love, who regrets that the "sin" of love is punishable, "by heaven's sore ban" (*Poems*, 176).

As Sonstroem had observed, Rose Mary has attacked and overcome not just the forces of evil, but the "whole system of good and evil that considers acts of love to be criminal. With the rebellious stroke of the sword she destroys the old 'heavy law,' and finds

---

[8]David Sonstroem, *Rossetti and the Fair Lady* (Middletown: Wesleyan University Press, 1970), p. 101.

herself in a new order, to be identified with the forces of good, where her old sin becomes an act of righteousness."9 Though not as systematically as Blake, Rossetti has relocated the redemption from the replacement of Judaism by Christianity, to the replacement of a perverse Christianity—a religion of mystery and chastity—by a religion of genuine and unrepressed love.

Earlier in the poem, when Rose Mary felt corrupted by sin, she had used an image that recalls the "gold bar of heaven" from "The Blessed Damozel," but only to say that not love, but "scorn leans over the bitter bar / And knows us now for the thing we are" (*Poems*, 161). Her idea of heaven was of a place where human love was scorned as degrading sin. But after destroying the beryl, she finds herself in the Rossettian heaven of "The Blessed Damozel," a heaven of love and of lovers:

> Warmed and lit is thy place afar
> With guerdon-fires of the sweet Love-star
> Where hearts of steadfast lovers are.
>
> [*Poems*, 176]

"Rose Mary" is among Rossetti's finest poetic accomplishments because of its sustained control of complex structure, its deft handling of layer upon layer of irony, its subtly significant imagery, but mostly because for once Rossetti did not simply take for granted the virtue of passionate love, but carefully balanced it against the traditional religious attitudes: "Redemption and damnation, heaven and hell, peaceful repose and terrible violence, pure innocence and guilty passion, these opposing elements are not often perfectly reconciled in Rossetti's work as they are, virtually, in *Rose Mary*. . . ."10 For once, Rossetti cannot be accused of simply not understanding that the Christian heaven of his vision is not the Christian heaven: he has made a comparison and justified, at least for himself, his own vision. Certainly he had no simple-minded belief in a heaven of lovers. His whole poem has demonstrated the impossibility of seeing

---

9Ibid., p. 102.

10W. S. Johnson, "D. G. Rossetti as Painter and Poet," *Victorian Poetry*, 3 (1965), 11n.

such a thing, but his happy ending is, he seems to suggest, as justifiable a hope as any Christian scheme can offer.

Bringing together two such different poems as "The Cloud Confines" and "Rose Mary" may at first seem odd, but the two considered together show what Rossetti, at the height of his confidence and powers, could and could not do. His poetry from 1870 to 1872, and especially in the summer of 1871, shows him boldly attempting to expand his poetic province by testing the limits of his vision. In "The Cloud Confines" he failed to transcend his own skepticism, but wisely and honestly accepted the limits of human percipience. In "Rose Mary" he accepted those limits, and explored the consequences of trying to see beyond them through a magic window or crystal ball. Like Blake—and also like Shelley and Swinburne—he attempted to show that ascetic Christianity, the current set of hypotheses about good and evil, was a life-destroying religion that must be replaced by more earthy, human values. The deceptively simple ballad structure is complicated with ironies that underscore the gap between the untried conviction of faith and reality, and the subtle imagery removes the point of mortal contact with immortality from some delusive external contact—symbolized by the beryl—to internal conviction and felt experience. "Rose Mary" is probably Rossetti's boldest denunciation of conventional moral values and boldest statement of his own belief in the sanctity of passionate human love, but its success compared with the relative failure of "The Cloud Confines" establishes the outer limits of his diminished province. He was not a visionary, and would not fake it, but he could write with conviction about what most nearly concerned him—love, guilt, and redemption—as long as he kept his emphasis on the reality of the material world, and remained too skeptical to try to see beyond the grave.

PART **III**

The Last Decade:
Classical Poetry and
Romantic Painting

8

Poetic Retrenchment

AFTER his youthful and enthusiastically confident Art-Catholic years of the 1840s and 1850s, Rossetti had allowed his poetic empire to diminish in breadth, but he showed, in the skeptical, brooding poetry of 1868–1872, that he could better govern a smaller realm. Once he rejected his casual aesthetic faith and accepted the implications of his skepticism, he became more and more limited to writing about his own sensibility, and so his poetry became increasingly introspective, even narcissistic. Finally, his confidence boosted by the reception of *Poems*, he had, like the fallen angels, set out to test the limits of his fallen state, and to make the most of it. With "Rose Mary" he had, seemingly, established the limit of contraction, had consolidated his position by exploring the basis for his skepticism and asserting, like Blake, Shelley, and others before him, a faith in human love. Nevertheless, after 1872 he continued to see his poetic empire diminish and even, quite self-consciously, began making statements about the necessity of diminution for modern poets. Not only did he give up hope of being the emperor of a vast poetic realm, he also became extremely careful about sweeping every last straw off his causeway. But now the nature of Rossetti's diminution was quite different—in addition to all but giving up the theme of love, he was no longer sharpening his introspective focus, but was becoming, surprisingly, a far less introspective poet. He was advocating an impersonal style in both poetry and painting, and, in terms that anticipated the lifeless poetry of the yellow nineties, was insisting upon a high finish for its own sake. The effects on his own poetry were disastrous since his new emphasis on a more impersonal art led him to abandon the theme that he had always been most successful with—himself. In painting, however, his critical dicta seemed to have little to do with his actual art, which remained extremely expressive and, if anything, became more expressive than ever.

Critical assessments of Rossetti's achievements during the last decade of his life have differed wildly, with some critics maintaining that his poetry greatly improved in his last years, others that it drastically declined, and still others that it remained of a piece with earlier work.[1] Similarly, opinion has greatly differed about whether the painting of the last decade represents the culmination, or the dissolution, of Rossetti's powers.[2] But though assessments of quality vary, certain changes in the style of both arts are generally agreed upon: the poetry, it is said, became more "objective" and "dramatic," and the painting became more "subjective," even "solipsistic,"[3] after Rossetti "lost his dramatic power."[4] And despite the seeming incompatibility of these often repeated judgments, they are, I think, quite accurate. Perhaps because Rossetti's critics have usually considered only one or the other of his arts, this rather obvious paradox has not been fully appreciated, and yet it is the

[1]For a brief summary of representative views, see Ronnalie Roper Howard, *The Dark Glass: Vision and Technique in the Poetry of Dante Gabriel Rossetti* (Athens: Ohio University Press, 1972), pp. 175–176.

[2]Timothy Hilton, for example, sees the late *Astarte Syriaca* as "the summation of Rossetti's career as an artist" in *The Pre-Raphaelites* (London: Oxford University Press, 1970), p. 187. John Nicoll, in his *Dante Gabriel Rossetti* (New York: Macmillan, 1975), sees Rossetti's career moving toward "the febrile indulgence and empty formalism of *Astarte Syriaca*," p. 18.

[3]*The Rossetti-Leyland Letters: The Correspondence of an Artist and His Patron*, ed. Francis L. Fennell, Jr. (Athens: Ohio University Press, 1978), p. xxiv.

[4]W. B. Yeats, *Autobiographies* (New York: Macmillan, 1927), p. 141.

most important single fact about the poetry and painting of Rossetti's last decade.

Rossetti, however, does not seem to have realized that his two
arts were going in opposite directions. In fact, during this last
decade he increasingly asserted that his painting and poetry were
compatible, and even that his painting was inseparable from his
poetry. He insisted that he was primarily a poet, and that "poetic
tendencies . . . chiefly give value to my pictures: only painting
being—what poetry is not—a livelihood—I have put my poetry
chiefly in that form."[5] During these years he wrote sonnets to
accompany, and interpret, almost all his major paintings. The completed work of art consisted of a painting and a poem—the poem
often inscribed on the frame or even painted on the picture itself.
Though this might seem the ultimate unity of the two arts, it
actually signals their divergence: Rossetti evidently needed the sonnets to provide the paintings with the "dramatic" quality that they
manifestly lacked, and the sonnets became more objective by actually being attached to the objects they describe. The irony, of
course, is that by putting his current poetic tendencies too literally
into his pictures, he was making them less "poetic" in the sense
that he intended the word—imaginative, suggestive, lyrical. Still,
the effect is probably precisely what Rossetti intended, since it is
wholly consistent with his many recorded comments that reveal his
new "objective" and "dramatic" aesthetic. Hall Caine, who observed that the "poet's dramatic instinct developed enormously"
during his final decade, claimed that, "conscious of this, Rossetti
used to say in his later years that he would never again write poems
as from his own person."[6]

The ultimate reasons for the shift in Rossetti's aesthetic views are
complex and, to an extent, unknowable, but some contributory
causes are apparent. Rossetti probably came to embrace an aesthetic that played down the importance of inspiration partly because he
found his own inspiration flagging. One correspondent reported

[5]*Letters*, II:849.
[6]Hall Caine, *Recollections of Dante Gabriel Rossetti* (London: Elliot Stock, 1882),
p. 171.

that Rossetti had said, "somewhat sadly, that he could now make no new departure in art, 'finding myself, as I grow older, more than ever at the mercy of my first sources of inspiration.'"[7] Probably by the word "art" Rossetti was referring to his painting, but a comment he made to Caine reveals that he did not depend on inspiration for his poetry either. Comparing himself with a far more copious bard, Rossetti said, "I am the reverse of Swinburne. For his method of production inspiration is indeed the word. With me the case is different."[8] But the reasons for Rossetti's increased objectivity clearly go beyond any sense he had of failing inspiration. Well before 1872 his poetry and painting, both extremely subjective, had come to be confined within ever narrowing limits; he had ceased to expect new sources of inspiration and had long ago begun to hoard his limited stock of poetic ideas.

Rossetti had evidently come to the conclusion by the mid-to-late 1860s that, in both arts, he must sacrifice breadth of scope to perfection of execution. In painting, as Caine observed, "Rossetti perceived that he must make narrower the stream of his effort if he would have it flow deeper; and then, throughout many years, he perfected his technical methods by abandoning complex subject-designs, and confining himself to simple three-quarter length pictures."[9] The setting of limits is more obviously the result of a deliberate, self-conscious decision in regard to his painting, but Rossetti's frequent comments on the subject after about 1868 show that he was just as self-consciously limiting himself in poetry. In 1871, for example, he observed that though lines might be thrown off rapidly in the "ardour of composition" they would later need to be corrected by "the humblest verbal labour."[10] In 1869 he com-

---

[7]John Skelton, quoted in *Letters*, IV:1815n.

[8]Caine, p. 220. Rossetti was still more emphatic, though playful, in discounting inspiration in painting. Caine records (p. 219) the comment that "'In painting, after all, there is in the less important details something of the craft of the superior carpenter, and the part of a picture that is not mechanical is often trivial enough. I don't wonder now,' he added, with a suspicion of a twinkle in the eye, 'if you imagine that one comes down here in a fine frenzy every morning to daub canvas?'"

[9]Ibid., p. 12.

[10]*Letters*, III:994.

plained to Jane Morris that "correction, when one suffers from the vain longing for perfectibility, is an endless task," and connected this longing for perfection with a poetic production necessarily limited in quantity and scope: "I have nothing of [Morris's] abundance in production," he said, and added that "the plan of any work, however small," must be rendered "faultless by repeated condensation and revision."[11] He took pride in confining his work within the narrowest possible limits, boasting to Caine that "probably the man does not live who could write what I have written more briefly than I have done."[12]

His deliberate limiting of poetic production, however, resulted not only from failing inspiration or delight in the virtues of condensation but also from his sense that as the world had grown old, most great poetry had already been written, and the modern poet must preserve his own resources. Consequently he prided himself on his somewhat small output—"I should never be a redundant poet"—in the same letter in which he made some extremely pertinent remarks about Tennyson: "The only man who has husbanded his forces rightly . . . is Tennyson. He has written as much as any poet ought now to write in a long lifetime after all foregone poetry. Self-scrutiny and self-repression will bear a very large part in the poetic 'Survival of the fittest.'"[13] And Rossetti's famous comments about Keats and Shelley also result from the belief that each poet has only a limited sphere in which he can work effectively:

> Keats hardly died so much too early—not at all if there had been any danger of his taking to the modern habit eventually—treating material as product, and shooting it all out as it comes. Of course, however, he wouldn't; he was always getting choicer and simpler, and my favorite piece in his works is *La Belle Dame Sans Merci*—I suppose about his last. As to Shelley, it is really a mercy that he has not been hatching yearly universes till now.[14]

[11]*Dante Gabriel Rossetti and Jane Morris*, ed. John Bryson in association with Janet Camp Troxell (London: Oxford University Press, 1976), p. 27.
[12]Caine, p. 221.
[13]*Letters*, IV:1857.
[14]Caine, pp. 169–170.

Certainly by the last two years of his life, when he made these various comments, Rossetti had arrived at a very clear sense of the limitations that a modern poet must place upon himself.

But although Rossetti's sense of his own failing inspiration and his sense of the necessary diminishment of the modern poet help to explain why he produced less poetry during his last decade, they do not suggest why his poetry became more objective, more dramatic. His praise for "La Belle Dame Sans Merci" is, I think, helpful here. Keats's ballad, as Rossetti misread it, was a masterpiece of poetic *pastiche*—the objective, carefully crafted reproduction of the inspiration of another age. For this kind of poetry not only was inspiration unnecessary, but the mass of "foregone poetry" became not a hindrance, but a source. After 1872, in fact, the bulk of Rossetti's poetry consisted of either mere exercises in craftsmanship, like the beryl songs he added to "Rose Mary," or ballads that are certainly little more than *pastiche*—"The White Ship" and "The King's Tragedy."

The most important reasons for Rossetti's becoming a more objective poet after 1872, however, are surely related to his nervous breakdown in the summer of that year. A brief look at that breakdown, its causes, and consequences, will not only help to explain Rossetti's changed poetic practice and theory, but will also suggest why his practices in painting veered off in the opposite direction. The breakdown, in June 1872, brought to an abrupt end a period of uncharacteristic poetic productivity that had begun at Penkill in the autumn of 1868, had supplied much of the material for *Poems* (1870), and had continued unabated—even with renewed confidence—for another two years. The most immediate cause of the nervous collapse was the appearance of Robert Buchanan's pamphlet *The Fleshly School of Poetry*, but as W. E. Fredeman has shown, even the "immediate causes of the breakdown were numerous and exceedingly complex."[15] The ultimate causes, including a decade of remorse and grief since the death, probably by suicide, of his wife, are more complex still. The causes, both immediate and

[15]W. E. Fredeman, *Prelude to the Last Decade: Dante Gabriel Rossetti in the Summer of 1872* (Manchester: The John Rylands Library, 1971), p. 19. I am indebted to Fredeman's study throughout this brief discussion of Rossetti's breakdown.

ultimate, have been well studied by Fredeman, and it is not necessary to review them here except to observe that all the symptoms preceding the breakdown—hypersensitivity to criticism, hypochondria and insomnia, with the effects of its "cure," chloral and whisky—evidently resulted from Rossetti's profound feelings of guilt. He plainly felt responsible for the death of Lizzie Siddal, felt guilty for betraying her with other women, both before and after her death, felt guilty for disinterring her coffin to retrieve the poems he had buried with her, and finally, felt guilty for his relationship with Jane Morris, a relationship not only adulterous, but traitorous to his one-time friend William Morris, and to his dead wife, Lizzie. Similarly, the symptoms following the breakdown—a sense of being haunted by spirits from the past as well as being persecuted by living men—can also be traced to guilt. Rossetti desperately feared public exposure, so the fame he had achieved with *Poems* must have seemed to him dearly bought when it resulted in Buchanan's humiliating and, as it seemed to Rossetti, well-informed public attack on not only his poetry, but his moral character as well.

Buchanan, who had only a slight knowledge of Rossetti's paintings, was forced to content himself with finding evidence of moral depravity mainly in the poetry. The feat was not difficult. Rossetti was plainly a deeply subjective, personal poet—many of the sonnets in *The House of Life* insist that poetry must be wrung from the personal experiences of the poet—so Buchanan naturally felt free to assume, for example, that in "Jenny" Rossetti was writing about his personal experiences with a prostitute (an incorrect assumption shared by some of Rossetti's friends).[16] Rossetti had been prepared

---

[16]George Augustus Sala, a nodding acquaintance of Rossetti's, believed that the model for *Mary Magdalene at the Door of Simon the Pharisee* was "a typically pre-Raphaelite model, immortalized by the artist in his poem, called Jenny" (*The Life and Adventures of George Augustus Sala, Written by Himself*, 2 vols. [New York: Scribner, 1895], 1:339). In other words he believed that Rossetti had written "Jenny" about his experiences with Fanny Cornforth, though in fact Rossetti did not meet her until long after the first version of "Jenny" had been written. Sala, who knew Buchanan, is one of the many people in the small and interwoven artistic and literary circles of London who might have gossiped with him about Rossetti, whose fear that Buchanan knew more than he ought to was surely not as unreasonably paranoid as has sometimes been suggested.

for an attack on "Jenny," a dramatic monologue that was obviously on the outskirts of conventional morality in its theme and treatment, and had the attack been solely on those works that were, in fact, dramatic utterances, he probably would have borne it. But he was deeply shocked by Buchanan's description of the view of love expressed in the most personal lyrics of *The House of Life.* Though carefully controlled and distanced by elaborate artifice, these sonnets laid bare Rossetti's, and his beloved's, souls. Buchanan had accused Rossetti of "wheeling his nuptial couch out into the public streets."[17] With the evidence of Buchanan's well-informed attack before him, Rossetti apparently believed the accusation, and was horrified to realize how much his poetry had revealed about him and, as he no doubt thought, about the women he loved. As Fredeman has shown, Rossetti very likely "saw in Buchanan's works unmistakable signs that news of the recovery of his manuscripts from Elizabeth Siddal's grave had 'oozed out' . . . or that his affair with Jane Morris was public knowledge and that her portrait stood out too prominently in *The House of Life.*"[18] If so, it is certainly not surprising that Rossetti, according to his brother, "thought that the pamphlet was a first symptom in a widespread conspiracy for crushing his fair fame as an artist and a man, and for hounding him out of honest society."[19]

Too much speculation along these lines is, of course, fruitless and, for my purpose, beside the point, but it is surely reasonable to suppose that Rossetti, dreading any close scrutiny of his personal life, would not be inclined to unlock his heart with a sonnet-key. Buchanan had said that Rossetti was "never dramatic, never impersonal,"[20] but from the date of the pamphlet on, Rossetti, as he told Caine much later, "would never again write poems as from his own person." His graphic art, however, had not only not been censured, but was almost immune to attack. Because of his close connection with a small group of patrons, Rossetti could make a living with his

---

[17]Robert Buchanan, *The Fleshly School of Poetry and Other Phenomena of the Day* (London: Strahan, 1872), p. ix.

[18]Fredeman, p. 45.

[19]*Dante Gabriel Rossetti: His Family Letters, with a Memoir by William Michael Rossetti,* 2 vols. (Boston: Roberts Brothers, 1895), I:305.

[20]Buchanan, p. 38.

painting without ever having to exhibit his work to the public. Paradoxically, writing poetry was, for Rossetti, a public act, though it was in practical terms merely an avocation; painting, though it made him a living, was essentially a private act. It has often been said that Rossetti ruined his art by the "ingloriousness of pandering"[21] to his patrons, but actually his relations with patrons enabled him to continue to do in private the kind of work in painting that he had previously done in both arts: to explore the new realms of poetic material that he alone knew. Before 1872, Rossetti—though he painted pictures—had perfectly fit Robert Browning's description of the subjective poet: "He does not paint pictures and hang them on the walls, but rather carries them on the retina of his own eyes: we must look deep into his human eyes, to see those pictures on them."[22] And when we look deep into those human eyes, as they are evoked in the poetry of 1868 to 1872, we see the equally mysterious eyes of Rossetti's beloved, of his vision of the soul. After 1872, Rossetti sought his vision almost exclusively by painting pictures and hanging them on the walls. Certainly he did not seek it in his poetry.

The most immediately obvious change in Rossetti's poetry after the breakdown of 1872 is quantitative rather than qualitative. From 1872 until 1878 he stopped writing poetry almost entirely, but the few poems written during this period seem, at first glance, to be stylistically and thematically consistent with those of 1868–1872. His obsession with love, death, and the separation of lovers is apparent even in the titles of some of the lyrics, such as "Parted Presence" (1875), "A Death-Parting" (1876), and "Adieu" (1876), and his agonized skepticism, his puzzled questioning of death, appears in three sonnets that would eventually be included in *The House of Life:* "The Heart of the Night" (1873), "Memorial Thresholds" (1873), and "The Trees of the Garden" (1875).[23] Rossetti's third and final productive spurt, from 1878 until his

[21]Robin Ironside, *Pre-Raphaelite Painters* (London: Phaidon, 1948), p. 89.

[22]"Essay on Shelley," in *Browning's Poetry and Prose*, ed. Simon Nowell-Smith (London: Rupert Hart-Davis, 1967), p. 673.

[23]For the dating of Rossetti's sonnets in *The House of Life*, I have relied on W. E. Fredeman's appendix to his "Rossetti's 'In Memoriam'. An Elegiac Reading of *The House of Life*," *Bulletin of the John Rylands Library*, 47 (1965), 298–341.

death, also included some new sonnets for *The House of Life,* including the beautiful "Ardour and Memory" and the famous three-sonnet series "True Woman," as well as some lyrics ("Insomnia," "Possession," "Spheral Change") that seem, at first, a part of Rossetti's painfully personal vision. But the great bulk of his poetry after 1872, and especially from 1878 to 1882, falls into three categories that, as Rossetti handled them, were relatively dramatic and descriptive, objective and impersonal; overwrought lyrics, ballads, and poems about poets, painters, and paintings.

Rossetti's style had always been elaborately ornate, but in his closing decade he exaggerated his mannerisms almost to the point of parody. A comparison of how his style worked at its best with the style of the late lyrics reveals the extent to which he eventually gave himself over to exercising his craftsmanship for its own sake, even in the most seemingly personal of the late poems. Earlier in his career, Rossetti's poetic style, particularly in the sonnets, had been the perfect vehicle for his limited vision. Coventry Patmore's comment that Rossetti gave "the impression of tensity rather than intensity"[24] is extremely appropriate for a poet who attempted to stretch his vision over the darkness of the grave. A more recent commentator, speaking of the poetry rather than of the poet, has made a similar observation with similar distaste: "his surfaces seem overwrought, not because they are, comparatively speaking, exceedingly ornate but because there is often no solid fabric beneath them."[25] The complaint, a common one, is that Rossetti's verse is too arduously full, that the fullness is of artifice rather than of content, that, in short, Rossetti's poetry is an elaborate camouflage to conceal his lack of anything to say. But since one of his most pressing concerns during his best period had been to camouflage the dark glass, his artifice has a thematic as well as formal purpose; his poems are deliberately overworked precisely because he wanted to draw the reader's attention to the poetic surface, and because he realized that his limited vision could not pass beneath the surfaces

[24]Quoted in Oswald Doughty, *A Victorian Romantic: Dante Gabriel Rossetti* (London: Frederick Muller, 1949), p. 89.

[25]Harold L. Weatherby, "Problems of Form and Content in the Poetry of Dante Gabriel Rossetti," *Victorian Poetry,* 2 (1964), 15.

of things. His obsession with the way his books were printed, his concern with the cover designs, the typeface, the spacing of lines on the page, were probably to some extent due to his respect for the symbolic value of the printed page.

Certainly all the characteristics of Rossetti's middle style seem designed to present an impenetrable surface. His highly artificial meters, for example, both draw attention to his artifice and, because his extraordinarily frequent spondees slow the verse down, force the reader to linger on the poetic surface. Because Rossetti was "never metrically spontaneous,"[26] his verses lack the freshness and immediacy of speech and substitute instead a deliberate, marmoreal diction. His love for spondaic feet, which frequently weigh down his lines with extra accents, adds to the heavy, opaque quality of the verse, as if his sonnets were literally carved "in ivory or in ebony." Or at least the words, like discrete stones, are heavily cemented together. Even his frequent use of hyphens to create compounds ("Silent Noon," for example, has seven hyphenated compounds) seems, like his use of extra accents, to add mortar to the words, cementing them together as tightly as possible into a cohesive, impenetrable surface.

The "tensity" of Rossetti's poetry is still more obvious in his overworking of imagery. Even the most sympathetic of comments on this subject indicates the extent to which he arduously filled his poems: "He hurries one symbol into another, he folds and enfolds them together; they are labyrinthine; yet if we pursue them, we reach at last their centre. . . . Then . . . all the involutions are understood. There is no one clearer than Rossetti."[27] This is excessively generous—Rossetti could, occasionally, lose control of his symbols, as in "The Stream's Secret"—but it effectively communicates the elaboration of his imagery, the way in which his poems are almost literally blanketed with images until they frequently seem to pose conundrums, defying the reader to make sense of the involuted and convoluted patterns. And since the images are almost always

---

[26]T. Earle Welby, *The Victorian Romantics, 1850–1870* (London: Gerald Howe, 1929), p. 32.

[27]Stopford Brooke, *Four Poets: A Study of Clough, Arnold, Rossetti and Morris* (London: Pitman, 1908), p. 137.

191

concrete, physical depictions of abstractions, the surface seems all the more opaque. The clusters of imagery in the sonnets, formally related to Rossetti's crowded watercolors, achieve much the same end of denying easy access to the work. The sonnet "Winged Hours" (1869) epitomizes the ways in which Rossetti, during his best period, could fill a sonnet to the point of bursting:

> Each hour until we meet is as a bird
>   That wings from far his gradual way along
>   The rustling covert of my soul,—his song
> Still loudlier trilled through leaves more deeply stirr'd:
> But at the hour of meeting, a clear word
>   Is every note he sings, in Love's own tongue;
>   Yet, Love, thou know'st the sweet strain suffers wrong
> Through our contending kisses oft unheard.
>
> What of that hour at last, when for her sake
>   No wing may fly to me nor song may flow;
>   When, wandering round my life unleaved, I know
> The bloodiest feathers scattered in the brake,
>   And think how she, far from me, with like eyes
>   Sees through the untuneful bough the wingless skies?
>
>   [*Poems*, 112]

The sonnet is certainly filled metrically: if "gradual," "loudlier," "every," "wandering" and "bloodiest" are all granted a full syllabic count, Rossetti has actually added five extra syllables to the 140 properly belonging to the sonnet. But the imagery, far more than the meter, draws attention to the poem's formal qualities. The controlling image, introduced in the first line, transforms the abstract idea of time into the physical image of a bird and enables Rossetti to develop a sonnet about love, forebodings of loss, loss itself, and even the projected memory of loss in graphic physical terms. The effect of this technique is difficult to define. Rossetti's elaborate simile would seem to enable him fully to exploit the emotional connotations of such phrases as "my life unleaved," "bloodiest feathers," "untuneful bough" and "wingless skies," and to a certain extent he does, but the poem, nevertheless, is more immediately striking for its artifice than for its emotion. The similes, with their various involutions, have completely covered the surface of the poem, but they seem also to have obliterated the emotional source of the sonnet. In "Winged Hours," as often in Rossetti's sonnets, the use of an elaborate simile or analogy displaces as much as it illustrates the theme; figurative language becomes a projection of the intellectual life of the artist on to his emotional concern. The formal order of art, in effect, crowds out the pain of the emotions; the manageable, physical characteristics of the simile crowd out the unmanageable abstractions. And adding to this effect, the dominant images of the poem are apparently inspired not only by the particular situation of the poet, but by literature. The image of the bird associated with love was common among the *stilnovisti*[28] and the "untuneful bough" seems a recollection of Shakespeare's "Bare ruined choirs, where late the sweet birds sang."

The near displacement of content by form, however, does not indicate that Rossetti was practicing Art for Art's sake. Rather he seems to be anticipating the golden bird upon a golden bough of Yeats, the need for an artifice that transcends the mire of the flesh. Form does not become important for Rossetti because he had nothing to say, but because it helped him to distance the painful things he did have to say. In "A Defence of Poetry" Shelley wrote that "poetry defeats the curse which binds us to be subjected to the accident of surrounding impressions. And whether it spreads its own figured curtain or withdraws life's dark veil from before the scene of things, it equally creates for us a being within our being. It makes us the inhabitants of a world to which the familiar world is a chaos."[29] One of the functions of poetry is to create order from chaos, art from life. Rossetti's "figured curtain" is painted with the colors of self-conscious artifice partly to separate it from the chaos of the familiar world and partly to emphasize its very nature as a "figured curtain." The relation of form to content in Rossetti's verse has been well described by Richard Stein, who writes: "His

---

[28]As Doughty (p. 338) points out, the image was a favorite of Dante's in *Paradiso*.

[29]*Shelley's Poetry and Prose*, ed. Donald H. Reiman and Sharon B. Powers (New York: Norton, 1977), p. 505.

'decorative' tendency is not manifested in an absence of controlling form but in an intentional formal complexity which denies the familiar illusion that structure grows organically from a poetic situation or the natural process of thought. Instead, Rossetti alerts us to the pressure of structure on statement, poetic form as an artificial scheme with which specific feelings and incidents must be aligned."[30] Rossetti's most personal utterances are aligned with rigid, unyielding forms because he felt that any "organic" form, attempting to imitate life, must imitate life's disorder, but as his sonnet on the sonnet indicates, he wanted his poetry to memorialize life—not to imitate it, but to embalm it. His poetic structures, especially his sonnets, deliberately create a surface impervious to the vicissitudes of life. His sonnets are filled not with incidents and feelings, but with artificial memorials to experience.

Perhaps it is partly the marmoreal quality of Rossetti's "moment's monuments" that has occasionally led readers to respond to *The House of Life* as to an elegy.[31] The poem has been called, not inappropriately, a "reliquary" containing the no longer living moments of a past life.[32] The full title of the work, *The House of Life: A Sonnet-Sequence*, implies that it is a work both about life and about the sequential passage of time. The poem itself exhibits a tension in which sequentiality suggests narrative, logical, rational development, but the parts, the individual sonnets, resist it. Each sonnet is an immortal artifact describing an eternal moment. The sonnets are removed from life into eternity, yet the sequence is a House of Life, not a mausoleum. The tension, perhaps, is meant to suggest time's point of contact with eternity, life's with art. For Rossetti, who saw the total of a man's life as the sum of his memories, and who saw memories as more or less static tableaux, this photo album style was a perfect way to embody, and perhaps more important, to formalize a total experience of life. But Rossetti was not, like Wordsworth, attempting to relive the past in memories, but to memorialize it in

[30]Richard Stein, *The Ritual of Interpretation: The Fine Arts as Literature in Ruskin, Rossetti, and Pater* (Cambridge: Harvard University Press, 1975), p. 198.

[31]See Fredeman, "Rossetti's 'In Memoriam,'" and Douglas Robillard, "Rossetti's 'Willowwood Sonnets' and the Structure of *The House of Life,*" *Victorian Newsletter,* 22 (1962), 5–9.

[32]Welby, p. 33.

art. The apparent disjunction between the wild passions memorialized in Rossetti's sonnets and their chiseled, Parnassian forms, their achieved stillness, calls to mind Eliot's conjecture that the "care for perfection of form among some of the romantic poets of the nineteenth century was an effort to support, or to conceal from view, an inner disorder," or Valéry's comment that all classicism implies a previous romanticism, that all order implies a disorder that must be controlled by form.[33] Though Valéry's remark may not describe all classicism, it does seem a fitting account of Rossetti's highly formal composition. Despite Rossetti's comment that sonnets, to him, meant insomnia, restlessness is surely not one of the characteristics of his finished products. Apparently by reducing his emotional struggles to formal order, he put his demons temporarily to rest. The "classical" characteristics of Rossetti's art do not, of course, correspond to the breadth of vision of the classical ages, but to a diminishment from Romantic art.[34] At their best, Rossetti's labyrinthine images do have a center in which a moment is preserved as in amber, is made eternal, but Rossetti, unlike Blake, never attempts to open a center to infinite vision.

The highly wrought sonnets of 1868 to 1872, then, are designed partially to enshrine experience, and partially as a buffer against experience. Everything about them suggests that their "tensity" is deliberately achieved to spread a veil—one might almost say a memorial shroud—over the dark glass of fear and hope. But for all his emphasis on artifice, on the painted veil, Rossetti was at that time a poet of life, not death. The painted veil itself is called "Life" by "those who live," and Rossetti focused his vision upon it precisely because it was the visible and apparent manifestation of life

[33]See T. S. Eliot's "Introduction" to Baudelaire's *Intimate Journals,* trans. Christopher Isherwood (New York: Random House, 1930), p. 14. See also Mario Praz, *The Romantic Agony,* trans. Angus Davidson (London: Oxford University Press, 1951), pp. 8–9.

[34]Rossetti's emphasis on craftsmanship and control is nearer to English neoclassicism than real classicism. Hazlitt's comment on Pope, in fact, seems neatly to describe Rossetti: "His mind dwelt with greater pleasure on his own garden, than on the garden of Eden; he could describe the faultless whole-length mirror that reflected his own person, better than the smooth surface of the lake that reflects the face of heaven": "On Dryden and Pope" in *Lectures on the English Poets and The Spirit of the Age* (London: Dent, 1910), p. 70.

and because he was too belated a Romantic to lift it and seek the imageless deep truth. Swinburne was quite right in saying that Rossetti's poetic form weaves a "veil and girdle of glorious words" over the "bitter sweetness of sincerity,"[35] and he was quite right also in calling such a form fleshly, for the woven artifice of Rossetti's surfaces veils the raw emotion in much the same way as flesh veils the soul.

But Swinburne was describing his friend's verse in 1870, before Rossetti became reticent about exposing himself with bittersweet sincerity even under a veil of glorious words. Even the most apparently personal poems of Rossetti's last decade seem strangely impersonal, seem to lack the "tensity" of the earlier work. The few additional sonnets written in this period for *The House of Life* exaggerate the artifice of the earlier sonnets, but without suggesting the same emotional tension. "The Heart of the Night," for example, closes with a string of emphatic, but somehow unconvincing, expostulations:

> O Lord of work and peace! O Lord of Life!
> O Lord, the awful Lord of will! though late,
> Even yet renew this soul with duteous breath;
> That when the peace is garnered in from strife,
> The work retrieved, the will regenerate,
> This soul may see thy face, O Lord of death!
> [*Poems*, 231]

William Rossetti's tentative comment about the poem is revealing: "This sonnet reads throughout as being an intense personal utterance: I assume it to be so." Paull Franklin Baum's response to William's comment is even more enlightening: "Except as such it has very little interest."[36] The poem appears anguished and intensely personal simply because the vaguely Calvinistic rhetoric and the insistent exclamations immediately suggest the anguish of the individual soul praying to its maker. But such a reading should

[35]"The Poems of Dante Gabriel Rossetti," in *The Complete Works of Algernon Charles Swinburne*, ed. Edmund Gosse and Thomas James Wise, 20 vols. (London: Heinemann, 1925–1927), 15:9.

[36]Baum, ed., *The House of Life: A Sonnet-Sequence* (Cambridge: Harvard University Press), p. 167.

make us pause—when was Rossetti even vaguely Calvinistic, after all, and when was he ever concerned with a "Lord of work and peace"? The impassioned rhetoric of the poem, in other words, does not seem to come from Rossetti's own passion, but is reminiscent of the somewhat facile posturing of his "Art-Catholic" period. At best, one could conceivably argue, his genuine struggle to reconcile love and life with death has been translated into another idiom, as though he no longer dared to express it directly. But the sonnet seems impersonal for stylistic as well as thematic reasons. Rossetti had always loaded his sonnets with artifice and controlled them with rhetorical structure, but in his best sonnets the genuine questions, the genuine passion, had seemed to strain against the tight, imposed control of the rhetoric. Here, the rhetoric is more of an outline to be filled in with appropriate phrases: the poem becomes an exercise in sonneteering not too different from the *bouts-rimés* that had kept Rossetti occupied in his youth. Within this mechanical structure such lines as "The work retrieved, the will regenerate" impress the reader not as the condensation or crystallization of complex thought, but as clever exercises in balance and patterning of sounds.

Not all of Rossetti's late poetry, of course, gives the impression that he was engaging in verbal exercises rather than attempting to say anything, but it is significant that the two sonnets associated in time and theme with "The Heart of the Night" are more impressive in their artifice than in their expressiveness. "The Trees of the Garden" faces the painful conclusion of skepticism, that some inscrutable "decree / Of some inexorable supremacy" conducts us to an unknowable and probably meaningless doom. But any emotional involvement that such a theme ought to entail is dissipated in complex, barely decipherable images. When the poet suggests, for example, that an answer may be sought from

> The storm-felled forest-trees moss-grown to-day
> Whose roots are hillocks where the children play
> [*Poems*, 234]

the reader is more likely to be impressed by the glut of hyphens than by the suitability of the image. The image is, of course, suitable—

197

Rossetti is contrasting the age-old, but decaying, trees with the still more obvious transience of the blithe children—but the intellectual effort needed to decipher it and fit it into the rest of the poem deprives it of any immediacy. And certainly squeezing seven accents into the line describing the trees is aesthetically uncalled for and seems an act of pointless virtuosity. It is significant that these two lines were mined from a notebook containing various felicitous phrases and first attempts at lines for sonnets. The sestet of "The Trees of the Garden," then, may have been constructed as a frame for the virtuoso lines.[37]

Even more clearly than "The Trees of the Garden," "Memorial Thresholds" is a poem that ought to be emotionally charged, but dissipates its emotional energy in perplexing images and overwrought artifice. Because the sonnet is the most apparently "personal" of all Rossetti's poems after 1872, and because it is almost impossible to paraphrase, it is worth quoting entirely:

> What place so strange,—though unrevealèd snow
>> With unimaginable fires arise
>> At the earth's end,—what passion of surprise
> Like frost-bound fire-girt scenes of long ago?
> Lo! this is none but I this hour; and lo!
>> This is the very place which to mine eyes
>> Those mortal hours in vain immortalize,
> 'Mid hurrying crowds, with what alone I know.
>
> City, of thine a single simple door,
>> By some new Power reduplicate, must be
>> Even yet my life-porch in eternity,
> Even with one presence filled, as once of yore:
> Or mocking winds whirl round a chaff-strown floor
>> Thee and thy years and these my words and me.
>
> [*Poems,* 233]

[37]Four notebooks in the British Library and several detached notebook pages in the Janet Camp Troxell Collection at Princeton University Library contain first attempts at passages later used in "Silent Noon," "Ardour and Memory," "Pride of Youth," "The Sonnet," "Soothsay," and other poems. The detached lines, which occur in identical form in both the Troxell notebook fragment and in the British Library notebook number two, vary only slightly from the published lines: "The

In its obscure way the poem is about the connection, as William Rossetti put it, of "some house" with "some event of supreme importance" in the poet's life, and about the hope that in the afterlife the same "event of supreme importance" will recur. The terms of William's description indicate that Rossetti's language points to nothing very precise, and in fact the language is not only imprecise but, in the opening quatrain at least, nearly meaningless, though we can, of course, force it to mean something by following Baum's example and connecting it with the "Innominata," Jane Morris. Once this information is imposed on it, it becomes at least movingly suggestive, if not clear. It becomes, at least, a poem about love, separation, and the hope for reunion after death, a poem about Rossetti's deepest emotional concerns. Still, the sonnet expresses nothing very clearly until the closing lines, in which the reverse of hope is poignantly described. If the hope of reunion is a false hope, life itself is a meaningless mockery. It is conceivable, at least, that Rossetti was no longer willing to risk a clear expression of his idea of spiritual love and his view of a heaven of love, and so he buried the hope under twelve lines of artifice and obscurity. The poem certainly seems to detach itself at a formidable aesthetic distance from the, presumably, genuine feelings, genuine love, that prompted it. And yet, in an odd way, the sonnet is extremely moving—the twisted, excessively condensed syntax of the first twelve lines is expressive in its very failure to express a clear hope; the clarity of the expression of despair in the last two lines is all the more powerful following the display of tongue-tied, thwarted hope. But of course what is especially moving is the plight of the poet, cut off from his sources of inspiration, and capable only of expressing orthodox despair, and not his one hope.

Though Rossetti's other late lyrics about love and separation are not as obscure as "Memorial Thresholds," they are generally more

---

upheaved forest-trees moss-grown today / Whose roots are hillocks where the children play." In general, an examination of Rossetti's late notebooks reveals the remarkable degree to which he milked his inspiration. Almost every stray thought jotted down in the notebooks was eventually incorporated into a poem, or a poem was built around it. Rossetti's patient craftsmanship is further evident in his use of prose outlines for many poems.

notable for ingenuity than for immediacy. In his best sonnets of this period, "Ardour and Memory" and "True Woman: I. Herself," he achieves not a passionate statement but an elucidation of ingeniously subtle images. An image used to describe the "sacred secret" of "True Woman," for example, is "the heart-shaped seal of green / That flecks the snowdrop underneath the snow" (*Poems*, 227). The single blade of grass, its tip bent over by the weight of the snow, would indeed impress a heart-shaped seal, though no one could ever see it. The image is certainly appropriate, even startlingly appropriate, but again the poet's ingenuity is more immediately impressive than his urgent need to express himself. The resulting sonnet is beautiful, but perhaps slightly precious: as a lyricist Rossetti seems to have become a creator of exquisite miniatures. I do not mean to disparage these sonnets—by any standards "Ardour and Memory" and "True Woman: I. Herself" are among Rossetti's finest—but to indicate that his poetry fundamentally changed after 1872, despite superficial similarities to earlier poetry. Generally, before 1872 his sonnets strain against their structural limits, stretching the verbal surface taut; after 1872 the "message" is more limited than the medium. In fact, the "message" of "Ardour and Memory" seems designed to justify the use of the beautiful imagery of the opening three lines, which were first written, again divorced from any context, in Rossetti's notebooks of verbal felicities.

That Rossetti had become more concerned with craftsmanship and artifice for their own sake after 1872 is even more evident in the late lyrics other than sonnets. Among the very few late lyrics, some, such as the beryl songs added to "Rose Mary," and "Chimes," are plainly little more than exercises in sound patterning. Others, like "Adieu," are about Rossetti's old themes, especially about the sadness of parting, but are overworked to the extent that they too become mere exercises:

> Waving whispering trees,
> What do you say to the breeze
>   And what says the breeze to you?
> 'Mid passing souls ill at ease,
> Moving murmuring trees,
>   Would ye ever wave an Adieu?

Tossing turbulent seas,
Winds that wrestle with these,
   Echo heard in the shell,—
'Mid fleeting life ill at ease,
Restless ravening seas,—
   Would the echo sigh Farewell?
       [*Poems*, 247]

Even "Parted Presence," a lyric with the same ostensible concerns as "The Stream's Secret," "Love's Nocturn," and many of the most moving sonnets of *The House of Life*, calls attention not to the pain of separation from the beloved, or the joyfully paradoxical union of the parted lovers, but to its own artifice:

Your heart is never away,
   But ever with mine, for ever,
   For ever without endeavour,
To-morrow, love, as to-day;
Two blent hearts never astray,
   Two souls no power may sever,
   Together, O my love, for ever!
       [*Poems*, 243]

William Rossetti's only comment on the poem was that "reverberation of sound . . . is very frequent in Rossetti's poems. . . . He was fond of the chiming—perhaps overmuch so" (*Works*, 670).

Although the complex reasons for Rossetti's apparent retrenchment as a poet probably involve such things as failing inspiration or, more likely, failing confidence and a need to safeguard his privacy, his belief that the latter-day poet must accept diminishment is also important. In his last public comment on poetry and poets, his review of Thomas Hake's *Parables and Tales*, Rossetti explicitly described and defended a limited order of poetry:

Of [the highest] order of poetry—the omnipotent freewill of the artist's mind,—our curbed and slackening world may seem to have seen the last. It has been succeeded by another kind of "finish," devoted and ardent, but less building on ensured foundations than self-questioning in the very moment of action or even later: yet by

201

such creative labour also the evening and the morning may be blent to a true day, though it be often but a fitful or an unglowing one.

Rossetti seems to be describing himself as well as his ostensible subject when he claims that "Dr. Hake is to be ranked with those poets who, in striving to perfect what they do as best they may, resolve to have a tussle for their own with Oblivion" (*Works*, 630). This notion of diminishment, however, is clearly of a different order from the one considered earlier. It is no longer a matter of abandoning immense themes to concentrate on the small, but poetically rich resources of the limited individual soul; it is an abandonment of any confident poetic stance at all. This emphasis on refinement of artifice in a "curbed and slackening world," in fact, leads to the often beautiful but generally vacuous poetry of the decadent nineties. Even in 1871 at the height of his confidence, Rossetti's advice to at least one poet of the coming generation reaffirms this debilitating idea: after reading Arthur O'Shaughnessy's poems, he advised the young poet to curb his Muse and heed "the inevitable inheritance of over-experience which no modern poet can ignore."[38] Nevertheless, his more excessively despairing comments in the essay on Hake sound more like a rationalization, a reaction to his own failure of confidence, than like a reasoned conviction. In fact, he indicates his dissatisfaction with this extreme version of diminishment with a comment that, he perhaps hoped, would let him slip out of the ranks of poets who depend exclusively on perfection of finish: "Not only with this second class, but even with those highest among consummate workers, productiveness must be found, at the close of life, to have been comparatively limited; though never failing, where a true master is in question, of such mass as is necessary to robust vitality" (*Works*, 630).

In his own closing years Rossetti certainly could not have hoped to base a reputation for "robust vitality" on his dainty, overwrought lyrics. In his most productive periods, however, he had written not only deeply personal lyrics, but also a number of ballads, and although he could no longer produce the kind of lyrics he once had, he could, for several reasons, return more easily to the ballad form.

[38]*Letters*, III:1041.

In fact, he reportedly looked back on his career from his deathbed, and saw its continuity in his devotion to the ballad. According to Hall Caine, Rossetti, in his last discussion of poetry, "talked long and earnestly. . . . He spoke of his love of early English ballad literature, and of how when he first met with it he had said to himself: 'There lies your line.'"[39] But a comparison of Rossetti's best early ballads with his late ones reveals a sharp turn in his line, a turn comparable to the movement toward objectivity and artifice in his lyrics.

Rossetti's ballads before 1872 had, of course, been concerned with the same themes as his lyrics, and were consequently open to the same accusations. Just as a Buchanan had accused Rossetti of wheeling his nuptial couch into the public street, a more recent, more sympathetic critic has, to a very similar effect, observed that the shared theme of "Sister Helen" and "Rose Mary" reveals Rossetti's "obsession with seduction and betrayal." In terms that seem to justify Rossetti's later fear of allowing his own sensibility to enter into his ballads, this critic has asserted that "the personal undertone appears in significant detail: Rose Mary has the heavy dark hair that in the paintings is associated with Jane Morris, while the rival woman has the golden tresses of Fanny Cornforth."[40] But of course it is not necessary to find specious biographical clues in the poems to see that they combine Rossetti's idiosyncratic concerns with elements of the traditional ballad form. Indeed, when Swinburne set out, in 1870, to praise Rossetti's ballads, he began by redefining the genre: "the highest form of ballad requires from a poet at once narrative power, lyrical and dramatic; it must hold in fusion these three faculties at once, or fail of its mark: it must condense the large loose fluency of romantic tale-telling into tight and intense brevity."[41] Swinburne is describing not the traditional ballad but a kind of lyrical ballad that absorbs the terseness and pace of the old ballads, but replaces their flat taciturnity with lyric and dramatic complexities. The definition is well adapted to "Sister Helen," the specific ballad Swinburne had in mind. In that poem

[39]Caine, p. 293.
[40]Lionel Stevenson, *The Pre-Raphaelite Poets* (New York: Norton, 1974), p. 61.
[41]Swinburne, "The Poems of Dante Gabriel Rossetti," p. 27.

203

the complication of the ballad stanza to include the three fully characterized, impassioned voices of Helen, her brother, and the speaker of the refrain adds the drama that Swinburne sees as part of the highest form of the ballad, and the emotional involvement of even the speaker of the refrain adds to the lyrical power. "Rose Mary," similarly, is complicated in terms of a plot that subtly examines the moral value of love. Both poems, moreover, depend upon a sophisticated symbolism that is certainly no part of the traditional ballad: in "Sister Helen" the waxen man suggests the destructive power of a literally consuming passion, and in "Rose Mary" the imagery of sky-reflecting water suggests the limits of mortal knowledge. In 1872 Rossetti's use of the ballad form was certainly not restricted to objective tale-telling but, as Swinburne said, was adapted to "hold in extract the very heart of tragedy, the burning essence distilled from 'Hate born of Love, and blind as he.' "[42] The ballad was a passionate lyrical form, well suited to express Rossetti's favorite themes: love, hate, the connection between sexual love and death, the paradoxical fusion of tenderness and violence in woman.

But the more traditional ballad must have seemed an especially attractive form to a man who evidently felt that his earlier verse had revealed too much about his personal life, but who also needed to produce "such mass as is necessary to robust vitality" in order to prove himself a "true master." It is traditionally a less expansive form than the love lyric and, in fact, partly depends for its success on making the poet disappear entirely—the ballad should appear to be the result of generations of oral tradition, as though it were the voice of the people, not the voice of the individual poet. At the very least, the form must have impressed Rossetti as an ideal way to camouflage his identity—it is surely no coincidence that in the last three years of his life, the years in which he most devoted himself to the writing of ballads, Rossetti came almost to idolize the "ardent and heroic" Thomas Chatterton, a poet completely hidden behind his own fiction of a poet, Rowley. He called Chatterton the "true day-spring of modern romantic poetry"[43] and even compared him

[42]Ibid., pp. 27–28.
[43]Caine, pp. 187, 185.

to the far greater chameleon poet, Shakespeare. It is significant that his sonnet in praise of Chatterton closes with an allusion to the well-kept secret of his identity: "thy grave unknown / And love-dream of thine unrecorded face." Here was a poet whose verse and name would live, but whose life could not be ransacked and defiled by critics.

Rossetti's admiration for Chatterton suggests one reason why he was attracted to the ballad, but it also suggests the danger posed by the form. Chatterton had attempted to write poetry that was essentially a hoax, literary *pastiche* so convincing that it would pass as genuinely medieval. Obviously any attempt to be too faithful to literary precedents is likely to become, like Chatterton-Rowley's ballads, mere antiquarianism. And the danger was especially great for Rossetti, who had always been disposed to overvalue all things medieval simply because they were medieval. His praise of Keats's "La Belle Dame Sans Merci," for example, completely overlooks the intensely personal, haunting qualities of that poem to make the strange and almost irrelevant comment that it showed "astonishingly real medievalism for one not bred as an artist."[44] And in fact even before Rossetti had any reason to worry about concealing his own identity, his ballads had occasionally come dangerously close to mere antiquarian *pastiche*. Rossetti himself considered the early ballad "Stratton Water" to be "successful only in so far as any imitation of the old ballad can be successful."[45] Swinburne, commenting on "Stratton Water," pointed out that the real danger of imitating the old ballads was that the result might be a bastardized form that was neither good *pastiche* nor good modern poetry: "The landscape of 'Stratton Water' is as vivid and thorough as any ballad can show; but some may wish it had been more or less of a compromise in style between old and new: it is now a study after the old manner, too close to be no closer."[46] In more general terms, if Rossetti used the ballad as a mask, he might produce excellent *pastiche*, but only *pastiche*, and if he aimed at more of a compromise

[44]*Letters*, IV:1711.

[45]The sentiment is recorded by William Sharp, *Dante Gabriel Rossetti: A Record and a Study* (London: Macmillan, 1882), p. 375.

[46]Swinburne, "The Poems of Dante Gabriel Rossetti," p. 29.

between old and new, it would be at the risk of exposing his own presence in the poem.

The ballads Rossetti wrote in his last decade indicate that he chose, whether consciously or not, to conceal his own identity behind artifice and antiquarianism. After completing "Rose Mary" in 1871, he did not write another ballad until 1878, when he began work on "The White Ship," which was followed by substantial revisions to "Rose Mary" and "Sister Helen" and by his last major poem, "The King's Tragedy," in 1881. The late revisions of "Sister Helen" and "Rose Mary" reveal a changed approach to the ballad, since in both cases the changes seem at first to emphasize the original lyricism of the poems, but in fact emphasize their nature as romantic tales. Rossetti's rather defensive letter to Hall Caine describes the changes to "Sister Helen," and the reasons for them, after Caine had protested that the poem was too perfect to meddle with. "Of course I knew," he wrote, "that your hair must arise from your scalp in protest. But what should you say if Keith of Ewern were a three days' bridegroom—if the spell had begun on the wedding-morning—and if the bride herself became the last pleader for mercy? I fancy you will see your way now. The culminating, irresistible provocation helps, I think, to humanize Helen, besides lifting the tragedy to a yet sterner height."[47] The idea, apparently, had been to increase the passion of Helen, to make her more comprehensible as an ordinary woman, and so to increase the emotional involvement of the reader. The result, however, of making Helen more human is that she becomes less impressive as a symbol, and further, the result of making the reader become more involved with her as a dramatic character is that he becomes less involved with the author—the dramatist is always more anonymous than the lyricist. Finally, the poem had originally been praised for condensing "the large loose fluency of romantic tale-telling into tight and intense brevity," but now the process of condensation is reversed. By providing Helen with further motives, Rossetti needlessly expanded the romantic tale and, by making it more easily comprehensible, made it also less mysterious and less moving.

The substantial addition to "Rose Mary," in 1879, of three long

[47]Caine, p. 128.

lyrics, each following a section of the narrative, changed that ballad in much the same way as the addition of eight stanzas had changed "Sister Helen." His main reason for adding the beryl songs was to clarify the narrative, as the additions to "Sister Helen" had clarified that story, and to avoid, again as in "Sister Helen," previously unexplained emotions. Even though he was adding lyrics to the narrative, he was emphasizing the poem's narrative, not lyric, structure. His second reason for adding the songs, however, is even more representative of the changes in his poetic ambitions at the end of his career. According to William Rossetti, the songs were written as a tour-de-force of poetic craftsmanship: "I have heard my brother say that he wrote them to show that he was not incapable of the daring rhyming and rhythmical exploits of some other poets" (*Works*, 660). Such an emphasis on craftsmanship, on poetic form rather than poetic meaning, was, of course, one way to avoid revealing any personal emotion or beliefs. But Rossetti's comments also reveal his rather sad attempt to remain in the top rank of modern poets without making himself vulnerable to the attacks that fame might bring. The result on "Rose Mary" of such tentative ambition was unfortunate—even Rossetti's Boswell, Theodore Watts, believed that the songs "turned a fine ballad into a bastard opera."[48]

In addition to tinkering with "Sister Helen" and "Rose Mary," Rossetti wrote two long ballads, "The White Ship" and "The King's Tragedy," during the last years of his life. As William's designation of these poems indicates, they are both "historical ballads" (*Works*, 660) based on chronicled events, and in both cases Rossetti was careful to base his narratives on known facts. He even boasted of his scrupulous fidelity to fact, saying of "The White Ship" that "every incident including that of the boy at the end, is given in one or other accounts of the event."[49] Obviously Rossetti was not looking deep within his own soul for inspiration. Further, both ballads are still more distanced from the personal experience of the poet by the use of a dramatic character as a speaker.[50] If any

[48]Sharp, p. 374.
[49]*Letters*, IV:1751.
[50]See Howard, p. 176.

psychological quirks are evident in "The White Ship," they can be attributed to Berold, the poor butcher of Rouen; if any moral view is manifested in "The King's Tragedy," it can be blamed on Kate Barlass. But no readily apparent philosophical or moral view does emerge from the poems beyond what is implicit in the recorded facts. Two recent critics, each trying to find the moral message of "The White Ship," arrived at absolutely opposed conclusions. One argued that the poem "presents something as close to a just world as occurs in Rossetti's canon";[51] the other, that the theme (Berold's, not necessarily Rossetti's) expresses the concept that God is "a fate which strikes down the powerful as well as the weak, which changes the course of human destiny in sudden disaster, which operates in despite of human hopes and plans."[52] Evidently the poem does not very emphatically express any one particular theme; the poet does not commit himself to any questionable moral stance.

Both the late ballads met with the enthusiastic applause of Rossetti's inner circle, and seemed sufficient proof, to him, that he was holding his own among modern poets. But though in sheer bulk the two poems together account for over two-thirds of Rossetti's poetry over the last ten years of his life, they express next to nothing of his own thoughts and feelings. They are, in some respects, well crafted, but they are nevertheless little more than versified accounts of old stories—in "The King's Tragedy" Rossetti actually reversifies parts of King James's poem *The King's Quhair,* changing the "ten-syllabled lines to eight syllables, in order that they might harmonize with the ballad metre" (*Poems,* 187). Unfortunately, though Rossetti carefully wrought each stanza, in a kind of poetic piece-work, he did not take as much care with the structure of the whole. Both poems are loosely organized, include far too much insignificant detail and, following the manner of the revisions to the earlier ballads, are too concerned with merely mechanical transitions. After finishing "The King's Tragedy," Rossetti described the pain and exhaustion involved in arduous composition

[51]Florence Saunders Boos, *The Poetry of Dante G. Rossetti: A Critical Reading and Source Study* (The Hague: Mouton, 1976), p. 178.
[52]Howard, p. 180.

with the dramatic remark that "it was as though my own life ebbed
out with it" (*Works*, 660), but certainly very little of his own life
seeped into the poem. The pain of composition must have been
wholly related to the patience required in meticulous craftsmanship, for there is no grappling with difficult intellectual or emotional issues in those late ballads.

Of all of Rossetti's late poetry, only the sonnets on poets and on
paintings—his own and other artists'—express very much about his
own feelings and attitudes, and even these poems remain curiously
detached. Though Rossetti had, as late as 1869, regarded poetry
about poetry as "intellectually incestuous,"[53] his 1881 volume *Ballads and Sonnets* included sonnets on Chatterton, Blake, Coleridge,
Keats, and Shelley, all grouped together under the general title
"Five English Poets." If, as has sometimes been said of him, Rossetti drew his inspiration from art, not life, such a topic might well
have inspired him. And since all these poets were among his particular favorites, and were among the greatest influences on him, he
might well have struggled with them in these sonnets. In attempting to define their achievements, he might well have begun to
define his own aspirations, but nothing very distinctive is said
about any of them. The sonnets on Chatterton, Keats, and Shelley
speak mainly of biographical facts and emphasize mostly the early
deaths of the poets. It is significant, however, that Rossetti concluded each poem with a reference to the enduring fame of a poet
who, necessarily, produced all his work when young.

The sonnet about Coleridge, similarly, calls attention to the
short period of youth in which his fame was earned:

Yet ah! Like desert pools that show the stars
    Once in long leagues,—even such the scarce-snatched hours
    Which deepening pain left to his lordliest powers:—
Heaven lost through spider-trammeled prison-bars.
    Six years, from sixty saved! Yet kindling skies
    Own them, a beacon to our centuries.

             [*Poems*, 253]

[53]*Letters*, II:728.

And in the earliest manuscript, the productive period had been still shorter: "Five years, from seventy saved!"[54] William Rossetti's remark that this poem revealed his brother's "love of Coleridge" but that it did not go "very far towards defining the quality of his excellence" is certainly correct (*Works*, 671), but probably beside the point. As in the sonnets on Keats and Chatterton, but more clearly, Rossetti had viewed the other poet not as an influence, but as an analogue to his own life—an analogue that suggested a hope for enduring fame. Rossetti could not very well see himself in Keats or Chatterton, but various notebook entries of the period indicate that he did see parallels between himself and Coleridge. He repeatedly complained that he had not had his just due from critics, so it is significant that he saw Coleridge as having to "endure through life" the attacks of "mediocrity in high places," and he regarded himself as plagued by critics for his very originality, so it is revealing that he says the same of Coleridge: "Invention absolute is slow of acceptance & must be so. This Coleridge and others have found." Further, Coleridge was analogous to Rossetti not only in his sufferings, but in his poetic style, as one of the notebook entries makes clear: "The sense of the momentous is strongest in Coleridge—not the weird & ominous only, but the value of monumental moments." The comment occurs within a few pages of notes for Rossetti's most famous artistic *confessio fidei*, the introductory sonnet to *The House of Life*, with its dictum that "A Sonnet is a moment's monument."[55] The reasons for Rossetti's apparent desire to see his own career reflected in Coleridge's can be guessed—like Coleridge he had become addicted to drugs, and for long periods had been indolent and unproductive. His many allusions in other poems to the phantoms of dead hours that would haunt him after death show that he had long felt guilty over his idleness—as Coleridge was wont to do. But more important, the imagery of the sestet of the sonnet on Coleridge is Rossetti's obsessive image for his own faint hope for immortality. It is exactly paralleled in a note-

---

[54]The manuscript is in the Ashley Collection of the British Library.

[55]The comments about Coleridge are all in the fourth of four notebooks in the Ashley Collection of the British Library. See also *Works*, 638. Hall Caine (p. 187) quotes Rossetti as praising Chatterton, not Coleridge, for battling against "merciless mediocrity in high places."

book entry: "As in a tract of lifeless land, the scattered pools of rain-water that for a moment catch the sky as the traveller passes, so are the far-apart intervals of living labour in the life of an idle man. After death, if the brief intervals be worthy, will all be sky-brimmed water, or all a desert of sand?" (*Works*, 642). Sadly, Rossetti seems to have realized that his best days as a poet were past, and to have hoped, consciously or not, that like these earlier poets he had built up a large enough stock of living poetry to enable his name to live on. Seen in this light, his late comments to Hall Caine that "Keats hardly died so much too early" and that Shelley mercifully died young seem not contemptuous, but terribly wistful.

The remaining sonnets in the series, those on Shelley and Blake, are less interesting for what they say about the two poets than for the type of poetry they represent. Neither poem is directly about the poet named in its title, but rather each is an inscription for an object. That for Shelley is an "Inscription for the couch, still preserved, on which he passed the last night of his life" (*Poems*, 253), and that for Blake is addressed "To Frederick Shields, on his sketch of Blake's work-room and death-room, 3 Fountain Court, Strand" (*Poems*, 252). The wealth of information in these comments, published parenthetically beneath the titles, is revealing. Rossetti's best work had always been accomplished when he kept his eyes on the material world, finding images there to suggest, faintly, the immortal nature of fear, despair, love, and hope, but at the close of his life he came more and more to depend on physical objects as symbols that he could moor his verse to—physical presences to anchor verbal abstractions upon. The objects that helped him to objectify his poetry were almost always pictures, but even the one exception, Shelley's couch, seemed to help him contend with skepticism and, however faintly, to assert hope. The Blake sonnet, a poem for a picture, seizes upon many of the objects represented in Shields's sketch to evoke something like Blake's, and his own, earlier sacramental vision in which the homely cupboard that housed Blake's works can be both an object of the material world and a symbol of the spiritual: "This cupboard, Holy of Holies, held the cloud / Of his soul writ and limned" (*Poems*, 252).

Rossetti's most famous and most important sonnet about poetry, his sonnet on the sonnet, also accompanies a picture, in this case his own work. Together, the poem, the picture, and his description of the picture, reveal a great deal about his aesthetic stance in 1880. The sonnet itself is, appropriately, described as a material object:

> A Sonnet is a moment's monument,—
>> Memorial from the Soul's eternity
>> To one dead deathless hour. Look that it be,
> Whether for lustral rite or dire portent,
> Of its own arduous fulness reverent:
>> Carve it in ivory or in ebony,
>> As Day or Night may rule; and let Time see
> Its flowering crest impearled and orient.
>
> A Sonnet is a coin: its face reveals
>> The soul,—its converse, to what Power 'tis due:—
> Whether for tribute to the august appeals
>> Of Life, or dower in Love's high retinue,
> It serve; or, 'mid the dark wharf's cavernous breath,
> In Charon's palm it pay the toll to Death.
>
> [*Poems*, 212]

The repeated emphasis on soul in art implies a highly introspective aesthetic, but as is characteristic of late Rossetti, the sonnet is not itself introspective—its subject is not the soul itself, but the monument to soul. In his best sonnets prior to 1872 Rossetti had attempted to enshrine memory and love in eternal art, but in this poem he tries only to enshrine the artifice itself. But the design that complements the sonnet attempts, though too schematically, to represent the soul. As Rossetti's description of the drawing makes clear, it is a rather allegorical representation of the ideas of the sonnet:

In it the soul is instituting the "memorial to one dead deathless hour," a ceremony easily effected by placing a winged hour-glass in a rose-bush, at the same time that she touches the fourteen-stringed harp of the Sonnet, hanging round her neck. On the rose-branches trailing over in the opposite corner is seen hanging the Coin, which is the second symbol used for the Sonnet. Its "face" bears the Soul, expressed in the butterfly; its "converse," the Serpent of Eternity enclosing the Alpha and Omega.[56]

Despite the painfully obvious allegory, however, the drawing illustrates the important point that Rossetti was willing to sketch the soul, but not to describe it verbally. Though it is certainly no radical break with tradition to depict the soul as the female *anima*, and though the winged female presented in this drawing is rather undistinguished, the drawing is nevertheless significant as one of Rossetti's many attempts, in the last fifteen years of his life, to paint the soul. His insistence on cluttering the drawing with the supporting images of a weak allegory, and on elucidating the allegory in prose and verse, is also characteristic of his late career as a painter. In this particular case the drawing was apparently made after the sonnet was written, and it is secondary in importance, but Rossetti's more usual practice in his late years was to draw or paint his vision of the soul, to include some incidental but unimportant supporting allegory, and then to interpret the picture verbally, in verse, or prose, or both. His apparent need to allegorize is symptomatic of prevailing Victorian aesthetics, but his imposing pictures of women, on a far greater scale than the *anima* of the drawing for "The Sonnet," reveal his most deeply felt artistic impulses.

[56]*Letters*, IV:1760.

9

The Feud of the Sister Arts

THE sources for Rossetti's late belief that the sister arts of painting and poetry could be indissolubly united may seem more obvious than they actually are. The origins of the Pre-Raphaelite movement were literary from the first. From childhood on, Rossetti was drawn to both painting and poetry, and he first came to appreciate Holman Hunt after seeing his painting from Keats's "Eve of St. Agnes." Similarly, his great admiration for Ford Madox Brown's painting must have been inspired in part by Brown's frequently literary subject matter. Further, Graham Hough points out that in Ruskin, who supplied the inspiration for Hunt, and through him for Millais, "we have a man of great literary powers who devoted himself mainly to art, and this in itself helped to draw literature and painting together." He adds that "even Hunt, who looked on himself and Millais as *par excellence* the professional painters of the group, regards 'the discipleship of the formative arts to that of letters' as 'a perennial law.'" His further statement, however, that "Rossetti's literary inspiration needs no underlining," must be qualified.[1] Rossetti was certainly the literary

---

[1]Graham Hough, *The Last Romantics* (1947, rpt. London: Methuen, 1961), p. 142.

man in the group, *par excellence,* and was certainly inspired by literature, but he did not see poetry and painting united in any easy symbiotic relationship. Rather, he vacillated among the notions that poetry might interpret painting, that painting might illustrate poetry, and that poetry could only end in rapt and ultimately mute awe before an essentially nonverbal art.

His earliest attempt to unite his own painting with poetry, in *The Girlhood of Mary Virgin,* had implied a belief that poetry could be frankly interpretive. The painting itself is filled with obvious symbols, and the accompanying poem simply explicates them: "These are the symbols." In this case the painting, conceived almost as a visual poem, preceded the sonnet, but in his next venture Rossetti wrote a poem, "Ave," which was later to be represented in a series of pictures. Similarly, he believed, for a time, that his poetry could be interpretive of another man's painting. In the first of his sonnets for pictures, "For an Annunciation (Early German)," he described a painting he had seen in an auction-room and extended its impression to affect not only sight, but also sound and touch; and by interpreting the expressions of the figures, he turned the painting into a narrative:[2]

> So prays she, and the Dove flies in to her,
>   And she has turned. At the low porch is one
>   Who looks as though deep awe made him to smile.
> Heavy with heat, the plants yield shadow there;
>   The loud flies cross each other in the sun;
>   And the aisled pillars meet the poplar-aisle.
> [Works, 166]

But the last line of the sonnet implies a limit to the interpretive power of poetry by simply describing a formal element in the composition that evidently "speaks" for itself.

The usual tendency of Rossetti's sonnets for pictures is, in fact, to describe and then stand back in unverbalized awe, as though to concede that the painting has its own untranslatable means of expression. His two sonnets for paintings by Memling both begin

---

[2]William Rossetti claims that this was the first of Rossetti's sonnets for pictures and dates it in 1847 (*Works,* 661).

with the same word, "MYSTERY," to show the independence of
the work from even the possibility of verbalized interpretation, and
the second of the two ends with an emphatic insistence on the
visual presentation of mystery:

> Whereon soe'er thou look,
> The light is starred in gems, and the gold burns.[3]

The clearest expression of Rossetti's doubts that painting can be
translated into words is the sonnet "For An Allegorical Dance of
Women by Andrea Mantegna (In the Louvre)," in which he explicitly rejects the idea that the sensual painting can be reduced to
allegory, and even that the painter can have been inspired by
intellectual purposes rather than by the pure beauty of rocks, and
sea, and the dancers. He concludes that Mantegna did not give

> ear to trace
> How many feet; nor bent assuredly
> His eyes from the blind fixedness of thought
> To see the dancers. It is bitter glad
> Even unto tears. Its meaning filleth it,
> A portion of most secret life: to wit:—
> Each human pulse shall keep the sense it had
> With all, though the mind's labour run to nought.[4]

Though he was himself drawn toward verbalizing and even moralizing upon the "meaning" of pictures, Rossetti was evidently
aware that the two arts of painting and poetry were essentially
different. Like poetry, painting could tell a tale or point a moral,
but its most profound meaning was in its formal beauty. As Richard
Stein has observed in his fine study of Rossetti's sonnets for pictures, speculation upon the significance of paintings always ends by
acknowledging the autonomous whole, complete in its own right
without the aid of words: "invariably his sonnets draw back at the

---

[3]Quoted from the earliest extant version, in the fourth issue of *The Germ*, May
1850.
[4]Ibid.

end to consider a picture as a formal, symbolic whole rather than as a collection of images and allusions."[5]

Rossetti, however, evidently changed his early views on the relation of poetry to painting, as the revisions to the most famous of his sonnets for pictures reveal. "For a Venetian Pastoral by Giorgione (In the Louvre)" was first published in *The Germ* in 1850, and was later much revised before inclusion in *Poems* in 1870. The first version had been more descriptive of the formal qualities of the painting, even including a brief prose description following the title. But like the prose descriptions of other pictures that Rossetti included in *The Germ*, this was dropped in 1870, and the revised sonnet itself, as Kenneth Ireland has shown, gives the reader considerably fewer hints about the actual appearance of the picture than does the original. The most obvious revision is in the final line: originally the sonnet had concluded

> Nor name this ever. Be it as it was:—
> Silence of heat, and solemn poetry.

But in 1870 the closing line became "Life touching lips with Immortality" (*Poems*, 138). The change is away from the mute awe of "Silence" (the word "poetry," I think, applies to a kind of sentiment, not a verbal art) to, as Ireland has said, greater "allegorical explicitness."[6] The painting is no longer left to speak for itself; the emphasis of the poem has shifted from appreciation to explication.

The revisions to the sonnet on Giorgione are representative of a larger shift in Rossetti's attitude toward the relation of painting and poetry. His last two sonnets for pictures by other artists, written in 1880, restrict virtually all description of the paintings to explanatory footnotes, and they do not end, as the earlier sonnets did, by drawing the reader's attention back to the pictorial form. Rather they emphasize the desire to read meaning into the pictures while acknowledging the unknowable mystery that can be embodied in visual but not verbal forms. The sonnet on Botticelli's *Spring* closes

[5]Richard Stein, *The Ritual of Interpretation: The Fine Arts as Literature in Ruskin, Rossetti, and Pater* (Cambridge: Harvard University Press, 1975), p. 135.

[6]Kenneth Ireland, "A Kind of Pastoral: Rossetti's Versions of Giorgione," *Victorian Poetry*, 17 (1979), 310.

with a series of questions that seem to lead the reader back to the picture, but actually only draw his attention to an epistemological question:

> What mystery here is read
> Of homage or of hope? But how command
> Dead Springs to answer? And how question here
> These mummers of that wind-withered New-Year?
> [*Poems*, 252]

The picture becomes the starting point for a meditation, but the particular formal qualities of the particular painting are not emphasized—the poem ends in generalized questions that are not closely related to the painting. The sonnet for Michelangelo's *The Holy Family* similarly establishes the sacred mystery embodied in the symbolic scroll held by the Virgin mother, but then goes on, in the sestet, to reveal the contents of the scroll. In so doing the sonnet extends beyond the confines of the painting into literary explication:

> Still before Eden waves the fiery sword,—
> Her Tree of Life unransomed: whose sad Tree
> Of Knowledge yet to growth of Calvary
> Must yield its Tempter,—Hell the earliest dead
> Of Earth resign,—and yet, O Son and Lord,
> The Seed o' the woman bruise the serpent's head.
> [*Poems*, 251]

As these two sonnets, and the revisions to the Giorgione sonnet, suggest, the change in Rossetti's attitude toward the sister arts is not toward greater union of the two, but toward a greater exaltation of the written word as the vehicle of meaning. The painting is no longer granted its own autonomous meaning but is made to stand in need of explication.

Since Rossetti's aesthetic beliefs shifted away from a faith in the autonomy of pictorial art at the same time that his artistic efforts were shifting more and more toward painting, rather than poetry, he was put in a somewhat uncomfortable position as an artist. In the latter part of his career he was essentially a painter, with the instincts of one, yet he felt a need to impose a "poetic" meaning on

218

his paintings. From the late 1850s on, Rossetti's paintings had become less and less literary in the obvious senses that they were no longer, normally, illustrations of scenes from literary works, and that they were far less concerned to capture a moment suggestive of a narrative line. They were, in fact, almost exclusively paintings of women, usually three-quarter-length portraits, and even when, as in *La Pia de Tolomei*, a picture was made to represent a literary scene, the scene was generally static, and the painting was of a woman in repose. But the more he abandoned literary or narrative meaning in his painting, the more he felt compelled to impose some such meaning with an explication in prose or poetry. Perhaps the most obvious examples of the ways in which verbal meaning is imposed upon formal beauty are the paintings and accompanying poems *Lady Lilith* and *Sibylla Palmifera*. Each is a portrait of a beautiful woman with accoutrements that suggest something about the nature of her beauty. Lilith, surrounded by roses, combs her hair and studies herself in a mirror. Her pose, her ample flesh, the curve of her mouth and her arched brow all reveal that she is vain, seductive, and dangerous. The accompanying sonnet, "Lilith" (called "Body's Beauty" when incorporated in *The House of Life*) provides a story to supplement the immediately apparent sensual impact of the painting:

> Of Adam's first wife, Lilith, it is told
> (The witch he loved before the gift of Eve,)
> That, ere the snake's, her sweet tongue could deceive,
> And her enchanted hair was the first gold.
> And still she sits, young while the earth is old,
> And, subtly of herself contemplative,
> Draws men to watch the bright web she can weave,
> Till heart and body and life are in its hold.
>
> The rose and poppy are her flowers; for where
> Is he not found, O Lilith, whom shed scent
> And soft-shed kisses and soft sleep shall snare?
> Lo! as that youth's eyes burned at thine, so went
> Thy spell through him, and left his straight neck bent,
> And round his heart one strangling golden hair.

[*Poems*, 142]

219

The sonnet is beautiful, and comes, presumably, from the same emotional sources as the painting, but it imposes a story on the picture that the picture itself does not tell. The significance of this can be best understood by looking next at the companion piece, *Sibylla Palmifera*, with its accompanying sonnet (called "Soul's Beauty" in *The House of Life*). Here again a beautiful woman is represented, this time staring sternly out of the picture, her expression accentuated, once again, by an expressively cocked eyebrow. But this woman is more demurely dressed, holds a plume, not a mirror, and is accompanied by two butterflies, meant, no doubt, to suggest Psyche. Her sonnet explains that she represents a more profound beauty, a beauty to be vainly aspired to:

> Under the arch of life, where love and death,
>   Terror and mystery, guard her shrine, I saw
>   Beauty enthroned; and though her gaze struck awe,
> I drew it in as simply as my breath.
> Hers are the eyes which, over and beneath
>   The sky and sea bend on thee,—which can draw,
>   By sea or sky or woman, to one law,
> The allotted bondman of her palm and wreath.
>
> This is that Lady Beauty, in whose praise
>   Thy voice and hand shake still,—long known to thee
>   By flying hair and fluttering hem,—the beat
>   Following her daily of thy heart and feet,
>   How passionately and irretrievably,
> In what fond flight, how many ways and days!
>
>   [Poems, 142]

Once again the sonnet is extremely beautiful in its own right, but here it does not so clearly proceed from the same emotional source as the painting. This painting also, after all, represents roses and poppies, though now less profuse and wild, more under the control of art. In spite of the plume and the butterflies, the viewer of the picture is more likely to be impressed with the seductive beauty, and the slightly threatening expression, of the woman than by her "mystery," and not surprisingly, it turns out that the sonnet, and even the title, of the painting were afterthoughts. The painting had originally been entitled simply *Palmifera* "to mark," as Rossetti explained, "the leading place which I intend her to hold among my beauties."[7] The addition of "Sibylla" to the title is an attempt to add prophetic meaning to the picture after the fact. So too, of course, is the sonnet, as Rossetti himself acknowledged. "I have somewhat extended my idea of the picture," he wrote, "and have written a sonnet to embody the conception—that of beauty the Palm-giver, i.e. the Principle of Beauty, which draws all high-toned men to itself, whether with the aim of embodying it in art or only of attaining its enjoyment in life."[8]

The problem implicit in the idea of a painter-poet first painting, and then explaining his painting, is a large one, related to the still larger question of whether an artist's explanation of his work in any medium should be accepted at face value. The answer, I think, is assuredly "no," since the artist as critic has an obvious bias, and since he will be eager to include in his criticism both a justification of his work and, more insidiously, just those elements that, for whatever reason, he failed to include in his original design but later suspects ought to have been part of it. In Rossetti's particular case the answer is still more definitely "no," for a number of reasons. First, his own moral vision, as he learned to his cost in 1872, was not compatible with Victorian mores, so his verbal criticism of painted works has a tendency to try to make them acceptable to conventional moral taste. His late paintings of women are most immediately impressive for their sensuality, but his explications of them, more often than not, seem designed to point a moral. Second, painting and poetry do not affect the reader or viewer in the same way: painting has greater immediacy since, however long a viewer may ponder a picture, his initial reaction will be to the whole composition, and will be nearly instantaneous, while the reader of poetry must follow the temporal sequence of language and arrive gradually at even a first impression. This is especially true of Rossetti's late work in both arts, since his poetry increasingly shifted away from aiming for immediacy of effect and toward formal

---

[7]Virginia Surtees, *Dante Gabriel Rossetti, 1828–1882, The Paintings and Drawings: A Catalogue Raisonné*, 2 vols. (London: Oxford University Press, 1971), I:111.
[8]Ibid., p. 112.

complexity, and his painting shifted more and more toward sensual immediacy and formal simplicity. And finally, Rossetti had much better instincts as a painter than as a critic of painting—as a detached observer of his own artistic life, Rossetti, in fact, ever but slenderly knew himself, since he vacillated between a view of painting as a literary art and his own practice of it as independent of verbal explanation. His best comments on paintings often acknowledge that they embody a mystery that lies beyond the reach of consciousness, and consequently, beyond the reach of language.

Rossetti's dilemma as a critic of paintings—his own or those of others—is characteristic of Victorian painters and critics in general. Until mid-century the criticism of painting, if not the actual practice, had stagnated, caught in a simplified version of Joshua Reynolds's academic aesthetics of the previous century, but the critical canons had been mainly in the hands of painters themselves. Nevertheless, there was considerable confusion about the proper role of the painter and the proper aims of painting. Lessing's argument that the doctrine of *ut pictura poesis* (as is painting, so is poetry) had conflated the two arts in ways unhealthy to both continued to fit the situation in the mid-nineteenth century: "in poetry it has engendered a mania for description and in painting a mania for allegory."[9] But Lessing's discussion had at least made the problem clear to painters, especially to the academic painters at the Royal Academy. Charles Eastlake, later to become president of the Royal Academy, was perfectly willing, in 1825, to limit the role of the painter to suit his medium: "Every art has its grand quality, its characteristic excellence, arrived at by a very simple process of reasoning, for its strength will obviously consist in that which is unobtainable by the other arts."[10] With the publication of the first volume of Ruskin's *Modern Painters*, and the subsequent turmoil inspired by the first Pre-Raphaelite paintings, however, expectations of what a painting ought to accomplish reverted to the literary ideal. Critical emphasis shifted away from formal design to mimetic accuracy, moral purpose, and, of course, literary significance. The

[9]Lessing, *Laocoön: An Essay on the Limits of Painting and Poetry,* trans. Edward Allen McCormick (New York: Bobbs-Merrill, 1962), p. 5.

[10]Quoted by David Robertson, *Sir Charles Eastlake and the Victorian Art World* (Princeton: Princeton University Press, 1978), p. 26.

extent of these changes becomes evident if one simply surveys a list of the major art critics following Ruskin: Sidney Colvin, H. Buxton Forman, and especially Swinburne and Pater were all, essentially, literary men. The common practice of art critics was to look for the story in a picture, so that by 1885 Oscar Wilde was scarcely exaggerating when he supported Whistler's attack on "the art critics who always treat a picture as if it were a novel, and try and find out the plot."[11]

Even those critics who sensed the inadequacy of literary criticism of painting during the mid-Victorian period were more often than not unwilling to separate themselves from the prevailing doctrines. Two essays that appeared in *The Nineteenth Century* in 1879 and 1880 reveal the issues and the confusion that prevailed about them toward the end of Rossetti's life. The first, "Is a Great Art School Possible?" by Mrs. E. I. Barrington, shows the perplexity of a thoughtful though now forgotten critic trying to determine what standards should be applied to art.[12] The second, "The Present Conditions of Art," by the important painter G. F. Watts, responds to Barrington's article, but only to reveal that the artist, like the critic, is uncertain about the proper aims of art.[13] Barrington expresses concern that the walls of the Royal Academy exhibitions do not show the high ideals of the highest art, do not show the work of the "poet-painter," but only the facility of the accomplished technician. Searching for causes, she finds that the nation has lost its sense of the beautiful, and finds the art critics responsible. Literary men, she argues, cannot judge the "painterly" qualities of art and have consequently misled the public. She seems to be calling for an

---

[11]"Mr. Whistler's Ten O'Clock," in *The Artist as Critic: Critical Writings of Oscar Wilde*, ed. Richard Ellmann (New York: Random House, 1970), p. 14. Singling out Ruskin as a primary source for the return to a literary aesthetic may not seem quite fair, for as George P. Landow has argued, Ruskin in many ways put the emphasis back on the visual, formal qualities of painting. But though Ruskin did indeed have a more sophisticated sense of pictorial form than most of his contemporaries, he was most noted for his *readings* of paintings. See Landow's "There Began to Be a Great Talking about the Fine Arts" in *The Mind and Art of Victorian England*, ed. Joseph L. Altholz (Minneapolis: University of Minnesota Press, 1976), pp. 124–145. See also Landow's book, *The Aesthetic and Critical Theories of John Ruskin* (Princeton: Princeton University Press, 1971).

[12]In *The Nineteenth Century*, 1879, pp. 714–732.

[13]In *The Nineteenth Century*, 1880, pp. 235–255.

art and an art criticism that go beyond the merely literary, and she regrets that Legros and Tissot, for example, do not produce pictures that give "food for thought."[14] She advocates poetic painting that will express "the close relation in feeling existing between what is best in all religions, and what is greatest in art"[15]—it is significant that her further explanation is entirely dependent upon examples from literature, and she concludes with a call for artists to paint, somehow, the feeling for nature, the moral fervor, and the special religious feeling of Wordsworth, Ruskin, and George Eliot. Barrington's essay perfectly illustrates the Victorian aesthetic dilemma that beset artists as well as critics. The art produced under the regime of Ruskinian criticism and the literary art criticism that it spawned are seen to be wanting, but the judge of art cannot bring herself to abandon the high moral ideals of Ruskin's criticism. Simply put, no nonliterary vocabulary was available to discuss the high moral purpose that was demanded of painting.

G. F. Watts, responding to Barrington, found himself in precisely the same position. Even more than Barrington, he accepted essentially Ruskinian principles about the moral purposes of art and even about the proper subjects for a picture. Possibly influenced by Ruskin's doctrine that the greatest art is that which communicates the greatest number of ideas, Watts attempted to describe what makes a good subject for the artist: "The man with the iron mask in his cell would make an ordinary potboiler, but the figure laid out in death, with Louis the Fourteenth, the mask in hand, looking at the dead man's face, perhaps for the first time, certainly for the last, would be suggestive of a host of ideas—"[16] Obviously, even artists were tempted to accept the narrative bias. Though he accepted the judgments on art of the literary men, however, Watts's artistic sensibility led him to recognize that ideas may be formal as well as

---

[14]Barrington, p. 725. Barrington was certainly following the Ruskinian line with regard to Tissot. Ruskin had panned Tissot's pictures in the Grosvenor Gallery in 1877: "Most of them are, unhappily, mere coloured photographs of vulgar society." At least Tissot didn't bring suit—Ruskin's attack on Whistler, which brought about the famous law-suit, appeared in the same letter of *Fors Clavigera*. See *The Complete Works of John Ruskin*, ed. E. T. Cook and Alexander Wedderburn, 39 vols. (London: George Allen, 1903–1912), 29:161.

[15]Barrington, p. 732.

[16]Watts, p. 251.

narrative: "heroic art must be noble in its treatment of the means at its disposition, line, colour and texture." But in addition to nobility of line, color, and texture, he conceded, heroic art "must have a correspondingly noble subject."[17]

In his own painting, Watts was at his best when he simply ignored any moral or illustrative purpose. His description of his own frescoes in the new Hall of Lincoln's Inn reveals the painter's triumph over the Ruskinian critic:

> the picture cannot be said to have a subject . . . I would call it suggestive, my intention being to produce a combination of forms and colour which should have a grand monumental effect, and pervade, so to speak, the building like a strain of Handel's music, becoming one with the architecture. This may seem too fanciful and vague to such as look upon art only as a means of illustrating actual events, or interesting by direct and exact imitation.[18]

Watt's juxtaposition of his practice, in this case at least, with the common expectations of the public distinctly establishes the two poles of the Victorian debate about the proper aims of art that began with Ruskin's attacks on the sterile formalism of the Royal Academy in 1846, and culminated in Whistler's attack, in his famous "Ten O'Clock Lecture," on Ruskin's literary standards in 1885. Throughout this period the critics, mostly literary men, insisted on painting that was both mimetic and narrative, and insisted on an art analogous to poetry; the best painters, on the other hand, were drawn to a formalism analogous to music, an analogy that led Whistler to name his paintings after musical terms—nocturnes and harmonies.

Watts himself, in 1880, was willing to compromise: "Art approximates nearest to poetry or music according to its subject and treatment."[19] But the two doctrines pulled in opposite directions, since they suggested opposed notions about the artist's relation to the larger society. Watts's discussion of the larger issues clearly estab-

---

[17]Ibid., p. 254.
[18]Quoted by M. S. Watts, *George Frederic Watts: The Annals of an Artist's Life*, 2 vols. (New York: Hodder, n.d.), p. 183.
[19]Watts, "The Present Conditions of Art," p. 254.

lishes the dilemma that beset all artists, and plagued Rossetti. Watts accepted the Ruskinian idea that art is intimately linked to such things as the condition of the laborer and a high level of national morality, since morality, in Ruskin's view, equals taste, but this led him to the conclusion that a great school of art "cannot exist unless beauty is cared for for its own sake, and this is not a consequence of modern civilization, certainly not in England."[20] The problem for the artist was that he ought to draw his inspiration from his own age, and contribute to the taste of his own age, but in an ugly age the artist is forced to separate himself from society: "great poetic ideas belonging to the past, present, and future, must either be expressed by the painter as a Greek or Italian would have rendered them, or he must invent a new method, or he must take what will suggest no noble effect whatever—modern costume and custom."[21] The same line of thought led Oscar Wilde to state the problem in even more extreme terms: since English dress is a disaster, the artist must paint masquerade, even though "all costumes are caricatures. The basis of Art is not the Fancy Ball."[22]

All of this, of course, is directly related to Rossetti's practice as an artist and to his custom of pairing paintings with sonnets. When he began painting, under the influence of Hunt and, indirectly, of Ruskin, he did not attempt exclusively to represent modern dress and customs, but he did accept the narrative and allegorical bias in art criticism—the beginning of his sonnet for *The Girlhood of Mary Virgin*, "These are the symbols," could be the beginning of one of Ruskin's explications of a painting, but it more significantly reveals that Rossetti's picture had been designed from the first as a work to be "read." His later work, however, can be better described by the musical than by the poetic analogy. Not only did he include obvious musical motifs in many of the late paintings, but his foremost concerns were with color and formal design, and he clearly rejected the mimetic ideal of super-realism that Ruskin had seemed to advocate and that the Pre-Raphaelite Brotherhood had insisted on. In fact, he concentrated on portraits of women in fancy dress. He

[20]Ibid., p. 240.
[21]Ibid.
[22]Wilde, "The Relation of Dress to Art," *The Artist as Critic*, p. 19.

certainly abandoned the idea, which he had never really put into practice, that faithful mimetic representation of nature was necessary to art. As Ruskin ruefully observed after Rossetti's death, he ceased to study nature and so "wilfully perverted and lacerated his powers of conception with Chinese puzzles and Japanese monsters, until his foliage looked fit for nothing but a fire-screen,"[23] but this only affirms the obvious shift in Rossetti's emphasis from a representational to a formal art. His detestation of Holman Hunt's *Isabella and the Pot of Basil,* a painting thoroughly faithful to Pre-Raphaelite and Ruskinian principles, shows how completely and energetically he rejected such principles: "His horrible daub representing apparently a half-crazed charwoman removing the chimney ornaments before a hard scrub, is appalling to every inner and outer sense. How grimy and sweaty is the poor thing's face, and how she must yearn for her beer."[24] And Rossetti's comments on his own paintings often reveal the radical shift in his aesthetic beliefs—he refers to the "harmonies" of color in his work, and seems to have conceived of some of his pictures as studies in color. He described *Veronica Veronese,* for example, as a "study of varied greens."[25]

Nevertheless, Rossetti, like Watts, obviously felt a need to justify his art in the terms of the prevailing art criticism. His struggles with the painting *Found* indicate the degree to which he was willing to try to reconcile his artistic career with the social commitment demanded of the artist. He began the picture in the heyday of the Pre-Raphaelite Brotherhood, and designed it upon clear Ruskinian principles. It would tell a story, and a socially significant one at that—the story of the young countrywoman, trapped into a life of sin in the big city, and unable to face her stern but forgiving country lover who has found her, and wants to rescue her. And it would be a faithful representation of nature. Rossetti searched indefatigably for the proper calf, to be painted in the middle distance, and still more tirelessly for the proper brick wall, to be painted brick by realistic brick in the foreground. But he never was able to finish

[23]Ruskin, *The Art of England,* in *Works,* 33:271.
[24]*Letters,* II:704.
[25]*The Rossetti-Leyland Letters: The Correspondence of an Artist and His Patron,* ed. Francis L. Fennell, Jr. (Athens: Ohio University Press, 1978), p. 29.

the picture, though he continued to work on it, off and on, for thirty years, and though it was the last major painting he worked on before his death. One of his reasons for wanting so desperately to finish it is revealing. As long as he was working only for the benefit of his patrons, as long as his work was not to be seen by the general public, he was not excessively concerned that his artistic practice deviated from the accepted dicta about the artist's responsibilities. But when he contemplated an exhibition of his paintings in 1879, he decided that he must finish *Found* in order to prove that he could "deal with what is real and human," and that his "preference of the ideal does not depend on incapacity to deal with simple nature."[26]

Rossetti was not, however, admitting that his "preference of the ideal" was a preference for the formal qualities of painting, though he was at least acknowledging that his usual practice had little to do with realism and social and moral purposiveness. Indeed, the one critical notion he could not bring himself to deny was that painting should be "poetic"—he even defined his "preference of the ideal" as "poetic painting."[27] Though his painting can be best described with the analogy to music, he himself usually insisted on the analogy to poetry. Nor is this surprising since, with the exception of Whistler, and occasionally Pater and Swinburne, the Victorians generally regarded poetry as the more exalted art. Watts, for example, confessed that poetry comes before painting and music,[28] and even Wilde, in direct defiance of Whistler, argued that "the poet is the supreme artist, for he is the master of colour and form, and the real musician besides, and is lord over all life and all arts; and so to the poet beyond all others are these mysteries known; to Edgar Allan Poe and to Baudelaire, not to Benjamin West and Paul Delaroche."[29]

Among the many ironies in Rossetti's career, perhaps the greatest is that he clung to the literary idea of painting even while his

[26]*Letters,* IV:1635. For a splendid discussion of Rossetti's efforts with *Found,* see Linda Nochlin's "Lost and *Found*: Once More the Fallen Woman," *Art Bulletin,* 60 (1978), 139–153.

[27]*Letters,* IV:1635.

[28]Watts, "The Present Conditions of Art," p. 254.

[29]Wilde, "Mr. Whislter's Ten O'Clock," p. 15.

own painting and his own influence were beginning to lead many Victorian critics toward a less constricted view. The most important art critics of the 1870s, Swinburne and Pater, were both literary men who often emphasized the subject of a painting rather than the painting itself, but both were far more willing than, say, Ruskin or Colvin to see the intrinsic merits of painting without regard to moral purposiveness and both tended more and more to see music, not poetry, as the analogous art. Swinburne, for example, could praise a picture for having "the interest of excellent narrative," but only to add that "a great picture is something other than this."[30] Appropriately, to praise the work of Whistler, he confessed the inadequacy of speech—though conceding that poetry might strike a similar note—and proceeded to musical analogies:

> no task is harder than this of translation from colour into speech, when the speech must be so hoarse and feeble, when the colour is so subtle and sublime. Music or verse might strike some string accordant in sound to such painting, but a mere version such as this is as a psalm of Tate's to a psalm of David's. In all of these the main strings touched are certain varying chords of blue and white, not without interludes of the bright and tender tones of floral purple or red.[31]

Likewise, he praised Simeon Solomon's Rossettian *Vision of Love Revealed in Sleep* because "throughout the whole there is as it were a suffusion of music."[32] But despite such comments, and despite his love for such painters of pure beauty as Albert Moore, Swinburne remained half committed to literary art criticism, to translating paintings into words. Pater, despite his famous observation that "All art constantly aspires towards the condition of music,"[33] also devoted his energy to translating color and line into languorous

[30]"Notes on Some Pictures of 1868," in *The Complete Works of Algernon Charles Swinburne,* ed. Edmund Gosse and Thomas James Wise, 20 vols. (London: Heinemann, 1925–1927), 15:202.

[31]Ibid., p. 210.

[32]Swinburne, "Simeon Solomon: Notes on His Vision of Love and Other Studies," *Works,* 15:446.

[33]Walter Pater, "The School of Giorgione," *The Renaissance: Studies in Art and Poetry,* ed. Donald L. Hill (Los Angeles: University of California Press, 1980), p. 106.

prose. The impulse of both Swinburne and Pater to love a painting for what it is, but to explain and justify that love by translating the painting into something else, is, I think, the impulse that led Rossetti to make stories and poems of his own pictures, both by loading them with "readable" symbols and by sending them forth with an exegesis in prose or verse.

The strong influence of Rossetti on Swinburne and, more indirectly, on Pater cannot be doubted. Swinburne, who nearly idolized Rossetti, must have discussed painting with him frequently, and certainly he must have been greatly influenced in forming his critical precepts both by such conversation and by his admiration for Rossetti's painting, which he regarded as second to the work of no man living.[34] He seems, moreover, to have formed his prose style for discussing painting on the model of Rossetti's "Hand and Soul." Pater, in turn, seems to have formed his style of describing paintings on the model of Swinburne's art criticism—as Pater admitted and as Rossetti and Swinburne both noted, after reading "Notes on Leonardo Da Vinci."[35] The usual assumption is that Pater's famous description of the *Mona Lisa* was strongly influenced by Swinburne's "Notes on Designs of the Old Masters at Florence," but it might, in fact, have been still more strongly influenced by his description of Rossetti's *Lady Lilith*, which appeared a year before Pater's article. Certainly Swinburne's description of Rossetti's picture, though less perfect as prose and more accurate as description, strangely anticipates Pater's rhapsodies on Leonardo's picture. Lady Lilith is "indifferent, equable, magnetic; she charms and draws down the souls of men by pure force of absorption, in no wise wilful or malignant; outside herself she cannot live, she cannot even see: and because of this she attracts and subdues all men at once in body and in spirit."[36] The tone of reverie and the emphasis on the fatal beauty of woman both suggest that Cecil Lang is right in saying that

[34]Swinburne, "Notes on Some Pictures of 1868," p. 211.

[35]See *The Swinburne Letters*, ed. Cecil Y. Lang, 6 vols. (New Haven: Yale University Press, 1959–1962), II:58. Swinburne, apparently responding to a comment by Rossetti, remarked: "I like Pater's article on Leonardo very much. I confess I did fancy there was a little spice of my style as you say, but how much good stuff of his own, and much of interest."

[36]Swinburne, "Notes on Some Pictures of 1868," p. 212.

"Pater, as an esthetic critic, owed more than his prose style to Swinburne."[37] Pater's debt to Swinburne, and indirectly to Rossetti, seemed obvious enough to them, at least if a comment by Theodore Watts-Dunton, the confidant of both men, reflects their feelings. Watts-Dunton regarded Pater as a "curious man, whom I never quite understand" and, with apparent resentment, observed that "Swinburne of course invented him—took him round to Rossetti, who disliked him extremely."[38] The purpose of this discussion, however, is not to criticize Pater, but rather to note the strong influence of Rossetti on both Swinburne and Pater, two major critics who helped prepare the artistic climate for the movement of British art toward a purer aestheticism in the last quarter of the nineteenth century. And certainly Rossetti's influence on Pater seems evident enough in the description of the *Mona Lisa*, a description that much more aptly fits a painting by Rossetti than it fits Leonardo's masterpiece.[39]

Nevertheless, though Rossetti contributed in important ways to the emerging aesthetic, his own conscious artistic aims remained literary as, to a great extent, did Swinburne's and Pater's. Like other major English painters of his time—Watts, Burne-Jones, Leighton, Alma-Tadema, Poynter—he remained committed to literary or classical subjects, painting beautiful women for their beauty alone, but attaching extraneous names, symbols, and descriptions to his works. It is, perhaps, because of the tenacity of the literary tradition of criticism in England that, with the important exceptions of Albert Moore, Whistler, and sometimes Watts, the major works of the period remained allegories or illustrations from litera-

---

[37]*The Swinburne Letters*, II:58 n.

[38]Quoted by William Rothenstein, *Men and Memories*, 3 vols. (New York: Coward-McCann, 1931–1940), I:232.

[39]James Sambrook, "Introduction" to his *Pre-Raphaelitism: A Collection of Critical Essays* (Chicago: University of Chicago Press, 1974), p. 14. Rossetti probably deliberately inspired comparisons of himself with Leonardo by, to some extent, imitating him. In 1874 he was looking for photographs "representing rocks and water, chiefly distant—something in the way of background to Leonardo's *Lady of the Rocks*" (*Letters*, III:1269). Rossetti's picture, never completed, was to be called *Madonna Pietra*. For a discussion of the relation of Rossetti to Leonardo, see K. J. Wilson, "The Leonardo Landscape of Rossetti's verse," *Studies in Iconography*, 4 (1978), 149–60.

ture, and nothing happened in English painting comparable to the brilliant formal innovations that were taking place in France. Rossetti himself was curiously blind to such innovation, even going so far as to refer to Manet as a "French idiot,"[40] yet in the most important respect, his painting itself, he at least partially liberated himself from the stifling expectations of the English critics and the English public. And despite his distaste for most French art, he was very likely influenced by his great admiration for Delacroix and Millet to use his pigments more freely and more sensually; ultimately his lack of English restraint helped to establish a new English sense of beauty.[41] It may be because his influence was most especially felt through his paintings and was, at least verbally, unconscious, that Rossetti's effect on the aesthetic movement has often been considered slighter than Pater's. Yeats's description of the feeling for beauty among the "tragic generation" clearly implies as much: "Woman herself was still in our eyes . . . romantic and mysterious, still the priestess of her shrine, our emotions remembering *Lilith* and *Sibylla Palmifera* of Rossetti. . . . If Rossetti was a subconscious influence, and perhaps the most powerful of all, we looked consciously to Pater for our philosophy."[42]

If the greatest effect of Rossetti's painting, and its greatest influence, were, as I have suggested, unverbalized, it is necessary to examine the paintings divorced from the literary apparatus that, naturally enough, usually guides discussion of his art.

[40]*Dante Gabriel Rossetti and Jane Morris,* ed. John Bryson in association with Janet Camp Troxell (London: Oxford University Press, 1976), p. 174.

[41]During a trip to Paris in 1864 Rossetti saw a retrospective show of the works of Delacroix, and also looked through the galleries. He wrote back to Burne-Jones: "Painting is bad enough in England but here really it is a solid stink & nothing else—I mean what goes on at present. Really Gerome is not a painter though a stunner of a sort. There is a man named Millet who is the best going by far. Old Ingres is done for. Delacroix is worth the coming with all his faults & I have looked a great deal at his collected works which are to close at the end of this month" (from an unpublished letter in the Fitzwilliam Museum, Cambridge).

[42]W. B. Yeats, *Autobiographies* (New York: Macmillan, 1927), p. 372.

10

Painting, 1859–1882

I F only because he wrote very few poems in the years from 1852
to 1868, Rossetti's careers as painter and poet did not coincide
after his initial Art-Catholic and Pre-Raphaelite phases. But
the little poetry he did write in the late 1850s, including his most
fleshly poem, "The Song of the Bower," reveals a change away
from the spiritual, aesthetically devotional idea of love toward a
more wholeheartedly physical and passionate view. A similar
change in the style and subjects of Rossetti's painting was initiated
with the production of *Bocca Baciata* (114) in 1859. He had begun
as a quasi-religious painter, working in oils, had changed his medium to watercolor and his concerns to chivalric themes, and was
now returning to oils to paint wholly different subjects. The transition was not instant and absolute, but from 1859 on he limited
himself increasingly to studies of women, usually either half- or
three-quarter-length portraits. Though Rossetti's most famous pictures remain the early oils of the life of the Virgin, and though
many modern critics regard the watercolors of his middle period as
his finest work, the late studies of women are the work of the
mature artist, and are certainly the paintings that were best known
in the nineteenth century. Rossetti was credited with discovering a

new type of female beauty, "a new ideal loveliness,"[1] and even, by Oscar Wilde, with creating, along with Burne-Jones, *the* new type of female beauty:

> Life imitates art far more than Art imitates life. We have all seen in our own day in England how a certain curious and fascinating type of beauty invented and emphasized by two painters, has so influenced life that whenever one goes to a picture view or to an artistic salon one sees . . . the mystic eyes of Rossetti's dream, the long ivory throat, the strange square-cut jaw, the loosened shadowy hair that he so ardently loved.[2]

Whether or not life imitated Rossetti's art, artists did. Burne-Jones was, of course, a devoted disciple, and many other, lesser, artists such as Simeon Solomon, Frederick Sandys, and Frederick Shields slavishly imitated him.[3] The paintings of Rossetti's final period, then, had a profound effect upon how nineteenth-century painters, critics, and consequently the cultured public saw both the arts of their own day and the arts of the past. The original Pre-Raphaelite movement had considerably altered the course of nineteenth-century art, but had left intact, or even strengthened, the contemporary love for narrative and genre painting and the critical canons that exalted pictures on moral and even "literary" grounds. The most significant and influential change in Rossetti's art was its shift in emphasis from illustrative literary painting to purely pictorial qualities.

The historical importance of Rossetti's paintings of women has long been appreciated, but the intrinsic significance of the works has not been fully studied—the issue has been obscured both by widespread feeling that the pictures are not worth study, that they are the "febrile indulgence"[4] of a painter merely pandering to his

---

[1]Percy Bate, *The English Pre-Raphaelite Painters: Their Associates and Successors* (1901, rpt. New York: Books for Libraries Press, 1970).

[2]"The Decay of Lying," in *The Artist as Critic: Critical Writings of Oscar Wilde,* ed. Richard Ellman (New York: Random House, 1970), p. 307.

[3]See Bate for an account, with illustrations, of Rossetti's numerous disciples.

[4]John Nicoll, *Dante Gabriel Rossetti* (New York: Macmillan, 1975), p. 18.

234

patrons,[5] and by a critical predilection for accepting Rossetti's sonnets for his own pictures as the definitive "reading" of them. In terms of his control of his craft, Rossetti certainly was a better artist after 1859 than before, partly because he was finally limiting himself to what he could do, and because it was only in the early 1860s that he really learned how to use oil paints differently from watercolors. Indeed, not only his handling of paint, but even his drawing improved over the course of his career. In 1874, Holman Hunt declared himself "surprised at the excellence of the later of Rossetti's works. They are so infinitely better drawn than anything I ever saw of his." Hunt went on: "It is clear withal that he is working with great earnestness, and undiminished power of improvement, and that he will yet be able to do great things."[6] Unfortunately, despite this improvement in his best work, despite many fine late paintings, Rossetti's reputation for slovenliness after the mid-1860s was only too well earned by many loosely and perhaps hurriedly executed works. The frequent slovenliness has, sadly, led to neglect of the work, and has only increased the biographical bias in Rossetti criticism. The biographical causes for his changed style—the sickness and death of his wife, his addiction to chloral—have been well studied, but the intrinsic significance of those changes has not.

In certain respects, Rossetti's art did not change radically after 1859. In terms of style, he remained a superb colorist and an only adequate draftsman, and he remained unconcerned with perspective, continuing to push all the elements of his pictures into the foreground. To a considerable extent, his subjects also remained the same. Rossetti had always been what Timothy Hilton has called

[5]The accusation of pandering is usually made on the basis of Rossetti's financially rewarding habit of making replicas, but as W. D. Paden has observed, this is not quite fair, since the making of replicas was traditional and only became objectionable with the rise of speculative buying and the "romantic view of the artist as an inspired creator" (*"La Pia de' Tolomei* by Dante Gabriel Rossetti," in *The Register of the Museum of Art,* The University of Kansas, Vol. II, No. 1, [Nov. 1958], p. 46). Unfortunately, however, Rossetti's practice of making replicas must be deplored simply on the grounds that the replicas are generally very bad work.

[6]From a letter of April 15, 1874, to Martin Tupper. I am indebted to Professor George P. Landow for showing me his transcript of a transcript in the Huntingdon Library, San Marino, California.

"the nearest thing we have to a love painter."[7] Even in the most ascetic of his early pictures, *Ecce Ancilla Domini!*, the viewer is more likely to be impressed by the huddled, almost sexually intimidated figure of the Virgin, and by her full mouth and entranced eyes than by the symbols: the haloed dove, the lilies, the flames around the angel Gabriel's feet. Similarly, the chivalric subjects of Rossetti's middle period are almost invariably love stories, not tales of war. At the centers of his crowded watercolors one repeatedly finds a pair of impassioned lovers, a fact that led one critic to comment that "Rossetti's Arthurian pictures and designs would give the impression that Malory was a great erotic poet."[8] Nevertheless, in addition to the changed medium, from watercolor to oils, two major changes appear in Rossetti's treatment of love in *Bocca Baciata*: the male lover disappears, and the picture no longer tells a story. Rossetti's canvases remained crowded after 1859, but usually with ornamentation, "floral adjuncts,"[9] wallpaper designs, and so on, rather than with incidents to be interpreted. Part of the reason for this may have been that Rossetti recognized his limits. R. L. Mégroz, one of many critics to feel that the straight lines and crowding of objects in Rossetti's watercolors may have been in part to disguise poor drawing, has observed that "Rossetti limited himself to three-quarter length single figures in the later work and so gained greater freedom in composition. In the earlier he wants to crowd poetic ideas, instead of a single half-mystical idea of the fleshly paradise, into each picture. Instead of the face of a woman, he has to crowd a closed space with dream symbols."[10] Mégroz's comment, however, implies not only a change in compositional techniques, but a change in Rossetti's idea of what his art should represent, no longer a narrative crowded with incident, but a single symbol, no longer an ethereal dream of paradise, but a *fleshly* paradise. Part of the reason for this may have been Rossetti's desire to

[7]Timothy Hilton, *The Pre-Raphaelites* (New York: Oxford University Press, 1970), p. 184.

[8]R. L. Mégroz, *Dante Gabriel Rossetti, Painter Poet of Heaven in Earth* (London: Faber, 1928), p. 300.

[9]*Dante Gabriel Rossetti: His Family Letters, with a Memoir* by William Michael Rossetti, 2 vols. (Boston: Roberts Brothers, 1895), I:203.

[10]Mégroz, p. 300.

consolidate his vision, for he realized that "thinking in all directions . . . is ruin" (*Works*, 639). But it is more significant that, in
his painting, as in his poetry, Rossetti became increasingly disillu-
sioned with the traditional symbols that pointed to worlds he could
not realize, and with the hackneyed forms mocked by Jules-An-
toine Castagnary in 1868, when he defined Romanticism in painting, "which illustrates the poets, exhumes the middle ages, restores
the bric-à-brac, mends the old armour and composes stews of artificial color."[11] Rossetti had contributed mightily to forming a taste
for just such Romantic painting in England, but by 1859 he was
increasingly drawn to the more private symbolism of his own experience, a symbolism dominated by the figure of woman. In both
arts, as he became more skeptical, he became more fleshly.

It was precisely the fleshliness of *Bocca Baciata* that struck Roset-
ti's contemporaries as the great change in his style. Swinburne
praised the figure in terms that raised moral questions: "She is more
stunning than can be decently expressed!"[12] More priggishly, Holman Hunt complained of the picture's "gross sensuality of a revolting kind, peculiar to foreign prints, that would scarcely pass our
English custom house from France."[13] Modern viewers would not
adopt Hunt's moral tone in discussing the picture, but would have
to agree that it is certainly sensual and perhaps, though on aesthetic
rather than moral grounds, that it is revolting. The canvas is dominated by the figure of Fanny Cornforth, whose features were indeed
somewhat coarse, and especially by the flesh of her upper chest, her
extraordinarily thick and elongated neck, and her full face, which
is set in sharp relief against the dark background of her hair, dress,
and the foliage of the marigolds that, though behind her, seem to
press into the foreground. Both the title, "the kissed mouth," and
the accessories, her jewelry, the rose she wears in her hair, and the
apple that hovers rather than sits in the foreground, reinforce the
impression of the model's features. She is clearly meant to represent

[11]Quoted in A. C. Hanson, *Manet and the Modern Tradition* (New Haven: Yale
University Press, 1977), p. 32.
[12]*The Swinburne Letters*, ed. Cecil Y. Lang, 6 vols. (New Haven: Yale University Press, 1959–1962), I:27.
[13]Virginia Surtees, *Dante Gabriel Rossetti 1828–1882, The Paintings and Drawings: A Catalogue Raisonné*, 2 vols. (London: Oxford University Press, 1971), I:69.

a seductress, the lure of physical passion. The rose and apple, especially, are consistently used in Rossetti's poetry for this purpose. Even the long, luxuriant hair is telling—the chaste damsels of Rossetti's earlier work almost always wear their hair back or covered; long rippling hair is reserved, usually, for such figures as Mary Magdalene, Dante's Francesca, and Keats's "La Belle Dame Sans Merci." Still more significant, the eyes of the model are wide open in contrast with Rossetti's earlier practice of painting women, almost invariably, with downcast or fully closed eyes. The nature of this change can be fully appreciated by comparing Rossetti's 1859 watercolor *My Lady Greensleeves* (113) with his 1863 adaptation of the same subject in oils (228). The early picture presents the full, kneeling figure, with downcast eyes and snooded hair; the later presents the head and upper body of a wavy-haired, full-mouthed, open-eyed seductress. The later figure appears older, more worldly, and infinitely more threatening, an effect enhanced by the staring, wide-open eyes. The viewer is now confronted with a woman capable of genuine confrontation rather than with a demure maiden incapable of meeting his gaze. The challenge wholly alters the aesthetic experience of the viewer, who is no longer invited to unabashed contemplation, but is challenged by a somewhat forbidding figure. The viewer can no longer "enter into" the picture unobserved, but is kept at a distance and almost forced to assess his or her pleasures in viewing the forbidden, frankly sensual flesh. The relation between the viewer and the work of art, in other words, becomes more reciprocal, more dynamic, and more emotional than contemplative and interpretive.[14]

The changed relation between viewer and picture in part accounts for Hunt's dislike of *Bocca Baciata*. Hunt admitted to "strong prejudices" based, apparently, on the picture having been described as "a triumph of our school," a triumph, in other words, of Pre-Raphaelitism.[15] As is well known, Hunt, with some reason, took

[14]For an intriguing discussion of Manet's contemporaneous use of an "impertinent stare" on his nudes, especially the *Olympia* (1863), and of the traditionally voyeuristic relation of viewer to picture, see Hanson, pp. 95–99. Hanson argues convincingly that the nude's gaze upsets the relation of the viewer to the picture by forcing the viewer to see the subject as a person, not an "art object."

[15]Surtees, I:69.

"Pre-Raphaelite" to mean "Huntian," and this the painting assuredly is not. Rossetti was never really a Pre-Raphaelite in Hunt's sense of going directly to nature, but he was in his early predilection for narrative and allegorical painting in which meaning is discovered by "reading" the picture. Very often such meaning was achieved in Pre-Raphaelite pictures by capturing the figures in some pose that suggests activity, a passing from one moment of the narrative of their lives to the next. The painting would depict one moment in a dramatic action, and suggest the rest. For this reason a "distinctive hallmark" of Pre-Raphaelite vision is, as John Dixon Hunt has said, "animated gesture."[16] Millais's *Mariana,* Hunt's *The Awakened Conscience* and *The Shadow of Death,* and the distorted postures of Rossetti's own *Ecce Ancilla Domini!* and of nearly all his Arthurian watercolors attempt to capture such moments. The woman of *Bocca Baciata,* however, is, like nearly all of Rossetti's major late studies of women, completely at rest, characterized not by action, but by repose. Her lack of meaningful activity is surely one reason why Hunt deplored the lack of moral significance in the picture—no lesson, it seemed, could be "read" from it. But Rossetti's changed style reflects, perhaps, his recognition of the inadequacies, for him, of the narrative mode. Though paintings in this style could stop time, they were nevertheless entrapped within time; like the figures on Keats's urn, the people caught forever in uncomfortable, distorted postures suggest eternal lack of fulfillment, eternal unrest. Yet as Rossetti's poetry makes clear, his ideal was repletion, as in "Nuptial Sleep," not ever-unsatisfied longing. An ideal of the early Pre-Raphaelites had been Giorgionesque moments, described by Pater as "a kind of profoundly significant and animated instant,"[17] and indeed Rossetti's early paintings had attempted to capture just such moments. His revision of an early sonnet on Giorgione's *A Venetian Pastoral,* however, suggests why he changed his style, since the poem, which had emphasized the

[16]John Dixon Hunt, "A Moment's Monument: Reflections on Pre-Raphaelite Vision in Poetry and in Painting," in *Pre-Raphaelitism: A Collection of Critical Essays,* ed. James Sambrook (Chicago: University of Chicago Press, 1974), p. 247.

[17]Walter Pater, "The School of Giorgione," in *The Renaissance: Studies in Art and Poetry,* ed. Donald L. Hill (Los Angeles: University of California Press, 1980), p. 118.

artifact, was revised to emphasize a moment outside of time, a sensuous culmination rather than a narrative moment stilled by art. *Bocca Baciata* represents a rejection of the Giorgionesque ideal, conceived by Pater as the perfection of genre painting.[18] The sensuous repose of *Bocca Baciata* and Rossetti's other late females takes such culmination as its subject, and achieves a timelessness that implies not only the immortality of the artifact but, as often in his poetry, the immortality of sensuous repletion, when the end of desire is the end of frustration in time.

One of the most notable characteristics of Rossetti's women after 1859 is that they are completely expressionless, no doubt for the same reason that they are physically at rest. But like "animated gesture," exaggerated facial expression was characteristic of Pre-Raphaelitism, a fact that Stephen Spender rather contemptuously noted: "Often one notes in Pre-Raphaelite painting that just when the painter should be endowed with transcendent imagination, the model is expected to supply it by assuming an expression which the painter then imitates, with perfect truth to nature. Much of the Pre-Raphaelite painting is just painted charades or dumb crambo by friends of the Pre-Raphaelites dressed up to fill the roles."[19] Though Spender's tone is unjust, his observation is correct enough and does suggest the limitations of such an art, but they are limitations that the painters themselves came to appreciate. After commenting on the "ghastly joy" of the woman in Hunt's *The Awakened Conscience*, Carol Christ makes the point that "because of the inadequacy of bodily posture and facial expression to convey states of extreme emotion, the Pre-Raphaelites turned to the use of landscape to convey the emotional intensity of their subjects."[20] Rossetti turned, however, not to nature but to formalist watercolors and then to expressionless faces—the very lack of expression a symbol to convey emotional intensity, since expression would provide an interpretive handle, a means to "read" or intellectualize a picture that ought to stir passion, not thought. As Christ has also said,

[18]Ibid., p. 99.

[19]Stephen Spender, "The Pre-Raphaelite Literary Painters," in Sambrook, p. 122.

[20]Carol T. Christ, *The Finer Optic: The Aesthetic of Particularity in Victorian Poetry* (New Haven: Yale University Press, 1975), p. 62.

"just as in Rossetti's view of love souls can know souls only through bodies, so in art the sensation of the image is an essential and self-sufficient part of our understanding of it."[21]

Rossetti's desire to emphasize the sensational impact of his painting led him to emphasize pattern and color in design rather than any poetic idea, an emphasis markedly changed from his earliest works. Strangely, critics have usually said the reverse, adopting the attitude of Rossetti's friend and commentator William Sharp, that "Rossetti seems to have reversed the conventional method, and thought first of his poetic *motif*, secondly of colour, and lastly of form."[22] Yet Rossetti's poems for pictures invariably were written after the picture was completed, and in one case he utterly changed the "poetic *motif*" of a picture from a representation of Beatrice to one of Solomon's bride, after establishing the form and color scheme.[23] Rossetti's paintings often have names drawn from literature, but the paintings are nevertheless not conceived as illustrating literary themes. In one case, for example, a painting, *La Bella Mano* (240), is named for a sonnet series but, Rossetti insisted, "the picture is . . . simply a painter's fancy and dependent on pictorial qualities alone."[24]

Whatever modern critics have made of Rossetti's late literary allusions, Holman Hunt certainly recognized the formal significance of Rossetti's changed thematic approach from the start. He

[21]Ibid., p. 51.

[22]William Sharp, *Dante Gabriel Rossetti: A Record and a Study* (London: Macmillan, 1882), p. 104. For a characteristic modern view, see Jerome Hamilton Buckley, *The Victorian Temper: A Study in Literary Culture* (New York: Random House, 1964). Buckley asserts that "As a painter [Rossetti] cared more for the content of a picture than for its construction; the pattern was at best incidental to the idea that had gripped his imagination" (p. 166).

[23]Surtees, I:104–105.

[24]Quoted in G. H. Fleming, *That Ne'er Shall Meet Again* (London: Hart-Davis, 1967), p. 350. And see also Richard Stein's comment in *The Ritual of Interpretation: The Fine Arts as Literature in Ruskin, Rossetti, and Pater* (Cambridge: Harvard University Press, 1975), "Rossetti's contemporaries tended to respond to the sensuousness of his painting and poetry, and modern critics have generally adopted the same perspective. But there are hints that his conception of art was more formalistic and abstract. As a letter of 1869 observes, 'The quality of complex structure in Art is more touching and pathetic to me always than even the emotional appeal of the subject matter.'" (p. 198).

praised *Bocca Baciata* as "remarkable in power of execution," and condemned it for "advocating as a principle mere gratification of the eye and if any passion at all—the animal passion to be the aim of art."[25] Hunt's moral tone can of course be dismissed, but he quite rightly saw that the artistic form designed to gratify the eye was closely related to Rossetti's sensual purpose. Rossetti had always been a painter of love, but in treating spiritual love he had earlier resorted to the conventions of medieval romance, which included even the painted figure of Love himself, and had designed his pictures around "narrative" elements. But as even the enthusiastic reviewer of the *Oxford and Cambridge Magazine* observed, we "cannot quite *believe* in" personifications of spiritual qualities. In a skeptical age, "even angels when they appear in material forms are to us, who live in these times . . . hardly credible; they are to us not angels, but only human creations with an impossible extra-machinery."[26] In his poetry, Rossetti's own skepticism had led him away from the celestial machinery of "The Blessed Damozel" toward a more sensual and more personal mode, toward an emphasis on flesh and blood. The same is true of his painting: after 1859 the Christian symbolism begins to disappear. But though Rossetti's women are certainly fleshly, they have always been rightly perceived as "half-mystical." The mystical element is assuredly toned down in *Bocca Baciata,* but one formal element is important in this respect. Like the women in a number of pictures that followed, including *Regina Cordium* (120), *Fair Rosamund* (128), *Girl at a Lattice* (152), and *Venus Verticordia* (173, and especially the studies for it, 173 A–C), the woman of *Bocca Baciata* seems to be enclosed behind a frame within a frame, as though looking out through a window. The fact is significant only because earlier in his career Rossetti had habitually used female figures peering from windows to suggest a mystic or heavenly realm (see especially *The Tune of Seven Towers* [92], *The Wedding of St. George and the Princess Sabra* [97], and the central panel of *The Seed of David* [105]). What had been a minor but suggestive detail in the earlier works now becomes the

[25]Quoted in Surtees, I:69.
[26]"Two Pictures," *The Oxford and Cambridge Magazine For 1856* (London: Bell and Dalby, 1856), p. 481.

whole picture, as though Rossetti had trimmed away the main "story" and left only the significant mystic symbol. Rossetti's great care over the proper framing of his pictures may well reflect a concern to make this personal symbolism more emphatic.

A far more clearly "mystic" treatment of woman is evident in the 1864 painting, *Beata Beatrix* (Plate 9), one of Rossetti's finest achievements. At first glance the picture seems more in Rossetti's earlier style than his later, perhaps because it was originally conceived "many years" before 1863.[27] The overt symbolism, the haloed dove, the sundial pointing to Dante's mystical number nine, and the figure of Love, all return to earlier elements in his work. Further, the posture of Beatrice, her head tilted back upon her outstretched neck, her bent, seemingly breathless pose, and her carefully studied cupped hands look back to the Pre-Raphaelite Giorgionesque moment—her apparent yearning suggests entrapment in time. And the fleshliness is very much toned down—the flesh tones are not as sharply relieved against a dark background, a far smaller proportion of the canvas is given over to flesh, and, significantly, Beatrice's eyes are closed. Most important, the subject is literary, and the treatment, as Rossetti's own description insists, is narrative.

> You will remember how much Dante dwells on the desolation of the city in connection with the incident of her death, & for this reason I have introduced it as the background, & made the figure [*sic*] of Dante and love passing through the street & gazing ominously on one another, conscious of the event, whilst the bird, a messenger of death, drops a poppy between the hands of Beatrice. She sees through her shut lids, is conscious of a new world.[28]

Such was Rossetti's intent, yet the impact of the picture, it seems to me, does not depend to any great extent on these elements. Though necessarily not to the same extent as *Bocca Baciata*, it is the

[27]The picture was not fully completed until 1870, but was begun at an unknown date, probably in the 1850s, and left unfinished. Surtees dates it in 1864, "the year in which it was probably taken up." For an account of the genesis of the painting, see Surtees, I:93–94.

[28]Quoted in Surtees, I:94.

Plate 9. Beata Beatrix. Oil, 34 × 26. By courtesy of The Tate Gallery, London.

face of the woman that attracts and sustains attention—indeed, some of the narrative elements, especially those in the background, are so inconspicuous as to be almost lost in the shadowy twilight.[29] Moreover, when external considerations are brought to bear on the picture, they are rarely literary, rarely concerned with Dante, but are biographical, concerned with Rossetti's memorial to his dead wife, Lizzie Siddal, who is cast as Beatrice. The intellectual symbolism, in short, is secondary to the emotional intensity communicated by the female figure.

The design of *Beata Beatrix* belongs to the same Rossettian class as *Bocca Baciata*. Though the fleshliness is toned down, Beatrice is clearly flesh and blood, and her flowing hair, yearning posture and parted, inviting lips are deliberately sensual. A study for *Beata Beatrix* (168B), represents a prim, well-combed damsel much like the Beatrice who denied Dante her salutation in an 1851 watercolor (50), but the final version shows Rossetti's deliberate rejection of such a portrayal. In fact, the closest analogue to it in Rossetti's works is a study for the fainting Queen Guenevere (Plate 10) which exhibits a similar posture, and almost identical hair and mouth. The similarity of *Beata Beatrix* to Guinevere does suggest deliberate sensuality, but it probably resulted more from a similarity of situation than of character—Guinevere is fainting, Beatrice is in a trance, "suddenly rapt from Earth to Heaven." The pose, expression, and other elements of the composition clearly suggest a "mystic" meaning even if we forget the imposed narrative and symbolism. Rossetti's intent was plainly to show the meeting of heaven and earth in the image of a woman; the ways in which he set about evoking soul from flesh are characteristic of his late art.

As in *Bocca Baciata* and other pictures, the face of the model is set in a frame within a frame. Beatrice's face is framed within an open window, above the top of the brick wall that cuts the picture in half, below the Ponte Vecchio, which runs parallel to the wall, near the top of the canvas, and between the vertical lines of a

---

[29]In the original painting, now in the Tate Gallery, the figures of Dantè and Love, and a woodside well, are dimly perceptible in the murky background. In some of Rossetti's copies, notably in the ghastly parody now hanging in the City Museum and Art Gallery in Birmingham, the background is much lighter, and the figures are plainly seen.

245

Plate 10. Study of Guenevere for *Sir Launcelot in the Queen's Chamber.* Pencil with some ink, 19 × 15-¾. By courtesy of The City Art Gallery, Manchester.

building and a well. The effect of this framing is both to emphasize the face, and to draw attention to the artifice of the picture, the subordination of all else to exalt the lady. In the words of Rossetti's sonnet "The Portrait," "Her face is made her shrine." In addition, the coloring and perspective, or lack of it, emphasize the spiritual quality of Beatrice. F. G. Stephens, Rossetti's friend and one-time Pre-Raphaelite brother, provided a fine description of the effect of Rossetti's technique:

> . . . the form of Beatrix is opposed to the dun evening light of the outer world, and so placed that the light shines through the outer threads of her dark auburn hair, and thus produces the effect of a saint-like halo, while the face itself, is to our sight, merged in the dimness caused by our looking at the splendour of the river. Accordingly, the figure appears partly outlined against the lustre, partly lost in the half-gloom of the chamber. It is thus visible in what may be called a twilight of brilliance and a twilight of shadow. . . . Her form is merged, not lost, in that shadowy space which, in Butler's happy phrase, is "of brightness made." Thus Rossetti happily showed that his subject was a mystery, not without life of this world, nor all unreal.[30]

The formal effects of the painting, especially the lighting, are designed to suggest the spiritual significance of the natural symbol. The artifice of form becomes, in effect, the soul of the work. The "poetic *motif*" is achieved much more by formal design than by the literary techniques of allusion, narrative, and interpretive symbolism. The appeal of the picture is far more sensual than intellectual.

Very early in his career, with the prose narrative "Hand and Soul," Rossetti had made clear his view that the proper pursuit of the artist was to paint his own soul. In the simplest terms, this affirms the Romantic injunction to produce art from one's inner self, from introspection, but for Rossetti the symbols of the soul were the female *anima*, the beloved, and the traditional symbol of the mirror or reflecting surface. His poem "The Portrait," which Cecil Lang has rightly observed is irresistibly associated with *Beata*

---

[30]F. G. Stephens, *Dante Gabriel Rossetti*, in *The Portfolio*, May 1894, pp. 62–64.

Beatrix,[31] opens with a collocation of the symbols of the portrait, the mirror, the beloved, and the living soul:

> This is her picture as she was:
>   It seems a thing to wonder on,
> As though mine image in the glass
>   Should tarry when myself am gone.
> I gaze until she seems to stir,—
> Until mine eyes almost aver
>   That now, even now, the sweet lips part
> To breathe the words of the sweet heart:—
> And yet the earth is over her.

The painting *Beata Beatrix* brings all of these elements together also. The model, Lizzie Siddal, is of course Rossetti's beloved—she was also dead by the time the painting was finished. The picture, moreover, captures both the living image of the beloved, and in its self-conscious artifice, the mirrored soul of the artist. It thus combines the image of the soul as the female beloved, and the image of the soul as a reflection of the artist's inner self.[32] In Rossetti's love poetry, the way to unite soul and body is to achieve complete union with the beloved; in his painting he attempts such a union by merging his subject, the beloved, with his formal technique, the expression of his soul. Importing Rossetti's poetry into a discussion of his painting, of course, can indicate only his aspirations, not his achievements. The poetry does, however, reveal the high value he placed on pictorial technique, and suggests a motive for the "mystical" elements of the design.

One element of the picture, which does not depend upon external reference but which clearly implies spiritual value, is the preoccupation with death. Rossetti himself insisted that the picture "is not at all intended to represent death, . . . but to render it under

---

[31]Cecil Y. Lang, *The Pre-Raphaelites and Their Circle* (Chicago: University of Chicago Press, 1968), p. 500.

[32]For an excellent discussion along these lines, see Susan P. Casteras, "The Double Vision in Portraiture," in *Dante Gabriel Rossetti and the Double Work of Art*, ed. Maryan Wynn Ainsworth (New Haven: Yale University Art Gallery, 1976), p. 11.

The qualities that make the pictures so striking are the design, the peculiar beauty of the faces themselves, and the lush, sensuous application of paint. Indeed, in this last respect *Beata Beatrix* is much more closely associated with the early oils and the water-colors of the middle period than with the simultaneously attractive and repellent females of the late period. The dry, brittle, thin surface of the paint on *Beata Beatrix* contributes to a sense of "ten-sity" that characterized the earlier periods—the paint seems almost stretched over the canvas, and the viewer is seemingly invited to look *through* the picture as he strains his vision toward the shadowy background figures, and still further beyond toward the light source behind Beatrice and seemingly behind the picture itself. The effect is almost the precise opposite of such pictures as *Bocca Baciata* or *Monna Vanna* (Plate 11), which provides a convenient contrast since it may be seen hanging beside *Beata Beatrix* at the Tate Gallery. Whereas the thin surface of *Beata Beatrix* invites the viewer into the picture, the richly textured *Monna Vanna,* painted in 1866, emphasizes the overwhelming massiveness of the figure and the sumptuousness of the clothing, and forces the eye to linger on its sensual surface. Further, the coloring creates a design that subtly blocks access, since the gold pattern of the dress swirls into the amber of the fan and on into the russet hair, drawing the eye into a kind of vortex that is, however, stilled by the sheer immovable bulk of the figure. Consequently the circularity of the design implies not the open-endedness of the spiral (as is often the case in paintings of G. F. Watts and, more notably, Turner) but the closed complete-ness of the circle. Any attempt to look beyond the sensual surface is rendered superfluous, and further, is blocked by the opacity of the background and even by the massive arm, or sleeve, posed rather like that of an offensive tackle. The overall effect of the rich, heavy paint is, in *Monna Vanna* as in most of Rossetti's late paintings, to suggest both the appeal and the threat of sensual beauty.

Rossetti's idea of seductive beauty places him squarely in the dark tradition of Romanticism traced by Mario Praz. His type is what Praz calls the fatal woman. In fact, Charles Baudelaire's definition of seductive female beauty seems perfectly to describe many of Rossetti's canvases. It is "intense and sad," so that a beautiful woman's head "makes one dream, but in a confused fashion, at

Plate 11. Monna Vanna. Oil, 35 × 34. By courtesy of The Tate Gallery, London.

once of pleasure and of sadness; conveys an idea of melancholy, of lassitude, even of satiety—a contradictory impression, of an ardour, that is to say, and a desire for life together with a bitterness which flows back upon them as if from a sense of deprivation and hopelessness. Mystery and regret are also characteristics of the Beautiful."[36] *Bocca Baciata, Fair Rosamund, Veronica Veronese,* virtually all of Rossetti's late studies of women, including even *The Beloved* (182), and *The Blessed Damozel* (244), are both voluptuous and sad, suggesting both the desire for life and the bitterness of death. They are characterized by melancholy, lassitude, and perhaps most important, satiety. Not only do they seem dangerous, inviting the viewer to a sexual experience that ends in death, but their own satiety suggests a condition outside of the desires that characterize time, a complete fulfillment often considered possible, as in Rossetti's, Swinburne's, and frequently Tennyson's and Keats's poetry, only in death.

The satiety of Rossetti's women suggests a heedlessness of others, a self-absorption that is especially evident in *Lady Lilith* (Plate 12). The picture is unfortunate in some respects, perhaps because Rossetti originally painted it from Fanny Cornforth in 1864, and later scratched out her head, substituting that of Alexa Wilding, which does not seem to fit well on Fanny's more than ample body. Nevertheless, Rossetti's intentions for the picture are clear enough. Lilith, the inhuman first wife of Adam, contemplates her own beauty in a mirror as she combs out her luxuriant, rippling hair. As Rossetti said in the painting's companion sonnet, "Body's Beauty," Lilith is both self-absorbed, "subtly of herself contemplative," and fatally attractive as she "Draws men to watch the bright web she can weave, / Till heart and body and life are in its hold." The idea is made still more clear in his prose description, in which he said the picture "represents a *Modern Lilith* combing out her abundant hair and gazing on herself with that self-absorption by whose strange fascination such natures draw others within their circle. The idea which you [Thomas Gordon Hake] indicate (viz: of the perilous principle in the world being female from the first) is about the most

[36]Charles Baudelaire, *Intimate Journals,* trans. Christopher Isherwood (New York: Random House, 1930), pp. 39–40.

Plate 12. Lady Lilith. Oil, 37-½ × 32. The Samuel and Mary R. Bancroft Collection of the Delaware Art Museum. By permission.

253

essential notion of the sonnet"[37] and, it might be added, of the painting. But once again, Rossetti's descriptions are superfluous. Lilith's self-absorption is evident enough in her actions and in her expressionless face; her sexual attraction is manifest in itself, though the roses and even the dressing table, which resembles an altar, symbolize her passionate nature. The important point, it seems to me, is that Rossetti should associate narcissism with sexual attraction, not only in the studies of women contemplatively admiring themselves, as in *Fazio's Mistress* (164), and *La Bella Mano* (240), and of women admired by others within the picture, as in *The Beloved* (182), but in virtually all the pictures in which a beautiful, self-absorbed woman dominates the canvas and compels the viewer's admiration. Even in *Sibylla Palmifera* (193), intended as the opposite of *Lady Lilith*, "soul's beauty" as opposed to "body's beauty," the central figure is an expressionless, contemplative beauty, apparently self-absorbed, and clearly sexually attractive, as the roses and the blindfolded cupid in the background attest.

The narcissism of Rossetti's women should not be surprising, since his ideal was to unite soul with body, to evoke a sense of soul from a portrayal of flesh. In his poetry he attempts this by repeated imagery of mirrors, reflecting pools, and even of portraits, for Rossetti recognized that narcissistic introspection is not an emblem of fleshly vanity, but of desire to unite the conscious self with the innermost soul. Moreover, the narcissism of these women suggests the fatality of love, both because the women lure men toward an ideal of repletion possible only in death, and because their own satiety, characterized by an expressionless lassitude, makes the women themselves appear almost lifeless. At one point Rossetti, engaged in an "experiment in method," attempted to achieve a "masklike quality" that would further emphasize the deathly character of the woman.[38]

In terms of form, Rossetti achieves the effect of narcissistic self-absorption that is both attractive and threatening by exploiting the techniques used in *Monna Vanna*. He so crowds his canvases that the viewer has no space to project himself into the picture, no

---

[37] *Letters*, II:850.
[38]Casteras, p. 13.

outlet on the canvas to draw his attention from the central figure. Commentators have frequently noted the "quality of inaccessibility" of these pictures.[39] Maryan Wynn Ainsworth, speaking of *Lady Lilith*, puts the case very well, arguing that we are drawn into the picture (Ainsworth says by the words of the accompanying sonnet, though the sexual attraction of the picture itself has the same effect), but "once having been drawn into it, we are repelled by the tightness of the enclosed space and the huge figure of Lilith, both of which make her own space inpenetrable. To the left a pleasant scene of woods appears as an outlet; but one soon realizes that this is a mirror of the reader-viewer's space. We are within Eden Bower, caught in Lilith's snare."[40] In various ways the same is true of most of Rossetti's pictures, which are not only dominated by the immense figure of a woman, but are filled with objects and ornamented backgrounds—flowers, wallpapers, tapestries—that, because of the lack of perspective, press suffocatingly into the foreground.

All these stylistic and thematic concerns appear in the magnificent *Astarte Syriaca* (Plate 13) of 1877, in many ways the apotheosis of Rossetti's artistic career. The painting has recently received, from Timothy Hilton, the high praise that is its due: "*Astarte Syriaca*," he wrote, "must be regarded as the summation of Rossetti's career as an artist; legend, religion, art and love are all combined in this awe-inspiring Hymn to Her. Alone in Rossetti's work, alone perhaps in the whole of Pre-Raphaelitism, it is one of those paintings that have a genuinely humbling quality."[41] But *Astarte Syriaca* has been at least as often loathed as loved. Though Graham Robertson was later haunted by the beauty that he felt Rossetti had "dreamed of" but had not attained, his initial response to *Astarte Syriaca* indicates the revulsion it often inspires. To him it was "a terrible work which, to my shocked and instantly averted gaze, announced itself as an unusually bad Rossetti. I saw—against my will—a lilac face with purple lips, huge lilac arms sprawling over

[39]Helene E. Roberts, "The Dream World of Dante Gabriel Rossetti," *Victorian Studies*, 17 (1974), 379.

[40]Maryan Wynn Ainsworth, "The Prince's Progress: Works from 1863 to 1871," in *Dante Gabriel Rossetti and the Double Work of Art*, pp. 78–79.

[41]Hilton, p. 187.

lumpy fulvous folds, distorted drawing, tortured, 'gormy' paint."
Robertson's revulsion and his subsequent sense of being "haunted
by a beautiful Presence"[42] reveal the extent to which *Astarte Syriaca*
both repels and attracts. The revulsion is due to the same causes,
though magnified, as in other pictures. The massive central figure,
dominating a huge canvas (72" × 42"), has all of the attractive yet
threatening characteristics of Rossetti's other fatal women. She is
expressionless, indolent, satiated. Her eyes, wide open, stare
straight out of the picture, her lips are exaggeratedly full, and the
flesh of her shoulders and arms is at least as alarming as appealing—
alarming because her body is simply so large—too large, in fact, for
her head. Her immense arms and shoulders give an impression of
physical power that represents quite the reverse of Rossetti's early
demure maidens, and even the full, flowing robe which, beneath its
contours, both reveals a massive physique and conceals its limits,
adds to the sense of superhuman size. Further, the leg, raised toward the viewer, has the same intimidating effect as the massive
arm of *Monna Vanna*. The drawing, moreover, is distorted. Not
only is the body too large for the head, but Astarte's neck is clum-
sily attached to her body. Further, the arms of the attendant angels
are too short, and their feet are so badly drawn as to provide a ready
explanation for Rossetti's usual custom of not painting people from
the knees down. And finally, the color is oppressive—the rich sea-
green robes of Astarte and her attendants and the lighter, yellower
green of the attendants' wings are relieved almost solely by the
somewhat unnaturally glowing flesh tones.

Rossetti is so commonly thought of as a premature *fin-de-siècle*
aesthetic dandy that the frequent ugliness of his pictures is assumed
to be simply a matter of artistic incapacity, but some of his comments as well as the consistency of his practice indicate his awareness, in his last period, that art must be willing to be, in some
sense, ugly. His comment, for example, that "Leighton's impasto is
scented soap & his surfaces violet powder" (*Works*, 637) reveals his
scorn for what he evidently considered the prettifying tendencies of
such painters as Leighton, Poynter, and Alma-Tadema. And his

[42]Graham Robertson, *Time Was* (London: Hamish Hamilton, 1931), pp.
86–87.

Plate 13. Astarte Syriaca. Oil, 72 × 42. By courtesy of The City Art
Gallery, Manchester.

willingness to produce "ugly" pictures is evident in his divergence from the new neoclassicism, which, like art nouveau, depended on high polish, on delicate drawing, and on an emphasis on an elaborated line rather than on the arrangement of masses. Rossetti never attempted the prettiness of elegant lines and delicate coloring that makes the nudes of Burne-Jones and Poynter so peculiarly sexless. Increasingly he concentrated on a bold use of paint that was rarely pretty and that might well be called ugly, but that nevertheless, as Robertson's experience shows, could startle and stimulate a viewer. Indeed, Rossetti's comments on works he had seen in Paris in 1864 indicate that he was quite consciously turning from the champion of the linear style, Ingres, whom he had formerly praised but now described as "done for," to the champion of the painterly style, Delacroix.[43] Though Rossetti never abandoned the notion that poetry is superior to painting, he was almost alone among his contemporaries to exploit painting's most obvious advantages, its directness and immediacy.

Despite all its repellent characteristics, and partly because of them, *Astarte Syriaca* remains a masterpiece, strangely commanding attention. In fact, that which repels also attracts. The relation of the viewer to the picture is similar to that of *Monna Vanna* and *Lady Lilith,* for while he is made aware of the dangers of Astarte's sexuality, he is nevertheless attracted to her

> Love-freighted lips and absolute eyes that wean
> The pulse of hearts to the spheres' dominant tune.
> [*Poems,* 260]

The oppressiveness of the coloring and the crowding of the picture, which prevent any escape, any resting place for the viewer's eyes, force his attention upon the flesh, and yet force him also, in effect, to keep his distance. Though Astarte is a temptress, clasping her twofold girdle as though about to undo it and stand forth naked, she is a sated temptress, self-absorbed and superior to those whom she attracts to their doom. She is, in fact, not human—hers is the

---

[43]From an unpublished letter in the Fitzwilliam Museum, Cambridge. See Chapter 9, note 40.

repletion of a fatal goddess, the repletion of the kingdom of death. Her evident fulfillment, her lack of desire and consequently her escape from time, is represented in part by the merger of the masculine sun and the feminine moon behind her (a conjunction, by the way, that helps to account for the unnatural light, the unnatural lilac glow of the flesh). But once again, though the subsidiary symbolism may help to point a moral, it is not essential to the impact of the painting, for the androgyny suggested by the conjunction of the sun and moon is fully apparent in the features of Astarte herself. The sheer bulk of her body, especially the heavy arms and broad shoulders, combine with the squared jaw and uncompromising gaze to produce an unquestionably masculine effect. The effect is, of course, deliberate and consciously achieved; Rossetti once wrote of the relation of beauty in man and woman that "the point of meeting where the two are most identical is the supreme perfection" (*Works*, 606). Rossetti shared the common nineteenth-century interest in androgyny, often expressed with the image of the hermaphrodite, for the common reason. For him, as for Shelley, Swinburne, and Gautier, the androgyne represented a fulfillment that puts an end to desires and to any sense of incompleteness and fragmentation. The expressionless, passionless, androgynous Astarte figures forth the union of the masculine and feminine within the individual, the fully integrated personality, the union of body and soul. The stylistic elements that seem to deny access to the picture reinforce the viewer's sense of its impenetrable completeness even more emphatically than does the circularity of design in *Monna Vanna*.

Yet *Astarte Syriaca*, like Rossetti's other paintings of women, paradoxically reinforces the viewer's sense of his own fragmented nature both by stimulating a desire for the fleshly paradise, the repose in sensuality that he sees embodied in the goddess, and by cutting him off from the completion with its very impenetrability. Certainly this was the relation of the artist to the picture. Throughout his mature life Rossetti had regarded complete union with the object of his love, with his ideal of woman, as just such a fulfillment. Perhaps for this reason he painted best and most frequently from models whom he loved—Elizabeth Siddal, Fanny Cornforth, Jane Morris. Such fulfillment could not, of course, occur in the

259

temporal realm of desire, but was possible, if at all, in memory, in the quiet introspective moment when the vision of past bliss could be summoned forth in peace. In such moments of memory the beloved was fully internalized, fully made one with the lover. It is significant that at the end of his life Rossetti produced an almost exact duplicate of the figure of Astarte, provided her with different symbolic accessories, and named the picture *Mnemosyne* (261).[44] But she represents an aspiration, not an achievement, a desire that the picture preserved in memory as in art should represent the fulfillment of life. Jane Bayard has said that Mnemosyne's "eyes reflect his dream with a fixed and melancholy look that is utterly self-absorbed."[45] The self-absorption implies both success, in self-completion, and failure, in isolation and inaccessibility. The painting at once suggests the calm of such completion and the sterile fruitlessness of it. The satiety that is suggested by Rossetti's women is the satiety of completed life; to wish for it is to wish for death.

Indeed, the most striking characteristic of Rossetti's satiated women, and especially of Astarte, is their lifeless, masklike countenance. The ultimate significance of the deathly countenance of these women may, I think, be understood in the terms of W. B. Yeats's comment on oriental religious art: "It is even possible that being is only possessed completely by the dead, and that it is some knowledge of this that makes us gaze with so much emotion upon the face of the Sphinx or Buddha."[46] Rossetti surely would not have consciously intended quite this effect, but he was concerned, quite consciously, with the mystery of death and with the desire to achieve complete "being." He did not need to be rationally aware that his work could be linked to religious or mythic art in this way, for he painted, as he always insisted, from his own inner, emotional experience—he generated his own myth.

Nevertheless, the myth generated is, in the painting as in the poetry, a limited one. Rossetti painted the same women, over and

[44]Rossetti painted *Mnemosyne* not directly from the completed *Astarte Syriaca*, but from a study for it. See Surtees, I:156.

[45]Jane Bayard, " 'Lustral Rites and Dire Portents': Works from 1871 to 1882," in *Dante Gabriel Rossetti and the Double Work of Art*, p. 102.

[46]W. B. Yeats, "Certain Noble Plays of Japan," in *Essays and Introductions* (New York: Macmillan, 1968), p. 226.

over again, and even when he painted an "outsider" he accommo-
dated her features to his "type"—even his sister-in-law was transformed. But also as in his poetry, limitation implies not failure, but
intensity of focus; Rossetti himself defended his practice on the
basis that what he saw as ideal beauty was unchanging, and that he
chose not to settle for less.[47] By confining and refining his art,
Rossetti, as Yeats put it, was like "an actor of passion who will
display some one quality of soul, personified again and again"—
with Titian and Botticelli, he depended "for his greatness upon a
type of beauty which presently we call by his name."[48] Further,
Rossetti was not, as he saw it, painting woman; he was painting his
own soul, "which he alone knew, exactly as he knew it." How he
painted his own soul while painting portraits of women can be
better understood by reference to a comment of Otto Rank's:

> When the Greek idea of the soul became that of the Psyche, man
> acquired living that soul which earlier had been something into
> which death changed him, and thereafter the art of human portrai-
> ture more and more depicts the soul of the living. This artistic free-
> dom in the representation of the living soul found its highest ex-
> pression in portraiture, which does not represent the actual, but the
> essential, man—that is, the soul. But whereas in pre-Greek art the
> dead man's soul could only be represented abstractly, and not as
> living, the representation of the living soul, which reached its
> culmination in portraiture, required a living soul for its very purpose
> of giving the picture life. And thus finally the living soul was no
> longer taken from the object depicted, but "added" by the working
> artist himself, of whom we then say that he has "put his soul into" the
> work and given it both life and immortality.[49]

Rank's discussion concludes with a description of the artist's endeavor that tallies well with Rossetti's own description of "The

[47]See Sharp, pp. 196–197: "In a sense, indeed, he became almost a slave to one
type; but his invariable defence of this was that it was to him an ideal face, or at
any rate the highest in all qualities that appealed to him which he had ever seen,
and that, therefore, not being a portrait painter, he could not do better than
accept it as his prevailing model."

[48]W. B. Yeats, *Autobiographies* (New York: Macmillan, 1927), pp. 154–155.

[49]Otto Rank, *Art and the Artist*, trans. Charles Francis Atkinson (New York:
Knopf, 1932), pp. 338–339.

Portrait," and with his own practice. The loving care with which Rossetti painted the women he loved is itself the soul of his work, and so it is both true and important that he painted best from the women he loved—his portraits of, for example, Alexa Wilding, are impressive, but they seem cold, hard and unimpassioned compared to his paintings of Lizzie Siddal, Fanny Cornforth, and Jane Morris. In the best sense, his finest painting, like his finest poetry, is narcissistic—the portrait of his own epipsyche, the vision of love that is the soul within his soul. Rossetti himself saw the painting of the soul as a strange technical challenge. He criticized the "later and more Academic Italian School" because "in Guido and these later men I have always thought the soul to be too visibly in a minor ratio, as compared to the body; and colour, which constitutes the pictorial atmosphere of beauty, is a sealed mystery to them." What these artists failed to achieve, and what Rossetti strove for, was a "rendering of the female type that would possess . . . that indescribable blending of familiarity with unexpectedness which brings home to our hearts the embodied visions of the great."[50] Painting of the "female type" should possess, in Freud's sense, a feeling of the uncanny, a sense of something rich and strange that unsettles comfortable famliarity, that suggests the presence of otherworldliness in worldly beauty.

Certainly Rossetti did not explicitly formulate all this about his painting, though the constant imagery of *döppelgangers*, of deceptive mirror images, and of uncannily living portraits suggests it, but indeed, my point has been that to the extent that Rossetti did rationalize about his late art, he did not do it full justice. His deliberately imposed symbols and especially the sonnets written for his pictures, though often beautiful in themselves, make the pictures too easily accessible in a limited, literary way, and reduce rather than reinforce the pictorial effect, which is, as I have said, more directly sensational than intellectual. If Rossetti had painted from literature and not from experience, he would probably have produced, though less well, something like the beautiful but scarcely provocative art of Burne-Jones. Burne-Jones's art, Timothy Hilton has justly said, "is the result of an interested study of mythology

50*Letters*, III:1328.

rather than its direct expression, and myth is at its height, artistically and socially, when it is expressed, not used."[51] Rossetti, with his mythic titles, his often conventional symbolism, his sonnets, and his occasional epistolary explications of his pictures, almost demands to be classed with the users of myth. Because he often regarded himself as essentially a poet, not a painter, he tended, in his comments at any rate, to undervalue the purely pictorial elements of his design. Yet it is the claustrophobic use of color, the crowding of canvases, enhanced by the lack of perspective, and especially the sensuous, yet androgynous, features of his women that make his late paintings so compelling. His late painting *is* the direct expression of his personal myth, an expression that is enhanced by the idiosyncracies of style, perhaps even by the failures of technique that his detractors deplore. Further, though his statements in prose and poetry about his paintings have occasionally been praised for allowing the reader-viewer into the picture, they actually constitute euhemeristic interference, secondary interpretation that mitigates the dynamic relation of the picture with the viewer, who is both repelled and attracted. The paintings themselves are the primary, unmediated vision; they appeal, at their best, to immediate, emotional sensation. Rossetti was at one with the critical spirit of his age that insisted on the verbal message of a painting, but his practice reveals the limitations of his own, and his age's, critical theories. His paintings, not his comments on them, contributed to the development of symbolist painting in France and England, and helped lead the way to a far less constricted view of art than that of the mid-Victorian period.

[51]Hilton, p. 195.

Conclusion

B ECAUSE of his Italian heritage, his medievalism, his antip-
athy to science, and his indifference to social and political
issues, Rossetti often seems an alien in the Victorian period.
But while it is true that much of what is usually regarded as characteristically Victorian was foreign to Rossetti's temperament, his
obvious importance at the center of a group of poets and artists that
included, at various times, Holman Hunt, Millais, Morris, Swinburne, Meredith, and Ruskin makes it clear that he was in tune
with the artistic, if not the public, temper of his age. Other poets
and painters of his time were more widely admired by the public,
but none received the same awed respect from fellow artists. Such
writers as Swinburne, Meredith, and for a time, Morris, regarded
him as, in Meredith's phrase, "our Master, of all of us."[1] Such
painters as Burne-Jones and Simeon Solomon were professed disciples. And two of the greatest critics of the Victorian period, Ruskin
and Pater, both sometimes regarded him as the foremost man of the
age. Pater is reported to have said that "of the six men then living

---

[1]*The Collected Letters of George Meredith*, ed. G. L. Cline, 3 vols. (London:
Oxford University Press, 1970), I:418.

264

who were destined to be famous—Tennyson, Browning, Ruskin, Matthew Arnold, Swinburne, and Rossetti—Rossetti was 'the most significant as well as the most fascinating.' "[2] Because of the biographical bias in Rossetti criticism, the remarkable admiration of his fellow artists is credited to his enormously attractive personality, but Pater, for one, scarcely knew him personally, and most of the others were first attracted to him by his work. Isolating the central characteristics of Rossetti's work, then, isolates something of central importance to the Victorian artistic imagination. Centering attention on Rossetti and his admirers provides a perspective on some Victorian issues that are generally seen from the viewpoints of Tennyson, Browning, and especially, Arnold.

Swinburne, Pater, and others most admired Rossetti's creation of new realms for the artist to work in, his "adding to poetry of fresh poetic material, of a new order of phenomena, in the creation of a new ideal."[3] The implication is that they, like Rossetti himself, feared that new material was desperately needed because previous generations of poets had used up all the material, that it had all been said. Admiration for an artist who could discover new sources for art was bound to run high in an age when Macaulay, for example, feared that poetry must inevitably decline for lack of material, and when John Stuart Mill actually feared that original musical composition would come to an end as all the possible mathematical variations were used up.[4] Certainly Rossetti's contemporaries constantly praised him for the originality of his imagination. Coventry Patmore admired his "extraordinary faculty for seeing objects in such a fierce light of imagination as very few poets have been able to throw upon external things";[5] Pater more pointedly noted that

[2]Thomas Wright, *The Life of Walter Pater*, 2 vols. (New York: Putnam, 1907), 2:23.

[3]Walter Pater, "Dante Gabriel Rossetti," in *Appreciations with an Essay on Style* (London: Macmillan, 1889), p. 242.

[4]Macaulay maintained in his essay "Milton" that "as civilization advances, poetry almost necessarily declines," and maintained almost everywhere that civilization, already much advanced, was advancing ever more triumphantly. See his *Critical and Miscellaneous Essays* (New York: Appleton, 1880), p. 12, and *Autobiography of John Stuart Mill* (New York: Signet, 1964), p. 114.

[5]Quoted by William Rossetti, in *Dante Gabriel Rossetti: His Family Letters, with a Memoir by William Michael Rossetti*, 2 vols. (Boston: Roberts Brothers, 1895), I:436.

"at a time when poetic originality in England might seem to have had its utmost play, here was certainly one new poet more, with a structure and music of verse, a vocabulary, an accent, unmistakably novel."[6] And indeed, Rossetti himself valued his originality above all else: "I was one of those whose little is their own."[7] But his self-effacing tone, due no doubt to becoming modesty, is revealing. Paradoxically, even while praising him for opening new realms, Rossetti's admirers praised him for his narrow range, for what Swinburne called his lack of "variety." The paradox that less is more in Rossetti's art can be better appreciated by taking a closer look at the comments of Patmore and Pater. Their suggestions that Rossetti's imagination worked with "minute and definite imagery," that "for Rossetti . . . the first condition of the poetic way of seeing and presenting things is particularization,"[8] seem to place Rossetti squarely in the Romantic tradition by their emphasis on both the value of what Blake called the "minute particular" and the value of imagination. But the heavy emphasis on the status of things, of objects, suggests Rossetti's diminution from the earlier Romantics, especially from Blake and Wordsworth, who saw particulars as a way to the general or absolute. Rossetti was always at his best when the objects of his vision were not translated into a realm of absolute value.

The characteristic Victorian handling of the minute particulars of experience is, in fact, an index of general diminution from the high poetic aspirations of the Romantics. The large Romantic themes, from Wordsworth's pantheism to Coleridge's metaphysics to Shelley's "yearly universes" provided an overall framework in which the details of vision could fit into a larger whole, but such themes were no longer available—the grand march of intellect had brought a relativism that resulted in too many possible perspectives and too many minute particulars without providing any final resting place from which to scan the whole. Like Rossetti's watercolors of the 1850s, the world presented too many details, each seeming to

[6]Pater, "Dante Gabriel Rossetti," p. 229.

[7]W. M. Rossetti, *Some Reminiscences of William Michael Rossetti*, 2 vols. (New York: Scribner, 1906), I:211.

[8]Pater, "Dante Gabriel Rossetti," pp. 230–231.

cry out for individual attention, but none crying out louder than others. As Carol Christ has convincingly shown, details in the relativistic world of the Victorians tend to remain discrete, isolated, and possibly meaningless, so that "conceiving of the universe as a mass of particulars led logically to seeing experience as wholly subjective and particular, which ultimately led to solipsism."[9] Most Victorians apparently felt, like Rossetti, that though the efforts of the Romantic poets to restore transcendent value to an age of unbelief had succeeded poetically, they had failed philosophically. The problem of subjectivism had remained; the solutions had not. The dilemma finds expression in Matthew Arnold's observations that the Romantics, for all their grandeur, had not thought enough, and that the nineteenth-century world view was too "multitudinous" to allow clarity and scope of poetic vision. Arnold felt that Clough had destroyed his poetry by giving in to multitudinousness, by failing to find an "*assiette,*" or fixed perspective, that would allow a limited but shaping view of the chaotic world.[10] But Arnold himself had similarly failed. *Empedocles on Etna* to some extent represents an effort to sweep aside the complexities of modern life and to diminish the realm of the poet to the rather empty lyricism of Callicles. Even Browning, who Arnold felt had been too much prevailed upon by the world's multitudinousness, had deliberately diminished his range. His dramatic monologues constitute a series of "*assiettes*" from which he could view the world without falling into the chaos of such early Romantic poems as *Pauline* and *Sordello.*[11] Even Tennyson, whom Rossetti thought the most abundant, least diminished, of his contemporaries had to find a form in *In Memoriam* to record short swallow flights of song, limited utterances from briefly held perspectives. Similarly, the medievalism of Morris, of Carlyle's *Past and Present*, of Tennyson's *Idylls of the King*, and, of course, of Rossetti represents an effort to find a point of

[9]Carol T. Christ, *The Finer Optic: The Aesthetic of Particularity in Victorian Poetry* (New Haven: Yale University Press, 1975), p. 32.

[10]*The Letters of Matthew Arnold to Arthur Hugh Clough,* ed. Howard Foster Lowry (London: Oxford University Press, 1932), p. 130.

[11]See the discussion of Browning in chapter 2 of James Richardson's *Thomas Hardy: The Poetry of Necessity* (Chicago: University of Chicago Press, 1977).

view that will make sense of the world, but at the expense of cutting off centuries of human experience.

With the exception of Swinburne, who held tenaciously to the high ideal of the prophet-bard, all the major Victorians accepted their necessary diminution to some extent. The tendency, clearly seen in Rossetti, was to begin on a large scale, founder on the rocks of relativism, and then take a limited *"assiette."* Ultimately Rossetti stayed closer to Romantic subjectivism than did most of his contemporaries, choosing for his limited theme what Pater described as "the just transcript of that peculiar phase of soul which he alone knew, precisely as he knew it."[12] As his constantly reiterated imagery linking mirrors, reflections in water, portraiture, and souls implies, Rossetti attempted, more literally perhaps than any other artist, to render his own idealized soul in art. But such a theme, depending as it does on what "he alone knew," comes perilously close to solipsism—a declaration of "I Am" without a corresponding "You Are." Part of Rossetti's appeal for Pater, I think, was the way in which his poetry both acknowledged and sought to escape what Pater called the "narrow chamber of the individual mind."[13] Both Rossetti and Pater directly confronted the problem of isolation within the self, and both looked for a way out in intense moments of apparent communion with the "forms and colours of the world."

Rossetti's way of attempting to escape from the closely related problems of multitudinousness and solipsism was to concentrate on the phases of the soul under the influence of love. Love, the thirst for union with otherness, elevates emotion over rationality, and simply denies, or seeks to deny, the rational assertion of separation. And because love intensely focuses on one limited object, it ignores the complexity and disorder of more objective perception. In terms of Rossetti's painting, it eliminates the multitudinous complexity of the watercolors by focusing on the single image of the ideal woman, an image that had previously been but one of many details competing for attention. If my argument that the preoccupation with the

[12]Pater, "Dante Gabriel Rossetti," p. 230.
[13]Walter Pater, *The Renaissance: Studies in Art and Poetry,* ed. Donald L. Hill (Los Angeles: University of California Press, 1980), p. 187.

theme of love as an escape from solipsism was an inevitable legacy of Romanticism is accepted, it should not be surprising that Rossetti was not alone in his choice of subject. Once again, what is especially evident in Rossetti's poetry is more indirectly manifest throughout the poetry of his age, for Morris, Patmore, Meredith, Swinburne, and even Browning, Tennyson, and Arnold all wrote more love poetry than their Romantic predecessors. Patmore, for example, was obsessed with man's relation to woman, the "Angel in the House," and saw such a relation as the paradigm of man's highest aspirations.

The greatest of the Victorian poets, Browning and Tennyson, wrote about a wide range of themes, but in some ways their careers follow the same pattern as Rossetti's. In the Shelleyan *Pauline*, Browning sought an immaterial, platonic realm, but, as William Irvine has said, "love bound him to sense, even to self."[14] Browning did not, by any means, restrict himself to love poetry after abandoning Shelleyan Romanticism, but he wrote a good deal of it, mostly concerned, like Rossetti's, to heal "the pain / Of finite hearts that yearn."[15] And like Rossetti's, his descriptions of the rare moments of fulfilled love indicate that they are attenuated and momentary, but nevertheless eternal and definitive, as in "By the Fire-Side":

> If two loves join, there is oft a scar,
>> They are one and one, with a shadowy third;
> One near one is too far.
>
> A moment after, and hands unseen
>> Were hanging the night around us fast;
> But we knew that a bar was broken between
>> Life and life: we were mixed at last
> In spite of the mortal screen.

Browning's love has more warmth, less fire than Rossetti's, but it has much the same significance, breaking down the bar between

---

[14]William Irvine and Park Honan, *The Book, the Ring, and the Poet: A New Biography of Robert Browning* (New York: McGraw-Hill, 1974), p. 36.

[15]"Two in the Campagna," ll. 59–60.

self and other, between "Life and life," and removing the "mortal screen" that normally entraps each person. And, as for Rossetti, the fulfillment of love is the definitive and defining fulfillment of the self, the completion of the self's potential and the sure sign of meaning in life:

> I am named and known by that moment's feat;
> > There took my station and degree;
> So grew my own small life complete.[16]

Browning's descriptions of love seem more warmly human than Rossetti's, but as the very title of "By the Fire-Side" suggests, the love he describes is sometimes almost too cozy, too serenely comfortable around the domestic hearth. Certainly Browning's conception of love was often both profound and lofty but because he was more comfortable with the values of his age, and because he believed in God, Browning did not have to make the most of his limited theme with the single-minded fervor of Rossetti.

Tennyson, on the other hand, was extremely troubled by the skepticism that nineteenth-century science seemed to make necessary. Toward the end of *In Memoriam* he acknowledges the futility of attempting to cast his vision beyond death in imagery that almost startlingly anticipates Rossetti's:

> What find I in the highest place,
> > But mine own phantom chanting hymns?
> > And on the depths of death there swims
> The reflex of a human face.

But unlike Rossetti, who was haunted by the image of the self cast on futurity, Tennyson briskly abandons it. His escape from the solipsism that oppresses the viewer of the dark glass was to ignore it:

> I'll rather take what fruit may be
> > Of sorrow under human skies:
> > 'T is held that sorrow makes us wise,
> Whatever wisdom sleep with thee.[17]

---

[16]"By the Fire-Side," ll. 228–235, 251–253.
[17]*In Memoriam, A.H.H.*, section 108.

Although Tennyson's real solace in *In Memoriam* comes from a mystic sense of contact with the spirit of his dead friend, he turns increasingly, toward the end of the poem, to the consolations of earthly experience and, in the end, to human love. The coda to Tennyson's great poem describes a marriage.[18]

The love poetry of both Browning and Tennyson suggests, in various ways, that the individual who does not love is isolated and fragmented. Mariana, the speaker of *Maud,* and King Arthur are all incomplete without their lovers. Furthermore, the contemplation of marriage at the end of *In Memoriam* leads directly to a rhapsody on evolutionary meliorism, implying that love and marriage are portents of the human progress toward completion and perfection. But despite the undercurrent of dissatisfaction with modern life expressed in their descriptions of the failure of love, both Browning and Tennyson were frequently able to describe a calm, comfortable, domestic love. Ultimately, I think, their faith both in some kind of an afterlife and, to an extent, in their age, enabled them to describe a love that was not called upon to suggest more than the completion of the mortal self by immersion in the common life of society. But for the agnostics, for Meredith, Swinburne, and Arnold as well as for Rossetti, the angel in the house could not easily provide the ultimate answers. The agonies of Rossettian love result from the effort to find meaning in the reflection that Tennyson ignored.

One of the Victorian period's fullest explorations of love, Meredith's *Modern Love,* examines the conditions that make love so necessary and so difficult for modern men and women. The highly cerebral Meredith's overriding concern in *Modern Love* is the interference of the dialogue of the mind with itself, of cerebration, in love. His ideals, courtly laws of love and faithfulness, are from a different age and do not fit the realities of his own. He expresses the dilemma by forcing confrontations between the old illusions and the new reality, by a deliberate and ironic primitivism that idealizes innocent lovers but undercuts their innocence by equating it with ignorance, their love with brute bestiality, and by playing off the passionate loves of Othello, Lear, Raphael, and Keats against the

---

[18]See W. S. Johnson, *Sex and Marriage in Victorian Poetry* (Ithaca: Cornell University Press, 1975), pp. 135–143.

paltry intellectual concerns of diminished modern man. The problem is with the age: thought interferes and mocks instinctive desires, but thought cannot be dispensed with. Meredith's most optimistic assertions are immediately undercut. When love, the crowning sun, is combined with intelligence,

> We are the lords of life, and life is warm.
> Intelligence and instinct now are one.
> But Nature says: "My children most they seem
> When they least know me: therefore I decree
> That they shall suffer." Swift doth young Love flee,
> And we stand wakened, shivering from our dream.
> Then if we study Nature we are wise.
> Thus do the few who live but with the day:
> The scientific animals are they.—
> Lady, this is my sonnet to your eyes.[19]

The irony of the final line clearly shows Meredith's distance from Rossetti, who wrote sonnets to his lady without ironic detachment. But Meredith's irony poignantly suggests what has been lost to the nineteenth century, and what Rossetti's archaism seeks to find again. Modern man's intellect has been divided from his instincts; his soul has been divided from his body.

The two finest nineteenth-century appreciations of Rossetti, those of Pater and Swinburne, both lavishly praise Rossetti's ability to unify body and soul. For Pater, the central quality of Rossetti's poetry is that "the two trains of phenomena that the words *matter* and *spirit* do but roughly distinguish, play inextricably into each other."[20] Swinburne observes that in all of Rossetti's poetry "there is no quality more notable than the sweet and sovereign unity of perfect spirit and sense, of fleshly form and intellectual fire."[21] Pater's and Swinburne's comments are especially interesting because they are only partially correct; they describe the artistic aspi-

---

[19]*Modern Love,* Sonnet XXX.

[20]Pater, "Dante Gabriel Rossetti," p. 236.

[21]"The Poems of Dante Gabriel Rossetti," in *The Complete Works of Algernon Charles Swinburne,* ed. Edmund Gosse and Thomas James Wise, 20 vols. (London: Heinemann, 1925–1927), 15:13.

272

rations of Pater and Swinburne better than the artistic success of Rossetti. Rossetti's poetry does not deny, but constantly acknowledges the separation of matter and spirit, and only rarely manages to fuse the two, and then in a limited way by fixing images on a surface. Rossetti's aesthetic detachment, like Meredith's irony, deliberately forces a disjunction between the emotional content of his poetry and the artifice imposed by the intellect.

Rossetti, in fact, was caught between two opposing ways of reconciling soul and body, the Romantic desire for loss of self in otherness, mergence with a universal soul, and the Victorian desire for perfection of the self, usually achieved—or attempted—through love. The one way seeks union with an outer soul, the idealized woman as *anima*; the other seeks a soul within the soul, or epipsyche, sought by Rossetti through introspection and symbolized by the reflecting surface. The two are not wholly at odds—they cannot merge utterly, but may meet at the boundary of self and other. The idea of becoming whole by perfecting the self, reconciling instinct and intellect, is evident in Browning's "By the Fire-Side" and Tennyson's *Idylls of the King,* but is still more obvious in the love poetry of Matthew Arnold. In "The Buried Life" Arnold makes it clear that the apotheosis of love is not union with the other, but union with the inner self:

> Only—but this is rare—
> When a belovéd hand is laid in ours,
> When, jaded with the rush and glare
> Of the interminable hours,
> Our eyes can in another's eyes read clear,
> When our world-deafen'd ear
> Is by the tones of a loved voice caress'd—
> A bolt is shot back somewhere in our breast,
> And a lost pulse of feeling stirs again.
> The eye sinks inward, and the heart lies plain,
> And what we mean, we say, and what we would, we know.
> A man becomes aware of his life's flow,
> And hears its winding murmur; and he sees
> The meadows where it glides, the sun, the breeze.[22]

[22]"The Buried Life," ll. 77–90.

Conclusion

As for Rossetti, contemplation of the beloved's eyes gives way to introspection, but for Arnold the introspection is more explicit and more complete. His image of the stream of past existence and his understanding of the meaning of life through the confluence of his past and present life is analogous to Rossetti's imagery of *döppelgangers* as past selves, but implies a greater integration of all the moments of existence. W. S. Johnson has rightly observed that in "The Buried Life" the "rare moment of true love is not essentially one of union, of marriage: it is a means of pursuing self-knowledge."[23] Rossetti explicitly used the same image of a "sunk stream long unmet" ("The One Hope") in a few poems, including "The Mirror," and implicitly in such poems as "Willowwood" and "The Landmark," in which he gazes upon his reflection in a well. But for Rossetti the image symbolizes, at best, a momentary and usually only partial integration of the conscious self and the subconscious inner self. The comparison with Arnold, however, sheds significant light on one of the Victorian period's most pressing concerns. The "buried life" surfaces constantly in Arnold's prose works as the "best self" that he repeatedly exhorts his contemporaries to cultivate. Arnold's prose is perhaps the fullest and most convincing of the Victorian exhortations to self-culture, the perfection of the self, as an antidote to the fragmentation of modern man and the multitudinousness of the age. The similarity of aims between his love poetry and Rossetti's suggests that Rossetti's narcissism is in some measure aligned with the Victorian concept of the "best self," and conversely, that the quest for the "best self" is in some measure narcissistic. Certainly Arnold's most famous poem, "Dover Beach," is self-absorbed, though ostensibly a love poem. As Anthony Hecht's fine parody, "The Dover Bitch," wittily demonstrates, the ostensible "beloved" is pretty well left out of the speaker's contemplation.[24] Arnold would have loathed the comparison, which may indeed be unjust, but his concentration in "Dover Beach" on the receding "Sea of Faith" and on the worthlessness of the external world combined with his constant desire to find his best self does remind one of Gautier's comment: "Perhaps . . . finding

[23]Johnson, p. 70.
[24]Anthony Hecht, *The Hard Hours* (New York: Atheneum, 1967), p. 17.

274

nothing in the world worthy of my love, I shall end by adoring myself, like the late Narcissus of egotistical memory."[25]

Rossetti certainly did not enthusiastically endorse the Victorian notion of self-culture. Indeed, he regarded self-culture, described by W. B. Scott as "this popular English Goetheism of the day," as ridiculously egotistical, an abandoning of responsibility for the benefit of such things as "enlarged views of Hamlet."[26] Self-culture for Arnold and for others was a way to perfect not only the self, but the morals of the age. Rossetti, who was torn between the morality of his strict Anglican mother and sisters and the desire to celebrate passionate love, could not find such broad implications in the idea of a fully integrated self. His failure, or refusal, to do so illustrates the flaw in Arnold's ethical system—the fully integrated self may or may not be a "best self" in the terms of conventional morality; the fully realized individual may or may not be compatible with a fully realized society. Though less bold than Swinburne, whose love poetry attempts to show the incompatibility of man's instincts with Christian ethics, Rossetti was drawn toward an idea of love that undercuts traditional moral values. Swinburne, like Nietzsche, went so far as to assert that Christian asceticism is responsible for the division of soul and body—the best self, like Nietzsche's *Übermensch*, would be beyond good and evil. The objects of Rossetti's love, often like the forbidding dark goddesses Mario Praz has called "fatal women," are frequently closer to a satanic than to a godly view of life. Like Swinburne, Rossetti objected to the moral view of the *Idylls of the King,* which set forth the perfect union of soul and body, of Arthur and Guinevere, as the foundation of a perfect civilization—his Guinevere would have been weighed against God "by another table of weights and measures."[27] After his earliest works Rossetti rejected the idea of a love that echoed God's love and endorsed the Christian ethical system. The "best self" found in love was too selfish to become a part of a larger society. The same, I think, might be said of Arnold's "best self," which could only

[25]Théophile Gautier, *Mademoiselle de Maupin* (Paris: Société des Beaux-Arts, 1912), p. 46.

[26]William Bell Scott, *Autobiographical Notes,* ed. W. Minto, 2 vols. (New York: Harper and Brothers, 1892), II:293–294.

[27]*Letters,* II:663.

275

remain, like Arnold's ordinary self, a *spectator ab extra* on the life of his time. Individualism, whether Rossetti's passionate quest or Arnold's cultured independence, led to isolation. Rossetti's agonized attempts to integrate the self reveal the darker side of the serene cultural humanism of Arnold.

Though "Rose Mary" perhaps achieved the same end, Rossetti never did write *God's Graal*, the poem that would have shown Guinevere's superiority to God, perhaps partly because Buchanan's outraged attack scared him away from such an "immoral" topic. Particularly toward the end of his life he was anxious to appear before the public as properly virtuous. His response to Buchanan emphasizes, in part, the morality of his poems taken as a whole, and later he befriended the young Hall Caine mostly because Caine had stressed, in a lecture, Rossetti's high moral purpose. Despite the bent of his nature, he remained closer to Arnold's morality than to Swinburne's, but his pursuit of a "best self" was less socially concerned. Like Arnold, Rossetti felt that the cultivation of art was the way to heal the fragmented self, but unlike Arnold, whose broad humanism was concerned with the ideas of art, Rossetti was mostly concerned with beauty, especially beauty of form. His comments on the works of other poets and artists almost always emphasize form above intellectual content, and in his own poetry and painting the serene perfection of form, the artfully covered surface, was the expression of the shaping soul of the artist. The moments commemorated were ephemeral and imperfect; the formal beauty was enduring and perfect. Rossetti never wanted to be associated with the idea of art for art's sake, but his emphasis on formal beauty shows some affinity with that movement—enough that Swinburne and, later, the advocates and artists of the Aesthetic and Decadent movements acknowledged him as their leader. But, in fact, Rossetti, like Pater, is closer to Arnold than the followers of both men realized. For Rossetti, Pater said, life was "a crisis at every moment" and his art is a commemoration of these crises.[28] As the "Conclusion" to *The Renaissance* argues, the ability to live in a constant state of crisis, to be always open to experience, is "success in life."[29]

[28]Pater, "Dante Gabriel Rossetti," p. 235.
[29]Pater, *The Renaissance*, p. 189.

dentalism and Victorian humanism, but his inability to achieve transcendent vision and his refusal to be concerned with humanist implications indicates that he is diminished both as a Romantic and as a Victorian. Nevertheless, as a "Victorian Romantic" his constant endeavor was to fuse Romantic spirituality with Victorian materialism, soul with body. His failure to be both fully Romantic and fully Victorian was inevitable, since soul and body seemed forever sundered once the sea of faith had fully receded. Rossetti's dilemma anticipates Yeats's remark that "we may never see again a Shelley and a Dickens in the one body, but be broken to the end."[31] Rossetti's limited success was to fuse intellectual form with passionate emotional content in art. The special domain of his art was the surface, the painted veil where the mysteries of the soul, or inner self, are in contact with the intellectual, shaping control of the artist. The special praise of Rossetti, as Swinburne and Pater appreciated, was that by limiting his scope he found new realms for poetry, for in seeking ways to describe this liminal area between matter and spirit he became, as Yeats recognized, an innovator in the symbolist mode that was to find its apotheosis in Yeats himself.

Certainly it is not entirely coincidental that Yeats shared with Shelley and Rossetti an obsessive interest in the image of the veil, or covering screen, that hides the spirit-world (a certainty to Yeats, though not to Shelley and Rossetti) from the world of matter. Yeats was more confident than either of his predecessors that the veil could be lifted, eventually and under the right circumstances, but in his early years at least he shared with them the inability to communicate openly with a spiritual world that could, as he claimed it later did, give him images for poetry. In fact, Yeats's continual dabbling in the occult may be seen as a sustained effort to escape from the inevitable diminishment of a poet without absolute values in a multitudinous age. His comments on Henley show that he was clearly aware of the need for diminution at the end of the nineteenth century. He said that Henley, "an ambitious, formidable man . . . showed alike in his practice and in his theory—in his lack of sympathy for Rossetti and Landor, for instance—that he never understood how small a fragment of our own nature can be

[31]W. B. Yeats, *Essays and Introductions* (New York: Macmillan, 1968), p. 296.

brought to perfect expression, nor that even but with great toil, in a much divided civilization."[32] Yeats evidently regarded Rossetti as the type of the modern poet, or at least his description of the poets of the nineties seems a remarkably apt description of Rossetti's aesthetic of diminution: "Their poems seem to say: 'You will remember us the longer because we are very small, very unambitious.' Yet my friends were most ambitious men; they wished to express life at its intense moments, those moments that are brief because of their intensity, and at those moments alone."[33] Like Rossetti, Yeats began in youth with a broad scope, and gradually learned to sort out the ideas and impulses that contributed to a kind of search for a diminished, or consolidated, "best self," to the "perfect expression" of a "small fragment of [his] own nature": "I had as many ideas as I have now, only I did not know how to choose from among them those that belonged to my life."[34]

Diminishment was, Yeats saw, painful but aesthetically necessary—like Pater and Swinburne, Yeats saw that Rossetti was especially to be praised for finding a new poetic realm within the narrow but certain grounds of the isolated and limited self. In this, Yeats saw, Rossetti was unlike his more celebrated contemporaries:

> Had not Matthew Arnold his faith in what he described as the best thought of his generation? Browning his psychological curiosity, Tennyson, as before him Shelley and Wordsworth, moral values that were not aesthetic values? But Coleridge of the *Ancient Mariner* and *Kubla Khan,* and Rossetti in all his writing made what Arnold has called that "morbid effort," that search for "perfection of thought and feeling, and to unite this to perfection of form," sought this new, pure beauty, and suffered in their lives because of it.[35]

But though Yeats points here to the difference between Rossetti and other Victorians, his own example indicates an important similarity. Ultimately Yeats refused the burden of diminution for though, like Rossetti, he looked introspectively for inspiration, he

[32]W. B. Yeats, *Autobiographies*, p. 364.
[33]Yeats, *Essays and Introductions*, p. 491.
[34]Yeats, *Autobiographies*, p. 103.
[35]Ibid., pp. 386–387.

279

affirmed that he examined not the ordinary, isolated self, but the *anima mundi*, that "age-long memoried self." In terms that seem to echo both Rossetti (as described by Pater) and Arnold, Yeats defined "genius" as "a crisis that joins that buried self for certain moments to our trivial daily mind."[36] Life was a crisis at every moment for Rossetti precisely because he constantly confronted his buried self, looking, as Arnold and Yeats in their different ways looked, for some kind of ultimate meaning. Both Arnold and Yeats saw, or convinced themselves that they saw, some link between their own deepest selves and a larger order, some possibility of wedding the self to a meaningful world. Arnold satisfied himself with finding in the abyss of his soul the "best thought of his generation," Yeats, with the quasi-mystical idea of the *anima mundi*, but Rossetti, seeing only the reflections of his own lonely identity, was unable to deduce from it any larger meaning. Yeats, for reasons other than his mysticism, was a far greater poet than Rossetti, but a comparison of the two raises the perplexing question of whether some faith, even an illusory faith, may not be necessary to give the poet confidence to speak for all men, rather than solely for himself. Certainly Rossetti, without the confidence of the visionary, was forced to be content with studying and describing only his own emotions, with affirming only the plaintive "I am" of the "narcissist." In all of this, of course, he was thoroughly Victorian—his sense of isolation in a multitudinous world led him to look within himself, and his insistence on empirical proofs prevented him from any leap of faith that would bring the isolated self into contact with anything else. But as Robert Langbaum has shown, such "subjective empiricism" is characteristic of Romanticism[37]—the peculiarly Victorian characteristic of Rossetti's Romanticism is its diminution. Perhaps the best description of "Victorian Romanticism" is in the discussion of Coleridge, a Romantic, by Pater, a Victorian sometimes thought of as a Victorian Romantic:

[36]Ibid., p. 337.

[37]See the "Introduction: Romanticism as a Modern Tradition" in Robert Langbaum, *The Poetry of Experience: The Dramatic Monologue in Modern Literary Tradition* (1957; rpt. New York: W. W. Norton, 1963), pp. 9–37.

To the intellect, the critical spirit, . . . subtleties of effect are more precious than anything else. What is lost in precision of form is gained in intricacy of expression. It is no vague scholastic abstraction that will satisfy the speculative instinct in our modern minds. Who would change the colour or curve of a rose-leaf for that . . . colourless, formless, intangible being . . . Plato put so high? For the true illustration of the speculative temper is not the Hindoo mystic, lost to sense, understanding, individuality, but one such as Goethe, to whom every moment of life brought its contribution of experimental, individual knowledge; by whom no touch of the world of form, colour, and passion was disregarded.[38]

Pater's discussion removes the transcendental ideal from Romanticism, removes also the tendency toward abstraction of the Victorian critical spirit, and leaves the Rossettian (and Paterian, of course) sense that every moment of life is a crisis, bringing "experimental, individual knowledge." In Rossetti and Pater, the two seemingly contradictory notions of empiricism and solipsism meet in the narrow chamber of the individual mind—solipsism establishing a barrier to the search for ultimate truth outside of the self, and empiricism a barrier to the search for ultimate subjective truth within. Rossetti's poetry, in its "intricacy of expression," its occasional preciosity in delineating "subtleties of effect," seems the inevitable result of a mind cut off from faith by precisely the "speculative instinct" that is thwarted. Speculation begins and ends in the momentary perception. Art is limited to memorializing the moment.

[38]Pater, "Coleridge," in *Appreciations*, p. 67.

Index

283

Dante Gabriel Rossetti and
the Limits of Victorian Vision

Designed by Richard E. Rosenbaum.
Composed by The Composing Room of Michigan, Inc.
in 11 point Goudy Old Style, 2 points leaded,
with display lines in Goudy Old Style.
Printed offset by Thomson/Shore, Inc. on
Warren's Olde Style, 60 pound basis.
Bound by John H. Dekker & Sons, Inc.
in Joanna book cloth.

Library of Congress Cataloging in Publication Data

Riede, David G.
   Dante Gabriel Rossetti and the limits of Victorian vision.

   Includes index.
   1. Rossetti, Dante Gabriel, 1828–1882.   2. Rossetti, Dante Gabriel,
1828–1882—Criticism and interpretation.   I. Title.
NX547.6.R67R53   1983   821'.8   82-22099
ISBN 0-8014-1552-7